LANGUAGE AND TRUTH

LANGUAGE AND TRUTH

GARTH L. HALLETT

Yale University Press
New Haven and London

Set in Baskerville with Avant-Garde type by
Keystone Typesetting Co., Orwigsburg, Pennsylvania.
Printed in the United States of America by
Thomson-Shore, Inc., Dexter, Michigan.

Library of Congress Cataloging-in-Publication Data
Hallett, Garth.
    Language and truth / Garth L. Hallett.
    p. cm.
    Includes index.
    ISBN 0–300–04012–1 (alk. paper)
    1. Languages—Philosophy.   2. Truth.   I. Title.
P106.H289   1988
121—dc19   87–16123
                                                                    CIP

*The paper in this book meets the guidelines for permanence
and durability of the Committee on Production Guidelines
for Book Longevity of the Council on Library Resources.*

10   9   8   7   6   5   4   3   2   1

CONTENTS

Preface   vii

PART ONE: THE CONCEPT *TRUE*
Chapter 1:   The Isomorphic Tradition   5
Chapter 2:   Critique of Isomorphism   17
Chapter 3:   Linguistic Truth   31
Chapter 4:   The Primacy of Linguistic Truth   47
Chapter 5:   Performatives, Avowals, and the
             Asymmetry of *True*   58
Chapter 6:   Cognitive Comparatives and *True*   70

PART TWO: THE DOMAIN OF *TRUE*
Chapter 7:   The Relativity of Linguistic Truth   91
Chapter 8:   The Concept *True* as Norm   108
Chapter 9:   A Paradigm Inquiry: Are Performatives
             True-False?   130
Chapter 10: Moral Truth   148
Chapter 11: Empirical Truth   165
Chapter 12: Trans-empirical Truth   177
Chapter 13: A Comparison with Tarski and Davidson 188

Notes   201
Index   228

PREFACE

What I have to do is as it were to describe the office of a king; in doing which I must never fall into the error of explaining the kingly dignity by the king's usefulness, but I must leave neither his usefulness nor his dignity out of account.
—*Ludwig Wittgenstein,* Remarks on the Foundations of Mathematics, *p. 160*

A concept as central to our culture as the concept *true* deserves a fuller, more accurate analysis than it has yet received. In part 1, I will undertake such an analysis; and in part 2, while continuing it, will attend as well to the norm implicit in the concept and will inquire whether the criterion that guides our unreflective use of *true* merits reflective acceptance as a rule of predication. Despite its basic importance, this practical inquiry, proceeding from the factual, has not previously been undertaken.

Attention has often centered on the means to truth, rather than on truth itself or its expression. Epistemological issues have appeared more significant than conceptual issues. Yet much can be said for the view, rightly understood, that "what makes a method of arriving at beliefs *justificatory* is just that the method tends to produce *true* beliefs."[1] In chapters 8–10, we will see that truth, as described in chapters 3–7, is a reasonable goal to strive for; hence any means that lead to this goal and do so effectively are to that extent also reasonable, instrumentally. The goal and its rationality, grounding that of the means, are the concern of this study.

Probing the concept *true* descriptively and normatively, in breadth and in depth, I shall be led to speak about the interplay among words, thoughts, and things; about performatives, avowals, cognitive comparatives, secondary senses, and figurative expressions; about empirical, trans-empirical, moral, and evaluative discourse. I shall say as much about language and its workings as I do about truth; hence the title.

Given the general interest of the topics treated, I have not written solely for specialists. In chapters 1 and 2 epistemologists and philosophers of language may find little that is new to them, but in subsequent chapters they should be better served. To my knowledge, no previous author has proposed or developed the analysis of linguistic truth introduced in chapter 3; or located *true* on the map of language, as in the three chapters that follow; or surveyed the class of cognitive comparatives, as in chapter 6; or formulated and defended the principle of relative similarity put forward in chapter 7 and applied in chapters 11 and 12; or systematically assessed the rule of rational discourse defended in chapters 8–10; or elucidated trans-empirical truth in the manner of chapter 12.

Though these undertakings have an un-Wittgensteinian air, my indebtedness to Wittgenstein is evident from the start. I am also grateful to Richard Blackwell, Arthur McGovern, T. Michael McNulty, and Eddy Zemach for their helpful comments on the whole work; to Francis Dinneen, Kevin Flannery, Thomas Givón, and Richard Swinburne for their comments on parts of it; and to John Muhlenbruch and Jean van Altena for countless stylistic improvements.

PART ONE

THE CONCEPT *TRUE*

Max Black once said that "the success of any philosophical investigation must be judged by the extent that it dispels initial perplexity and permits a perspicuous view of a complex territory."[1] Of perplexity concerning truth there has been plenty, as the opening chapters, especially, will attest. To dispel that perplexity and attain a clearer view of the conceptual terrain from which it arises, I shall not attempt an essential definition of truth in the manner of old; nor shall I substitute the technique of "explication" now widely favored as an alternative to definition.

"The primary difference between explication and definition," a popular text observes, "is that the criterion of accord with intuitive understanding is weakened in the former case."[2] The concept or reality to be clarified may be variegated and complex, but explication, because it does not pretend to capture it entirely or exactly, is less readily shown to be incomplete or inexact. Yet, paradoxically, precision is cited as the procedure's principal virtue. Thus the same text continues:

> In seeking an explication for a term, we wish to capture as much of the meaning as we can characterize precisely. Thus, while we do insist on accord with intuitive understanding, we permit some deviation in the interest of gaining precision. For example, if we wish to explicate "true," we might try as an explicatum the phrase "in correspondence with the facts," even though this explicatum does not capture the meaning of "true" as it is used in, say, "a true Rembrandt" or "a true woman."[3]

From even this brief, introductory account, one can sense why in practice, explication tends to generate more confusion than it dissipates. It is unclear, first of all, why the meaning of "a true Rembrandt" or "a true woman" cannot be spelled out as exactly as the meaning of "a true proposition" or "a true statement." It is unclear why preference should be given to "a true statement" (or the like) rather than to "a true Rembrandt." It is unclear why the result should be proposed as an explication of "true" rather than of "true statement." It is far from evident, finally, why and in what sense a phrase like "in correspondence with the facts" might be termed precise.

None of the thinkers whose views I discuss in part 1 would disagree that in some sense true statements, beliefs, and the like "correspond with the facts"; yet their accounts of the correspondence would diverge notably. Isomorphists would all stress mental contents, but some would articulate them essentialistically, others empirically, and others atomistically. John Austin would cite linguistic conventions. Peter Strawson would reject a descriptive account of *true* in favor of a performative interpretation. Even William James would acknowledge that true ideas "correspond with the facts," although he would equate their correspondence with their utility.[4] A formula that admits such diversity is hardly precise. Nor does it illuminate this tangle of conflicting viewpoints or permit one to decide among them.

The like holds for Alfred Tarski's famed explication of truth and for Donald Davidson's derivative account, both of which I assess at the end of the book. Here, at the start, I merely wish to suggest in preliminary fashion why my approach will be less formal and less theoretical than some may consider desirable, and why, in place of succinct, precise-sounding theories or explications, I have opted instead for the virtues of perspicuous representation. A summarizing formula may prove helpful now and then; but my principal aim in this first part is to achieve an overview of the large and complex domain—of the facts, theories, and varied word uses—that has engendered such confusion concerning the concept *true*.

My procedure will therefore resemble one favored in biology. "The biological explanation of a phenomenon," writes Agnes Arber, "is the discovery of its own intrinsic place in a nexus of relations, extending indefinitely in all directions. To explain it is to see it simultaneously in its full individuality (as a whole in itself), and in its subordinate position (as one element in a larger whole)."[5] Conceptual and theoretical phenomena can be illumined in like fashion, intrinsically and extrinsically. Thus, rather than explicate or define the concept *true*, I shall explore its inner structure, situate it on the larger map of language, and relate my account to the accounts of others, dialectically.

Chapter 1 sketches a long-dominant viewpoint which lines up words, thoughts, and things in parallel and relies on mental contents of various kinds to explain the reference, meaning, and truth of both speech and thought. Chapter 2 indicates some principal problems with this viewpoint. Chapters 3 and 4 offer solutions to these problems, first by detecting in the agreement of word uses the key to linguistic truth, then by explaining mental truth in terms of linguistic truth, rather than the other way around. The last part of chapter 4 and all of chapters 5 and 6 further clarify the concept *true*, internally and externally, by relating it to other expressions with secondary senses, to other asymmetrical concepts which, like *true*, function both descriptively and nondescriptively, and to the large class of descriptive expressions labeled *cognitive comparatives*.

CHAPTER 1

THE ISOMORPHIC TRADITION

Thought, language, now appear to us as the unique correlate, picture, of the world. These concepts: proposition, language, thought, world, stand in line one behind the other, each equivalent to each.[1]

Wittgenstein's own early theory, which he here had in mind, and other theories back through the centuries have played innumerable variations on the same central theme: words, thoughts, and things are seen not just as being causally related to one another, but as running parallel. One way or another, words are paired with thoughts, and thoughts with things.

In this traditional conception, the correlated items need not resemble one another; for instance, words need not resemble the ideas they express or the realities they thereby denote. Nor does the ordering of words always resemble that of thoughts, or the ordering of thoughts that of things; grammar may be deceptive and thoughts may err. Assertions and judgments, depicting things, may depict them as they are not. Still, if there is to be any depicting at all, accurate or inaccurate, there must be matching. Hence, an apt name for this conception and for the state of affairs it assumes is *isomorphism*, not *correspondence*, for the latter usually signifies something more than mere matching.[2]

To pinpoint this notion of isomorphism, as distinct from resemblance, consider, for example, the relationship between the notes on a sheet of music and the keys struck by a pianist playing the music. To each mark on the sheet, with its specific location (higher or lower, on this line or that), there corresponds a specific ivory key, which is struck by the pianist's finger; a specific string, which is set vibrating; a specific vibration, excited in the air; and a specific sensation, registered in the hearer. Yet the mark does not resemble the ivory key, nor the key the string, the string the vibration, the vibration the consequent sensation, or the sensation the original mark on the paper. What we observe instead is perfect correlation: this mark paired with this key, this string, this vibration, and this sensation; another mark with another key, string, vibration, and sensation; and so on—one-to-one matching.

So it is for speech and thought, as many have conceived them: with one reality, one thought or word is paired; with another reality, another thought or word; and so forth. Clement of Alexandria, for example, gave classic expression to such a view when he wrote, "In language three things should be distinguished: first of all names, that are essentially symbols of concepts and, consequently, of objects. Second, concepts, which are images and impressions of objects. . . . Third, objects, which impress the concepts in our minds."[3] In more elaborate versions of isomorphism, the lineup may rival the comparison just made using mark, key, string, vibration, and sensation. Thus a specific reality may be seen as being correlated with a specific idea, and the idea with an inner word, and the inner word with a spoken word, and the spoken word with a written word.

In this tradition as a whole, the correlations between verbal signs and mental signs and between mental signs and things serve as preconditions for verbal or mental truth. Truth depends on meanings, and meanings are isomorphic. The nature of this dependence and of the distinction between truth and mere matching can be suggested in first approximation (ignoring for a moment the details of specific theories) by means of the musical illustration given above. For typical isomorphists, truth in speech or thought resembles correctness in playing. If a score has F after C and the pianist's fingers strike F after C, the playing is correct; otherwise it is not. If the score joins the two notes in a chord and the pianist plays them together as a chord, again, the playing is correct. And so forth. One combination corresponds with the other, or it does not. There could be no correspondence, however, without the correlations. If this note on the musical score were not the mark for that specific key (the note C for the key C), and this other note for that other key (F for F), there would be neither correctness nor incorrectness—or any such practice as playing the music.

Similarly, isomorphists suppose, mental or sensible signs would have no meaning, nor would there be any such activity as speaking or writing, were the signs not somehow correlated with particular thoughts or things. If, in addition, the arrangement of the signs agrees with that of their correlates, then truth is achieved. Thought or speech joins what reality joins or separates what it separates or otherwise orders things as they are ordered in fact.[4] In any case, though, there must be matching; for without that, there can be neither meaning nor communication. Thus the isomorphic structure, present in falsehood as well as in truth, is broader than truth and more fundamental.

On this basic common theme many variations have been played. Platonic or neo-Platonic versions, for example, matched words with "forms" recollected from a former life or intuited in the present one. Aristotelian variants hooked up words with concepts, or intellectual representations, and concepts, in turn, with essences, natures, and properties. Empiricist theories replaced concepts with images and essences with concrete particulars in the world. Wittgenstein's early philosophy had recourse to atomic names, linked by thought to atomic objects. These are the major variants which I shall now sketch.

To my knowledge, the family resemblance among various isomorphist theories has not been fully charted; so a full-scale mapping of the phenomenon might be desirable. However, in this chapter I shall aim not at completeness or fine-grained analysis, but at perspicuous representation by means of key examples chronologically arranged. At each step in the historical sequence I shall start with truth as correspondence, as seen by that author or school; then indicate the dependence of truth, so conceived, on a broader, isomorphic scheme of language, thought, and things; and then spell out briefly how and to what extent for that conception "language, thought, world, stand in line one behind the other, each equivalent to each." An overview of the series will follow, then refinements of the initial accounts, so as to permit a realistic assessment of this viewpoint.

Essentialist Versions

The dialogues of Plato convey a conception of truth which profoundly influenced subsequent treatments. The details are not clear, and no single work gives the whole picture, but the general impression that emerges is the following. Whether in thought ("the inward dialogue carried on by the mind with itself without spoken sound") or in speech ("the stream which flows from the mind through the lips"), a judgment requires a verb (for example, "sits") to indicate an action, and a name (for example, "Theaetetus") to indicate its agent. The joining of name and verb results in truth or falsehood. For example, "Theaetetus sits" may state a truth, whereas "Theaetetus flies" clearly states a falsehood.[5] Just how and why the first combination results in truth, when it does, and the second in a falsehood, Plato does not spell out. But his doctrine of subsistent forms, one for each general term, suggests that each statement asserts a relation between Theaetetus's current action and a form (for example, sitting or flying)—a relation of participation, say—and that when the relation obtains, the statement is true, and when it does not, the statement is false. "The statement, therefore, has a meaning, but the statement as a whole does not correspond with the fact as a whole."[6]

Although Aristotle conceived the correlates of universal terms rather differently from Plato and replaced subsistent forms with immanent natures or essences, his account of truth was basically similar. A judgment is true, he explained, if the one who makes the judgment is related to things in a way which corresponds to them, and is false if he or she is related to things in a way which is contrary to them. "He who thinks the separated to be separated and the combined to be combined has the truth, while he whose thought is in a state contrary to that of the objects is in error."[7]

Aquinas took much the same tack. "Properly speaking," he said, "truth is in the intellect in its function of affirming and denying one reality of another; and not in sense, nor in the intellect knowing the meaning."[8] The judgment "Socrates sits" represents Socrates and sitting with equal fidelity, whether the judgment and its verbal expression are true or false; its truth or falsehood depends on whether the two things—Socrates and sitting—are in fact conjoined, as asserted and thought—that is, on whether Socrates is in fact sitting.[9]

In Locke, some centuries later, the illustrations differ, but not the basic viewpoint.

> The mind, either by perceiving, or supposing, the agreement or disagreement of any of its ideas, does tacitly within itself put them into a kind of proposition affirmative or negative; which I have endeavoured to express by the terms putting together and separating. . . . When ideas are so put together, or separated in the mind, as they or the things they stand for do agree or not, that is, as I may call it, *mental truth*. But *truth of words* is something more; and that is the affirming or denying of words one of another, as the ideas they stand for agree or disagree.[10]

Here the underlying isomorphism is quite explicit: the words "stand for" ideas, and the ideas "stand for" things; and without these correlations there could be neither truth nor falsehood, in either thought or verbal expression. Something similar is evidently true for Aquinas, Aristotle, and Plato. There can be no affirming or denying, no joining or disjoining, of Socrates' sitting or Theaetetus's flying or the like, without verbal or mental signs for the people and the actions. It is these correlations that permit judgments and assertions to be false as well as true. Even though the judgment should err in regard to Socrates' sitting, one sign is the sign for him, and the other the sign for sitting; even if the corresponding statement is false, *Socrates* is the name for that person, and *sitting* the name for that action or position. Hence the statement is meaningful, thanks to its parts; but their conjunction does not mirror reality.

For Plato, Aristotle, Aquinas, and Locke, the typical correlate in reality for a general term or general idea is the sort of thing called a *universal.* But this umbrella term conceals a well-known divergence. For Plato and his successors the extra-mental correlate is one in number, as well as in kind; whereas for Aristotle and his followers, including Aquinas and Locke, it is one in kind, but many in number. For the latter, billions of human essences dot the globe, for example, perfectly similar in each person; whereas for Plato and Platonists, there is but one humanity, as there is but one justice, one beauty, one goodness—eternal and unchanging—mirrored more or less imperfectly in unstable beings like ourselves.

"Plato seems to have been mistaken in this matter," wrote Aquinas,

> since, holding that all knowledge is had by means of a certain similarity, he believed that the form of the thing known must be in the knower just as it is in the thing known. But the form of the thing intellectually known is, he realized, present in the intellect universally, and immaterially, and unchangeably. . . . So he supposed that things which are known intellectually must exist in the same way, namely immaterially and unchangeably. But this is not necessary; for even in the sensible realm we see that a form is present differently in one sensible thing than in another, for instance when whiteness is more intense in one thing, less intense in another, and when whiteness is joined with sweetness in one thing and not in another.[11]

It is the intellect that singles out each form, abstractively, by means of an immaterial likeness.[12] In the resultant isomorphic matching, each general term has its own representation, and each representation its extra-mental correlate. Images may be many and various, as whites and persons are; but the concept *human* or the concept *white* is invariant, as is its correlate in reality, present in the various instances.

Locke thought no differently. "Ideas become general," he wrote, "by separating from them the circumstances of time and place, and any other ideas that may determine them to this or that particular existence. By this way of abstraction they are made capable of representing more individuals than one; each of which having in it a conformity to that abstract idea, is (as we call it) of that sort."[13] "That then which general words signify is a *sort* of things; and each of them does that, by being a sign of an abstract idea in the mind, to which idea, as things existing are found to agree, so they come to be ranked under that name, or, which is all one, be of that sort."[14] Once again, words, ideas, and realities run parallel.

It is not immediately clear, however, whether the ideas parallel the words in each linguistic act, or whether the mind is simply stocked with ideas from past abstractions, which it recalls when necessary, to guide or validate the words. In which of these two senses are words signs "of an abstract idea in the mind"? Though essentialists have seldom attended to the analysis of individual speech acts, the view that they typically hold is clear enough. Speakers, they would say, are not robots. They think when they talk and think what they say, before or while they say it. "What we call speech," wrote Aquinas, "is simply the manifestation of an interior word, which we mentally conceive."[15] "Because it is the nature of our intelligence to receive from the senses, sensible signs are used to express our interior concepts, and by these signs we manifest our heart's thoughts."[16] "Some," it is true, notes Locke, "not only children but men, speak several words no otherwise than parrots do, only because they have learned them, and have been accustomed to those sounds. But so far as words are of use and signification, so far is there a constant connexion between the sound and the idea, and a designation that the one stands for the other; without which application of them, they are nothing but so much insignificant noise."[17]

The "constant connexion between the sound and the idea" extends, ideally, to the recipient as well. Locke speaks for the same strong tradition when he writes: "The chief end of language in communication being to be understood, words serve not well for that end, neither in civil nor philosophical discourse, when any word does not excite in the hearer the same idea which it stands for in the mind of the speaker."[18] Such a transfer is normal, he believes, at least in the case of simpler words. Thus, "to slide, roll, tumble, walk, creep, run, dance, leap, skip, and abundance of others that might be named, are words which are no sooner heard but every one who understands English has presently in his mind distinct ideas, which are all but the different modifications of motion."[19] It is as though the speaker hears a note in his mind and strikes the right key, and the recipient now hears the same note in his mind. Insofar as speech succeeds, the parallel is perfect. Item matches item, in speaker, speech, and hearer.

This transpersonal isomorphism obtains whether the message conveyed is right or wrong, truthful or mendacious. It is the ordering of the items that makes the difference between truth and falsehood, veracity and mendacity. Thus Locke, faithful spokesman for the tradition, itemizes the constituents of a lie as follows: "(1) Articulate sounds. (2) Certain ideas in the mind of the speaker. (3) Those words the signs of those ideas. (4) Those signs put together, by affirmation or negation, otherwise than the ideas they stand for are in the mind of the speaker."[20] Here too, as in the preceding analysis of falsehood, but now in the relation between ideas and words, rather than ideas and realities, isomorphism holds, though correspondence fails. It has to. How, in either case, error or mendacity, could correspondence fail if there were no items—no correlated items—to compare?

Empiricist Versions

With Bishop Berkeley's critique of abstract general ideas[21] and the growing prevalence of similar thinking, isomorphist conceptions did not vanish from the scene but tended to substitute concrete images for abstract ideas.

Bertrand Russell, for example, suggested that in certain cases we can give the following very simple account of correspondence:

> We can say that true propositions actually resemble their objectives [the realities they describe] in a way in which false propositions do not. But for this purpose it is necessary to revert to image-propositions instead of word-propositions. Let us take again the illustration of a memory-image of a familiar room, and let us suppose that in the image the window is to the left of the door. If in fact the window is to the left of the door, there is a correspondence between the image and the objective; there is the same relation between the window and the door as between the images of them.[22]

From this simple illustration, "the general nature of the formal correspondence which makes truth or falsehood can be seen":

> The *phrase* "A is to the left of B" means the image-proposition, and is true when this is true, false when this is false; on the other hand, the phrase "A is not to the left of B" is true when the image-proposition is false, and false when it is true. Thus for this simplest case we have obtained a formal definition of truth and falsehood, both for image-propositions and for word-propositions. It is easy to see that the same *kind* of definition can be extended to more complicated cases.[23]

In this account, as in the preceding one, isomorphism is clearly requisite for such correspondence or lack thereof. Truth and falsehood build on meaning, and meaning is conceived isomorphically. "A word-proposition, apart from niceties, 'means' the corresponding image-proposition, and an image-proposition has an objective reference dependent upon the meanings of its constituent images."[24] Thus the door and the window, in Russell's example, cannot be rightly or wrongly ordered in the imagination unless there is an image for the door and another for the window; and these images then correlate with words.

Many suppose, as Wittgenstein observed, that this correlation occurs at the very moment of speech, that is, "that using a sentence involves imagining something for every word."[25] St. Augustine, despite his Platonism, illustrates the tendency. What an unnoticed marvel it is, he exclaimed, that the things we have experienced—the high mountains, the great rivers, the vastness of sea and ocean, the movements of the stars—are present in our minds when we talk about them, just as they are outside the mind ("with the same vast spaces between them"). Were they not thus present, he believed, we could not speak of them.[26] Indeed, whether we speak of remembered realities or of things never experienced, we must have images in our minds to guide our choice of words.

> I mention a stone or the sun, when the things themselves are not present to my senses, yet images of the things are present in my memory. I mention bodily pain, which is not present when I am not in pain; yet unless there were some image of it in my memory, I should not know what to say of it or how to differentiate it in

thought from pleasure. I name bodily health, when I am in bodily health, and the thing itself is present in me; all the same, unless there were some image of it in my memory, I could not possibly recall what the sound of the name signified; nor would sick people know what was meant by the word health, in the absence of the thing itself from the body, unless some image were preserved by the power of memory.[27]

Russell acknowledged that sheer habit may sometimes take the place of images. A child recounting an incident may, for instance,

only have the habit of the appropriate words, as in the case of a poem which we know by heart though we cannot remember learning it. And the hearer also may only pay attention to the words, and not call up any corresponding picture. But it is nevertheless the possibility of a memory-image in the child and an imagination-image in the hearer that makes the essence of the 'meaning' of the words. In so far as this is absent, the words are mere counters, capable of meaning, but not at the moment possessing it.[28]

An Atomist Version

In other writings, Russell envisaged direct matching of words and things, without the intermediary of images. In the case of simpler propositions, he suggested, the "objective" (that is, the reality which would verify a proposition) can be obtained by replacing each word by what it means.

For example, if the proposition is "Socrates precedes Plato," the objective which verifies it results from replacing the word "Socrates" by Socrates, the word "Plato" by Plato, and the word "precedes" by the relation of preceding between Socrates and Plato. If the result of this process is a fact, the proposition is true; if not, it is false. When our proposition is "Socrates does not precede Plato," the conditions of truth and falsehood are exactly reversed. More complicated propositions can be dealt with on the same lines.[29]

With this quotation from Russell, we enter the perspective of Wittgenstein's *Tractatus Logico-Philosophicus*, where "one name stands for one thing, another for another thing, and they are combined with one another. In this way the whole group—like a *tableau vivant*—presents a state of affairs" (4.0311).[30] Here too, if we replaced each name by its referent and each relation of names by its correlative relation (whether spatial, temporal, or other), and if the result then agreed, or coincided, with reality, the proposition would be true; if not, it would be false.

At the level of "elementary" propositions, composed (Wittgenstein supposed) of the simplest possible names for the simplest objects, it is especially obvious that the propositional sign is a picture, a sort of verbal blueprint, of what it signifies. However, according to the *Tractatus*, the truth of complex, everyday propositions depends entirely on the truth of such elementary propositions (5.3), so that in the final analysis all truth or falsehood receives the same explication. Whether in a *tableau vivant,* a mental representation, or a written or spoken proposition, the fact that the elements of a picture are related to one another in a determinate way represents that things are related to one another in a determinate way (2.15). And the agreement or disagreement of the pictured relationship with the real one constitutes the picture's truth or falsity. "In order to tell whether a picture is true or false we must compare it with reality" (2.223).

Here again, as with piano playing or the conjunction of concepts or the combination of images, such comparison and such truth or falsity presuppose a matching of elements. How, we might wonder, can a picture be a picture of *reality,* yet fail to portray things as they *really* are? What is the difference between a false picture and a picture of nothing, between a false proposition and a fable? The *Tractatus* answer, simply put, is that the fable does not name real things, whereas a statement about the real world does. A proposition is a *picture* of reality by virtue of the way its elements are arranged, its logical form; it is a picture of *reality* by virtue of its names (2.1– 2.1515).[31] Even when a proposition corresponds to no existing state of affairs, its names still have reference. For the atomic referents of atomic names are simple and indestructible. Thus "the possibility of propositions is based on the principle that objects have signs as their representatives" (4.0312).

It is conceivable, and sometimes desirable, that genuine, atomic names should appear in the spoken or written expression of a proposition, "in such a way that elements of the propositional sign correspond to the objects of the thought" (3.2)—that is, to the objects thought designates. But in any case, such thinking-out is necessary for the propositional sign to have meaning. "We use the perceptible sign of a proposition (spoken or written, etc.) as a projection of a possible situation. The method of projection is to think out the sense of the proposition" (3.11). When, for example, we say that a book is lying on a table or that a table is a yard long, what we *mean* is quite determinate.[32] At the very moment of utterance, "proposition, language, thought, world, stand in line one behind the other, each equivalent to each."

Like many exponents of the two previous points of view—the essentialist and the empiricist—Wittgenstein was inclined to extend his account beyond statements and their contents to all forms of thought. This resulted in a still broader picture theory, which I have elsewhere described as follows:

> Just as a command says that *you,* and no other, should close *this* door, and no other, foreshadowing the whole thing through its logical form and naming names, so too in expectation the picture is already there before the event. And "the wish or will to do something is of the same sort as expecting, believing, and so on" (Man. 108, 250). "It is as though the thought were a shadow of the event"

(Man. 108, 230). The names show *where* to look, the form shows *what* to look for, and it thereby becomes possible to determine whether an assertion is verified, a command obeyed, an expectation met, a wish fulfilled. If the indestructible objects are lined up as represented by their names within the assertion, command, expectation, or wish, then the answer is affirmative, there is correspondence; otherwise not. Such is the crucial role required of names in a consistent extension of the picture theory; they solve the problem of falsehood, which, in a system that puts a proposition at the heart of every linguistic and psychological act and requires of every proposition that it be capable of falsehood, is all-pervasive.[33]

Overview

The three viewpoints just sketched differ so significantly that their basic affinity may easily escape notice, and often has. Yet in all three:

1. Utterances receive their meaning from mental contents (concepts, images, or atomic names, in judgments, thoughts, or mental projections) and are true if and only if these are true.
2. The truth of the mental contents consists in their correspondence with reality.
3. More precisely, it consists in agreement between the ordering of the contents' constitutive elements (the concepts, images, or atomic names) and the ordering of the realities with which they correlate (the essences, things, or atomic objects).
4. The correspondence therefore presupposes and requires the correlations.
5. Both the matching and the ordering typically accompany the words to which they impart meaning and truth. Speakers think what they say as they say it—essentialistically, empirically, or atomically—and hearers duplicate the process.

None of this agreement can be taken for granted. Each of these five points has been contested, and some accounts of meaning and truth deny all five.

The three isomorphist positions differ principally in their conceptions of the mental contents and of their correlates. For essentialists, general, abstract concepts correlate with essences, which they mirror. For empiricists, concrete images correlate with concrete particulars. For atomists like Wittgenstein, atomic names in the mind (or equivalent mental hookups pinpointing referents) correlate with atomic objects. Such are the typical, most basic constituents of thought in each account.

From this overview of similarities and dissimilarities and from the sketches it summarizes, it is possible to form an initial estimate of both the importance and the validity of the isomorphic viewpoint. However, before undertaking such an appraisal, in chapter 2, I should first note several respects in which my sample résumés simplify the complexity of isomorphic thinking:

1. Other versions—some fuller, some skimpier—have not been mentioned. (Extensive isomorphism, but of a different kind, is found, for example, in William James's *The Principles of Psychology*, where he links words not with images or concepts, but with characteristic "feelings."[34])

2. Accounts like those cited may fit within a broader, more varied treatment. (For example, Aquinas, while treating the mind's agreement with reality as the prime notion of truth,[35] speaks also of the "truth" of the things with which the mind conforms and of the "truth" of effects which reveal the things' truth to us.[36])

3. The three versions cited vary considerably from author to author. (Some essentialists, for example, add extra entities outside the mind or within it or in language, over and above those we have noted. The correlations multiply. Thus Locke, like many, distinguished between two kinds of essence, one "nominal", the other "real."[37] Aquinas introduced an "interior word," on which the outer word is modeled, between the concept, or "word of the heart," and the spoken word.[38] Aristotle, distinguishing between the spoken word and the written word and between one language and another, asserted still fuller parallelism: "Spoken words are the symbols of mental experience and written words are the symbols of spoken words. Just as all men have not the same writing, so all men have not the same speech sounds, but the mental experiences, which these directly symbolize, are the same for all, as also are those things of which our experiences are the images."[39] Isomorphism is thus transcultural and intercultural.)

4. A standard conception—essentialist, empiricist, or atomist—is not applied indiscriminately across the board. No thinker of any stature has extended his parallelistic account to cover all words without exception. (Augustine, for example, argued in *De Magistro* that *nihil* does not resemble other words, since it has no reference. Aquinas distinguished equivocal terms from univocal terms, and analogous terms from both. Locke noted that, "besides words which are names of ideas in the mind, there are a great many others that are made use of to signify the *connexion* that the mind gives to ideas, or to propositions, one with another."[40] In the *Tractatus*, Wittgenstein insisted that whatever signs—logical constants like "or" and "not" or Ts and Fs in truth tables—were used to build up compound propositions from elementary ones, they would not "stand proxy" for logical objects; they would not function in the same way as the other signs, the names.[41])

5. Some isomorphists mix their accounts. (It has already been noted, for instance, that Augustine the neo-Platonist gave a non-Platonic account of thought and speech when they concerned mountains, waves, stars, and the like. Had the categories been Platonic favorites like beauty, goodness, unity, and truth, his analysis would have followed a different bent.)

This chapter's sketches, then, are just that—sketches. These thumbnail accounts of the essentialist, empiricist, and atomist viewpoints do not cite all versions of isomorphism or fill in details or mention all variations, exceptions, and combinations. Nevertheless, they retain their utility. A quotation from G. E. Moore illustrates why.

"Questions as to the nature of general ideas," Moore observed,

> have . . . played an immensely large part in philosophy. There are some philosophers who say that there are no such things at all: that general ideas are pure fictions like chimaeras or griffins. . . . But a majority of philosophers would, I think, say that there are such things; and *if* there are, then, I think there is no doubt that they are one of the most important kinds of things in the Universe. *If* there are any at all, there are tremendous numbers of them, and we are all constantly thinking and talking of them.[42]

There speaks the true isomorphist. *If* there are "general ideas," as Platonists, Aristotelians, and others have believed; *if* there are image-propositions, as Russell and so many have supposed; *if* there are atomic names for atomic objects, as logical atomists have alleged; then, in each case, most proponents of the view would agree, there are tremendous numbers of them, and they dominate our thinking. The existence of exceptions, variations, amplifications, fluctuations, and uncertainties detracts little from the force and importance of the model.

CHAPTER 2

CRITIQUE OF ISOMORPHISM

For the most part, the isomorphic view of speech, thought, and reality is not based on argument but is taken for granted.[1] Various pre-reflective influences powerfully suggest it. For example, the sameness of the appearance of single words on various occasions suggests a similar sameness in their meanings. Or the singular form of abstract nouns suggests a single referent (knowledge is one thing, beauty is one thing, and so forth). Or the association of proper names with single, constant referents (Churchill, Chicago, the Taj Mahal) serves as an implicit model and suggests a similar function for general names: no doubt they too pick out some one entity—if not a single concrete referent, then a single essence or nature common to the various things called by the common name. After all, do not all horses, say, have at least this in common, that they are horses? And are not all books books, all people people, all laws laws? Again, feeling in our bones—correctly—that truth is some sort of correspondence, we assume without question that where there is correspondence, there must be matching. How could a photo, model, or map correctly or incorrectly portray the way things stand in reality unless it represented the things individually and arranged them in this way or that? And isn't it obvious that in our imaginings we often do so picture things—a sofa here, a table there, a lampstand in the corner?

Possibly, therefore, some readers experienced a certain puzzlement in the preceding chapter as I traced the various versions of isomorphism. The recital may have seemed comparable to recounting in detail, century by century, the strange and striking conviction that water is requisite for most forms of life, that the sun affects the seasons, or that humans have their origin in sexual intercourse. Why all the fuss? Isomorphic theories may have erred in details, as theories of life, the seasons, and procreation have; but surely the general conception is correct.

To the contrary, in all its versions, isomorphic thinking is seriously misleading. That is one reason why it deserves critical attention. Another is its prominence in Western thought. A third is the continuing influence of the same forces that propagated it in the past. A fourth motive, finally, for undertaking a somewhat detailed critique is the great significance of such an all-embracing viewpoint. Typically, the isomorphic mind-set shapes a person's conception of speech as a whole, of thought as a whole, and of everything and anything thought of or spoken of. Furthermore, since speech and thought are among the things we speak and think about, they get doubly cast in the isomorphic mold: as verbal and mental correlates of reality, and as realities correlated with. Indeed, the influence of such an optic is even more pervasive: it determines not only what views we take of things, but also what kinds of questions we ask about them, what knowledge we value, what types of inquiry we consider feasible and important. Accordingly, the web it weaves is so vast, so intricate, and so tight that there seems no escaping it. Tug on a single strand, and half a dozen others hold it fast, and with it the whole conception.

Consider, for example, the influential, widely held version that populates the mind with universal concepts and the universe with corresponding essences. "Any use of language," declares David Ross,

> involves the recognition, either conscious or unconscious, of the fact that there are such entities; for every word used, except proper names—every abstract noun, every general noun, every adjective, every verb, even every pronoun and every preposition—is a name for something of which there are or may be instances. The first step towards the conscious recognition of this class of entities was, if we may believe Aristotle, taken by Socrates when he concentrated on the search for definitions; to ask for the meaning of a general word was a step from the mere use of such a word towards the recognition of universals as a distinct class of entities.[2]

Rather, I would say, the Socratic inquiry reflected a conception already formed, unreflectively, and now operative at every turn: determining this specific form of query, requiring a specific sort of answer. When, for instance, in Plato's dialogues Socrates asks what knowledge is and Theaetetus cites various kinds of knowledge, or when he asks what piety is and Euthyphro mentions various instances of piety, Socrates brushes these answers aside.[3] He did not ask for many things, he insists, but for a single thing: knowledge, or piety. Surely the singular term designates some single entity.[4] Surely word, thought, and thing are lined up one to one.

The subtle power of essentialist presuppositions appears with equal clarity in the passage from G. E. Moore quoted at the end of chapter 1. Why did Moore suppose that if there are *any* "general ideas" (conceived in the essentialist manner), then there must be a huge number? How, despite his acknowledged ignorance of their exact nature, could he so readily pass from "any at all" to "tremendous numbers of them"? Well, if some general terms have such meanings, will not all? For are they not all *general terms?* Do they not all belong to a single class and merit the single label "general term"? Thus, in the very act of assessing isomorphism, Moore revealed his innately isomorphic mind-set. Little wonder that he sided with the essentialists and held that there are indeed multitudes of general ideas, and that they are in fact "one of the most important kinds of things in the Universe."

Such illustrations attest the prevalence, importance, and power of isomorphic thinking.[5] If it is mistaken, the error is momentous. If it requires correction, the remedy will prove difficult. The schematic critique that follows may not succeed in weaning convinced isomorphists from their views. It may, however, raise doubts in their minds by revealing unnoted difficulties, and may thereby prepare acceptance of the alternative viewpoint presented in the following chapters. In addition, both for isomorphists and for nonisomorphists, this chapter's negative comments will complement the positive account to come. Truth set against error stands out more sharply, as does white from black. And to say how things *are* is only half the story; it is equally instructive to make clear how things *are not.*

A thorough critique of all varieties of isomorphism, however, is beyond my present intentions. To simplify matters, I shall note only some principal objections to the major variants sketched in chapter 1. After indicating some fairly obvious difficulties for the empiricist form of isomorphism, I shall pass to the essentialist version, which resolves some of the difficulties, then to the atomist formulation, which enjoys certain advantages over both the others. When atomism in turn proves hopelessly deficient, no isomorphic options will remain, and it will be clear that solutions must be sought elsewhere.

Empiricist Versions

"The popular notion," wrote William James,

> is that a true idea must copy its reality. Like other popular views, this one follows the analogy of the most usual experience. Our true ideas of sensible things do indeed copy them. Shut your eyes and think of yonder clock on the wall, and you get just such a true picture or copy of its dial. But your idea of its "works" (unless you are a clock-maker) is much less of a copy, yet it passes muster, for it in no way clashes with the reality. Even tho it should shrink to the mere word "works," that word still serves you truly; and when you speak of the "time-keeping function" of the clock, or of its spring's "elasticity," it is hard to see exactly what your ideas can copy.[6]

As a critique of correspondence through *images,* James's remarks seem basically valid. A great many things of which we speak we do not imagine as we utter the words; a great many we could not imagine as we utter the words; and many we could not imagine even if we fell silent and gave the task our undivided attention. We could not imagine works we mention but have never seen. We could not mentally portray their resembling the works in thousands of other watches, their having been made in Switzerland or marketed in the United States, their being more expensive or efficient than the works in rival brands, and so forth. Such events or states of affairs we readily state but could not possibly imagine in full detail, as correspondence would require. At best the bits and pieces that drifted through our minds would resemble the illustrations in a book: possible, but hardly necessary or supplied for every word.[7]

If we pass from simple, declarative assertions to negative, disjunctive, or hypothetical statements, the difficulties for an imagistic account of truth become still more evident. How is it possible to *imagine* works *not* being made in Switzerland, or being made in Switzerland *or* in the United States? How is it possible to imagine that *if* works are made in Switzerland, they are more expensive, or that *when* they are made in Switzerland, *then* they are more reliable? Does each such word—*not, or, if, when, then, still, and, but, therefore*—have its own special image? What of modal or deontic terms (*ought, should, can, may, must*)? What about *fortunate, helpful, gratuitous, likely, coincidental,* and countless other expressions?

When Augustine asserted the need for images (of mountains, waves, pains, and so on) in order to know what we are talking about and to use words correctly, the examples he cited made his claim sound somewhat plausible. But suppose, instead, that we wish to speak about patents or marketing or Switzerland. What images might come to mind to represent such things, and how might they guide us? What inner picture might we form, for instance, of Switzerland? We could not represent so much as a single canton or a single city. And even if the image of some single street, say, stood proxy for the country as a whole, how would that image guide our choice of words? What expression would it instruct us to use: "street"? "narrow street"? "northward view"? "photo by Peterson"? "night-time exposure"? "the old quarter"? "Geneva"? "European city"? "Switzerland"? How, for that matter, could a mere image dictate any phrase whatever? How could we pass from the nonverbal picture to words?

The same difficulty arises in even the simplest examples. It is often supposed that if I see a flower and correctly call it blue, a supplementary image, in addition to that of the flower, must enable me to pick the correct color predicate. How else, it is argued, would I know what word to employ? But the answer is simple. If I don't know the name of the blue before my eyes, how will a murky specimen in my imagination enlighten me? How will

I know *its* name? (Does the imagined blue, unlike the seen blue, come with a label attached: "Call this and like shades 'blue' "?) Images do not and cannot work in the manner often supposed.[8]

A related difficulty is the problem of invariance. It can hardly be supposed that identical images, unvarying from person to person and from occasion to occasion, accompany our words, as isomorphic matching would require.[9] To grasp the gravity of the problem, consider the account offered by an ardent advocate of images. According to Titchener, the general idea of triangularity, when closely examined, turns out to be "a flashy thing, come and gone from moment to moment; it hints 2 or 3 red angles, with the red lines deepening into black, seen on a dark green ground. It is not there long enough for me to say whether the angles join to form the complete figure or even whether all 3 of the necessary angles are given."[10] It is highly dubious whether Titchener himself consistently had this identical image every time he uttered or heard the word *triangularity*, and still more evident that people in general do not.

These criticisms go beyond James's. For he did not consider the common conviction I have just critiqued, that there must be images, in large numbers, guiding our speech. Nor did he (in the work cited) assess the idea that images correlate one to one with words. He attended only to the notion that images might correspond with what we describe and might thereby reveal the nature of truth. And even within this narrow focus, he was too kind to the opposition. The empiricist view of truth fails more completely than he realized.

First of all, James conceded too readily that an *accurate* image or copy would be *true*. We do not generally call images *true*, any more than we call photos, portraits, or other pictures true. We call them "accurate," "faithful," "clear," perhaps even "true to life." And if someone points to a portrait and says, "That's an excellent likeness," we may call this statement true or false. But rarely if ever do we say, "The photo was true," "Her portrait was true," "Michelangelo's statue was false," or the like. For this difference, which James ignored, there are important reasons. It is significant, for instance, that statements consist of words, whereas pictures do not, and that the words are used to make assertions, whereas pictures or images typically are not.

Second, not even an image of a clock forms a replica of the clock; nor does an image of the dial show the whole dial, four-dimensionally (back and front, inside and out, past and present). This may seem a trivial point, but it is not. For one thing, it shows that though images may serve as signs of things, they do not copy them. But words, too, are signs. So why do we need a second set of signs to accompany our words?[11] Must every word an actor speaks be first whispered by a prompter? Furthermore, even if our words were amply supplied with inner illustrations, the illustrations would never fill out the full sense of the words. Nor, therefore, would the illustrations' correspondence with reality establish the truth of the words.

Consider the same illustration as before. In order for the statement "The clock just struck the hour" to be true, there must, for instance, be a *clock* of which it is true, and not a mere clock appearance: there must be a front and a back and sides and works and chimes and a past as well as a present—far more, that is, than appears in even the most faithful representation of some one side or part at some one instant. Thus the representation might be accurate as far as it goes, but the statement might nonetheless be false. (For example, the image might depict exactly the clock casing, yet the casing might be empty. And in that case it would be false that a *clock* struck the hour, as alleged.) But if images account, at best, for so little of the correspondence that verifies a statement, perhaps they are quite superfluous. Perhaps what covers the missing sides and parts and instants, regardless of what some image happens to depict, is what accounts for the total correspondence that makes a statement true. Such, as we shall see in the next chapter, is in fact the case.

Third, even with regard to the aspects or parts that fall within our vision, James was too lenient; he too readily assumed that our ideas of sensible objects "do indeed copy them," if only partially. Philosophical debate from Descartes via Berkeley and Kant to the present has centered on this very question, and it has not been kind to the naive assumption expressed by James. If you and I see the clock face from different angles, so that its appearance differs—elliptical for you, circular for me—does the clock then have both shapes? If I see it from close up and you from far away, so that the images differ—large for me, small for you—is the clock then both sizes? Or is there some privileged position at which the apparent size and shape correspond to the real size and shape—despite the fact that one term of the comparison is a physical object and the other is not? What might it *mean* to say that the clock image is the same size as the clock? Can the image be measured in feet or inches?

Finally, given the fuzzy incompleteness of most images, the problem of reference also proves perplexing. What makes my clock image the image of this particular clock, the one spoken of, the one that chimed the hour? Is the image such a perfect representation, down to the knots in the wood and the scratches on the varnish, that it picks out this and this alone as the clock in question, from among all those produced by the same manufacturer? But even if the image were that detailed, why might it not be an *inexact* image of some *other* clock? If perfect similarity determined reference, how could thought or speech ever err?[12]

The answer is that nothing *in* the image conclusively identifies its referent—the one with which comparison would have to be made to determine correspondence or lack thereof. Hence the image in and of itself cannot establish truth by correspondence. And if it does not do so by itself, then, once again, perhaps it does not do so at all. Whatever picks out the referent may do the rest as well.[13] Images may be neither a sufficient nor a necessary condition of truth by correspondence. And in fact we have already noted convincing reasons for believing that they are not.

To be sure, we do have images. To be sure, they may have referents, and we may know what the referents are. To be sure, they may resemble their referents, at least to some extent, and may illustrate true thoughts, expressible by true statements. Indeed, on occasion, they not only illustrate our thoughts, but may account in part for the thoughts' accuracy or inaccuracy. However, even then, their resemblance to their referents does not adequately explain the truth of the thoughts, any more than the resemblance of pictures fully explains the truth of statements in which they play a similar, more than illustrative role.

Suppose I make a sketch of someone and say, "This is how he looks." The statement may be true. And its truth may depend on the accuracy of the sketch. But the sketch itself is not true or false. Nor by itself does it make the statement true. For suppose I had said, "This is *not* how he looks." Then the sketch's very accuracy would make the statement false. Or suppose I had said, "This is how *she* looks." Then its faithful portrayal of some other, masculine referent would not save the statement from falsehood. Even in this most favorable situation, therefore, where the picture does not merely illustrate but replaces some words, the accuracy or inaccuracy of the picture does not adequately explain the truth or falsehood of the statement.

Transfer this whole scenario to the mind—make the sketch a mental image, and the statement a thought—and nothing changes. If the thought is expressible by "This is how he looks" and the image is accurate, the thought is true. If the thought is "This is not how he looks," the thought is false, despite—indeed, because of—the perfect accuracy of the image. If the thought is "This is how she looks," the thought again is false, despite the image's accuracy vis-à-vis some other referent. Thus, even in this most favorable hypothesis, where the image does not merely illustrate a thought but figures in it, the image and its accuracy fail to explain the truth or falsehood of the thought. The empiricist account leaves something out, and what it leaves out may be more important than what it includes. Indeed, generally speaking, truth and falsehood may have no need of images.

Essentialist Versions

Having refuted to his satisfaction the equation of truth with copying, James inquired: "Where our ideas cannot copy definitely their object, what does agreement with that object mean?" His reply was: "To 'agree' in the widest sense with a reality, *can only mean to be guided either straight up to it or into its surroundings, or to be put into such working touch with it as to handle either it or something connected with it better than if we disagreed."*[14] It is this function or process of agreeable leading that, quite generally, constitutes truth.[15] What else might truth be, when the ideas in question are of the clock's works or its time-keeping function or the spring's elasticity? How could we picture such things?

In so arguing, James ignored the standard essentialist solution to the problem of correspondence. We may not be able to *imagine* the unseen works, essentialists would reply, but we can form an abstract concept, or mental representation, of works in general and can use the concept to make a truthful judgment without having to picture any particular works in detail. After all, a statement like "The clock's works need cleaning" does not specify the number, shape, and disposition of the inner parts; nor, therefore, does the thought so expressed fill in these details. In order for the statement and the judgment it expresses to be true, it suffices that the words in the sentence—*clock, works, need, cleaning*—express concepts in the judgment; that the concepts in the judgment match essences in reality; and that the overall configuration in the mind agrees with that in reality—that is, that the clock's works need cleaning as averred.

Essentialists would extend this account to the other items cited by James: the clock's time-keeping function and the spring's elasticity. These words too, they would say—*time, keep, function, spring, elasticity*—express general concepts with which we can form judgments that will then agree or disagree with reality. In each case, truth is indeed correspondence, in the straight-forward sense of similarity. The mental union or separation, in affirmation or negation, mirrors the union or separation in reality.

What, though, of Switzerland? What, for that matter, of the Boer War, the Pacific Ocean, RCA, the Bible, the United States, or the French Foreign Legion? These are all individual things or conglomerates of things, not classes; hence they have no essences, at least of the kind so far considered. It would therefore appear that either you picture them whole or you do not picture them at all; no abstract representation can come to your assistance. Yet they obviously cannot be pictured whole. So the truth of countless thoughts and statements, it would seem, cannot be explained in the essentialist manner. Even a mental snapshot of some single individual pictures him or her at one moment, in one position, from one side, in one set of clothes, and so forth; it does not portray brain, heart, liver, lungs, memories, preferences, or life history before and after that instant.

Particular things in general, and not just those with proper names, pose a problem for the essentialist viewpoint, as they do for the empiricist conception. For essentialism succeeds no better than its empiricist rival in explaining reference. Consider so simple a statement as "The clock needs cleaning." How does the corresponding judgment—the inner affirmation and representation expressed by these words—pick out the clock in question? Not by means of the abstract concept *clock,* applicable to all members of the class. Nor by representing some essence peculiar to this clock. Nor by means of the clock's individuating traits, faithfully portrayed in the empiricist manner. (As noted earlier, if reference depends on perfect similarity, then falsehood is impossible: the clock in the image would never have scratches its referent doesn't have, would never chime when it doesn't, would never be where it isn't, and so on.)

I imagine that an essentialist might suggest a solution like the following: "In the statement's specific context, the expression 'the clock' would be shorthand for some definite description—for instance, 'the clock just mentioned' or 'the clock we are both observing.' And each of these words—*we, just, mention, observe,* and so on—expresses a general concept, so that the essentialist explanation works as well for 'The clock needs cleaning' as it does, say, for 'Clocks have works' or 'Clocks tell time,' where no specific clock is referred to."

A similar solution might be suggested for Switzerland, RCA, and the rest. Switzerland, for example, might be verbally defined as "a country with three principal official languages, each spoken in a neighboring country" and might be mentally represented by the corresponding concepts—*country, three, principal,* and so forth. These, then, might serve both to uniquely identify the country in question and to formulate true judgments about it, expressible in true statements.

Let us therefore consider how well the essentialist account succeeds even for general terms. Is there an essence of countries, languages, or speaking; of clocks, needing, cleaning, having, telling, time, or works; of mentioning, observing, elasticity, functions, patenting, producing, marketing, and all the rest? If not, then no universal concepts mirror such essences; nor can universal terms express the missing likenesses. Without essences—abundant essences—the whole essentialist structure collapses.

To be sure, thought is not sensation. Intellect has its own operations. It distinguishes and divides, compares and contrasts. Thus, if there were something common to all the varied members of a class (for example, to clocks or springs or works), the intellect might spot it. But if there is in fact no such common essence, the mind cannot discern what is not there or store its likeness in memory.

To be sure, all clocks have the property of being clocks, all elastic things are elastic, and so forth (as essentialists are wont to urge). But the same would hold true no matter how uniform or disparate were the realities called "clocks" or "elasticity"; in a critique of isomorphism what we want to ascertain is whether the realities designated and the representations expressed by works like *clock* and *elasticity* are as uniform as the spoken or written words. Is the relatively uniform sound or visual configuration *clock* or *country* or *language* matched by an equally uniform referent or an equally uniform nonverbal representation in the mind?

What grounds do we have for supposing such isomorphism? None, really. No thorough research or careful examination of cases accounts for belief in uniform essences captured by uniform thoughts and expressed by uniform words. Unexamined assumptions and question-begging arguments chiefly explain their vogue: "Why would we speak of 'knowledge,' in the singular, if knowledge were not some single thing?"[16] "Why would we use the same term for the members of a class unless they all had something in common?" "Don't words like *bike* and *game* and *corporation* obviously have the *same meaning* on various occasions, when applied to quite disparate specimens?" "Don't they abstract from the various things' peculiarities; and if they do, mustn't they pick out a common essence? What else is there for the words to denote, once all variations are omitted?"

"Don't *think*," said Wittgenstein, in his well-known response to such queries, "but look and see." Examine, for example, the things called games. No trait or set of traits possessed by games and by them alone sets them off from other activities and accounts for our use of the word. Many games, it is true, have rules; many involve competition; many have winning and losing; many require skill, create interest and excitement, lack a practical purpose, or engage two or more people. But not all do. And many other activities exhibit one or the other of these features (business involves competition, trials have rules, dancing entertains, translation calls for skill, and so on). What we discover in games, as in many another class covered by a general term, is not some single, distinctive essence, but what Wittgenstein dubbed "family resemblances": "for the various resemblances between members of a family: build, features, colour of eyes, gait, temperament, etc. etc. overlap and criss-cross in the same way."[17]

Once accepted as a pattern that recurs, the family-resemblance structure suggests possible answers to the essentialist's queries. "Why might we use a single term for many disparate things, unless they had an essence?" Perhaps because they cluster closely in this family fashion. "Doesn't the term have the *same meaning* in its various applications?" Yes, it ascribes membership in the family. "Isn't it *abstract*?" Yes, for it does not ascribe any single family feature, since any one may be lacking; much less does it indicate less characteristic features—for example, how long the game lasts, how many people play, how close the score may be, or the like.

Other words suggest other possibilities. A concept like *blue*, for example, reveals quite a different configuration; for no one shade of blue overlaps with any other or shares family traits with its neighbors. Nor do blues necessarily resemble other blues more than they do shades of other colors. A deep blue just this side of purple, for example, may resemble a nearby purple more closely than it resembles some chalky blue off near the border with white; and that pale blue may resemble a neighboring white more than it does a deeper shade of blue that shares the common label. The simple structure is this: blues fall within one stretch, purples within another, and so forth. We divide the color territory somewhat as we divide nations into states or states into counties, by means of boundaries that are largely arbitrary. (A house just across the street may lie in another country, whereas a house three thousand miles away may not.)

This new configuration, neither essentialist nor of the family-resemblance type, suggests a new set of answers to the essentialist's doubts. "Why else would we use the same term, if not to indicate a common essence?" Perhaps to locate the shade (taste, touch, sound, and so forth) within a single stretch of some continuum. "Doesn't the term have the *same meaning* each time?" Yes, it indicates the same stretch of the same continuum. "Isn't the term *abstract*?" Yes, it names no single shade, say, within the varied lineup, much less the shade's brilliance or saturation. If, for instance, I say, "The book's cover is blue," you learn nothing save the range of shades the cover falls within. It may be turquoise or cobalt or aquamarine or . . . .

Other examples reveal further possibilities, each attesting in its own fashion how groundless is the supposition that general terms must function essentialistically, and how frequently they in fact do not.[18] Indeed, I can think of no word in English or any other language that operates in the manner typically supposed by essentialists—that is, with such rigid uniformity that a single mental likeness might mirror the single content as we utter the word. The supposed rule is not even the exception; for the supposed necessity is not even a practical possibility. Given the world as it is, words *could not* function in the way it is thought that they must. Color words, for example, cannot pick out "pure blue" amid the various blues or "pure red" among the reds; for there is no such thing. And for them to designate single, indivisible shades, the whole populace would have to learn thousands of color words in place of the familiar dozen or so and apply them with pinpoint precision.

Accordingly, it is false to suppose and misleading to assert that single words match single conscious contents, and that the contents mirror extramental correlates, one to one. The one word *blue*, for example, denotes dozens of different shades. The one word *game* denotes hundreds of different activities, each variously combining a set of family traits. And these are typical single terms. A phrase like *yellow ochre*, achieving near-essentialist uniformity by combining *yellow* and *ochre*, is a rarity even among compound expressions.

The *Tractatus* Version

Young Wittgenstein did not suppose that existing terminology in natural languages like English and German mirrors thought or reality. But he did believe that we think out the words we utter, and that an analysis of the thinking, if laid bare, would reveal a perfect parallel between the analytic signs and the realities they stand for, with one name for this object, a second for that, a third for a third, and so forth, and the relations between the signs matching those between the objects.

There need not be essences, then, or concepts that capture them. We need not even form images. All that is required is that we think out the sense of the signs, correlating them with the realities that we think or speak about. "*That* is how a picture is attached to reality; it reaches right out to it. It is laid against reality like a ruler" (*Tractatus*, 2.1511–2.1512). "If you exclude the element of intention from language, its whole function then collapses."[19]

This theory, as mentioned earlier, was meant to solve the problem of reference. What makes our thought of something a thought of that thing and no other? How is the connection made? When we try to explain it, the later Wittgenstein reportedly observed, "we imagine at first a connection like strings. . . . If I said 'My brother is in America'—I could imagine there being rays projecting from my words to my brother in America." "But," he added, "what if my brother isn't in America?—then the rays don't hit anything."[20]

"Yet surely," it might be objected, "when I think of him, it is *him* I mean, wherever he may be!" Well, suppose he has just burned up in an auto accident or been vaporized by an explosion. In that case there is no "him" for you to mean (in the manner imagined). However, the *Tractatus* was ready with an answer. The mind's target is the logical atoms—the logically simple items—of which he was composed before his demise; and those still exist, somewhere in the atmosphere, perhaps, beyond the explosion site or round about the burning car. It is *these* that thought picks out, even when it errs concerning his whereabouts or his present existence.

I say that the logical atoms are *perhaps* where the physical atoms are, in the clouds or on the earth, because Wittgenstein never decided what would count as logical atoms. He never discovered any items that could serve as referents for truly atomic names in the manner prescribed by his theory. So he gradually came to realize that speech and thought do not function as he imagined. The postulated atoms and the rays that pick them out are mythical—as mythical as the pure, invisible colors that G. E. Moore supposed for our color terms or the phantom pains Augustine required to guide our use of the word *pain*. In each case, supposedly there *have* to be such things; yet in no case do they, or could they, exist. "The more narrowly we examine actual language, the sharper becomes the conflict between it and our requirement."[21]

Suppose we speak of Napoleon's invasion of Russia. Presto, while the words are still on our lips, our thinking pinpoints all the logical atoms in all the people, all the movements, all the rifles, horses, pots, and carriages. Napoleon and his army no longer exist, but we accurately identify the indestructible bits that composed them and put them all back together again in just the way required to make the statement true. But what way is that, and what are the bits? We haven't a clue! Yet we frequently run off such statements, a dozen or so per minute. There must be some other explanation, then, for the statements' meaning and truth.

Broader Perspectives

In broad outline, we can see that the isomorphic viewpoint is caught in a dilemma. To match words, ideas, and referents and make them correlate one to one, it must either reduce the too numerous referents by postulating essences or multiply the signs and thoughts in the *Tractatus* manner. Middle-of-the-road empiricism, leaving things much as they are, clearly will not work. There are too many different shades of blue, too many different kinds of works, too many different varieties of games (to cite our previous examples), for a single word or correlated image to match them one to one. There must either be a single essence to match the single word or many signs and thoughts to match the many things. Time and again, however, there is no such essence, and the mind does not send out feelers to a trillion mysterious items each time someone mentions Napoleon or a visit to Switzerland. Saying it must be so does not make it so.

Truth-by-correspondence, based on, but going beyond, the mere matching of items, encounters further problems. Correspondence, it is thought, must occur in the mind, for written or spoken words seldom resemble the realities named or described. Thought, not speech, must be the prime locus of truth. However, if there are no uniform essences and no mental contents that picture them, the demands thus put on the mind seem to exceed its capacities. How can a mental act duplicate the vast, complex realities—the campaigns, cities, countries, corporations, cultures, and the like—that we so often speak about? How, too, can a replica in consciousness reach beyond consciousness and attach to a specific referent as the reality represented?

In this connection a second dilemma appears. On the one hand, complete accuracy may seem to be the likeliest way to assure reference for a mental representation, linking it to a particular referent; the more exactly the mental picture depicts the object, the more certainly (we think) is that the one meant. Surely nothing else looks *exactly* that way. On the other hand, the possibility of falsehood for any factual judgment requires that referents not necessarily look as asserted and represented. The house that we falsely think is engulfed in flames and so represent that way must still be the house in question, despite the lack of resemblance between it and our representation. The street that we mistakenly describe and picture as bending to the right must, nonetheless, be the street described, despite this serious misrepresentation. And so forth. Hence isomorphists must choose.

Does resemblance determine reference, or does it determine truth and falsehood? It cannot do both. One and the same thought cannot simultaneously resemble a thing so perfectly that it picks it out as its reference yet resemble the thing imperfectly and therefore be false. Once the choice has been made, however, either reference or correspondence is left unexplained. We are forced, then, to take a different tack if we wish to understand meaning and truth.

CHAPTER 3

LINGUISTIC TRUTH

In order to appreciate a solution, a person needs to have experienced and grappled with the problem it solves. It is to be hoped, therefore, that the preceding chapter will have rendered more likely an appreciative hearing of the account of meaning and truth now to be presented. The critique in that chapter made evident, I trust, that the way in which people naturally conceive the working of speech and thought is illusory. Words do not line up with thoughts, and thoughts with things; nor does the conjunction of verbal or mental correlates mirror the conjunction of things; nor, accordingly, can truth be explained by such mirroring. The traditional viewpoint, which puts truth within the moment, in the mind, leads to a dead end. Yet, what better explanation can be given?

The later, post-Tractarian Wittgenstein indicated both a reason for past failures and a new direction for inquiry when he remarked:

> If you are puzzled about the nature of thought, belief, knowledge, and the like, substitute for the thought the expression of the thought, etc. The difficulty which lies in this substitution, and at the same time the whole point of it, is this: the expression of belief, thought, etc., is just a sentence;—and the sentence has sense only as a member of a system of language; as one expression within a calculus. Now we are tempted to imagine this calculus, as it were, as a permanent background to every sentence which we say, and to think that, although the sentence as written on a piece of paper or spoken stands isolated, in the mental act of thinking the calculus is there—all in a lump. The mental act seems to perform in a miraculous way what could not be performed by any act of manipulating symbols. Now when the temptation to think that in some sense the whole calculus must be present at the same time vanishes, there is no more point in *postulating* the existence of a peculiar kind of mental act alongside of our expression.[1]

This emphasis on the "system of language" and "manipulating symbols" contrasts with traditional stress on mental correlates and mental correspondence on the one hand and with James's stress on consequences and "agreeable leading" on the other. Yet the account it suggests will turn out to agree in important, though differing, respects with both of these antecedent, antithetically related viewpoints. It will appear, that is, as a synthetic solution, retaining the truth both of isomorphist views and of James's position, while avoiding the errors or oversights of each.[2]

A Linguistic Account of Linguistic Truth

Most people would agree that statements or assertions, in the sense of declarative utterances or speech acts (as I shall understand the terms *statement* and *assertion* in this study), figure among the things that may be called true or false, even if they are not, for some, the primary "bearers" of truth.[3] Most would likewise agree that the truth of such utterances depends on the meanings of the expressions—words, names, numerals, and so on—that they contain,[4] and that the meanings of these constitutive expressions depend on their established uses (in the language as a whole, in the given context or milieu, or in the linguistic practice of the particular writer or speaker). From these combined premises it follows that the truth of statements or assertions depends somehow on the established uses of their constituent expressions. Here, then, is a worthwhile lead to follow, in keeping with Wittgenstein's general advice that we turn from the contents of the mind to the manipulation of signs.

To profit from this lead requires attention, first to the nature of the "established uses" on which meaning and truth depend, and then to the nature of the dependence. The uses, to start with, reveal the following traits, all germane to truth-assessment: generally speaking, they are *varied, comprehensive, specific,* and *language-wide.*

Varied. The established use of one expression differs from that of another, and the difference is often notable. Hence the phrase "established word uses" cannot be sharply defined. If someone insists, "But what *precisely* do you mean by the 'established use' of expressions?," the answer will have to be: "What precise expression do you have in mind?" Just as a single, uniform account cannot be given of the use of hammers, nails, vices, bevels, and cranes, so a single account cannot be given of the use of *if, maybe, sugar,* and *amen.* Some words refer, some do not; some have descriptive criteria, some do not; some are indexical, some are not; and so forth.

Word use may vary notably, not only from word to word, but also word *by* word. Thus Waismann's cautions concerning "*the* ordinary use of language" are applicable to the phrase "*the* established use of a word":

There are *uses*, differing from one another in many ways, e.g. according to geography, taste, social standing, special purpose to be served, and so forth. This has long been recognized by linguists who distinguish between use in writing and use in talking, or (in a different sense) between speech and language, between poetic and prose expression, elevated and every-day diction, literary style and more colloquial speech, slang and idiom, or again between jargon, cant and argot; not to mention shoptalk, college lingo, etc. All these are particular ways of using language, loosely revolving around a—not too clearly defined—central body, the standard speech.[5]

This "central body" itself is usually varied, with the dictionary often citing, for example, both noun and verb uses for a single term and numerous varieties of each.

Comprehensive. The "uses" of expressions—those on which meaning and truth depend—consist of much more than phonetics or grammar. The use of *I*, for example, can no more be explained without mentioning the speaker, or the use of *see* without mentioning eyes and light, or the use of *rain* without mentioning clouds and drops of water, than the use of a hammer can be explained without mentioning people, hands, nails, boards, movements, and the like. The importance of this observation will appear later, when I deal with the common impression that an account of truth in terms of word uses leaves out the "facts," or "reality."

Specific. Though relatively comprehensive, word uses are nonetheless restricted vis-à-vis other expressions in an utterance or in the language. Each has its own specific job to do. Thus the role of *rained*, for example, in "It rained hard last night" is not that of *it, hard, last,* or *night;* nor is its customary use in the English language the same as theirs.

Language-wide. Because the established uses of expressions are specific, not embracing all aspects of any given speech act, and because they vary, they are not confined to this or that species of utterance. A given word—a verb, noun, particle, numeral, proper name, or other—may appear in statements, questions, commands, or exhortations; in active or passive constructions, indicative or subjunctive, negative or affirmative; concerning past, present, or future events; in historical, logical, scientific, philosophical, or everyday discussion.

It follows, and is worth noting briefly at this point, that if the truth of a statement is to be judged by the established uses of its constituent expressions, it cannot be determined from some one assertion in the past, no matter how often repeated by how many speakers. The past assertion is particular; established word use is general. And indeed, mere consensus is not treated as establishing the truth of a statement. I shall return to this topic later, when discussing the neutrality of language.

To achieve a synoptic view of the preceding features of established word uses, it may be helpful to consider typical dictionary entries that encapsulate such uses—for example, Webster's entry for *mug:*

> **mug** (mŭg), *n.* **1.** A kind of earthen or metal drinking cup, with a handle,— usually cylindrical, with no lip. **2.** The quantity a mug holds. **3.** [Perh. a different word.] *Slang.* **a** The face or mouth. **b** A grimace. **c** *Brit.* A dupe.—*v.t. & i.;* MUGGED (mŭgd); MUG'GING. **1.** *Slang.* To grimace; make faces (at). **2.** To photograph;—esp. used of photographing criminals.

These details are all relevant for judgments of truth or falsehood, and they reveal the four traits just enumerated: (1) variety: noun uses are listed, then verb uses, and a variety of each are given; (2) comprehensiveness: besides the brief grammatical and phonetic indications, mention is made of materials, shapes, contents, faces, photographs, criminals, and so forth; (3) specificity: no other word in the dictionary has an entry identical (or anywhere near identical) to this one; (4) breadth: as thus standardly employed, *mug* may appear in the most varied utterances: in statements or requests, descriptions or inquiries, instructions or imprecations. It may be used to affirm or to deny—indeed, to affirm or to deny the same thing.

The same traits that characterize a dictionary entry reporting standard usage may characterize a stipulation of meaning, made perhaps in similar form, or an established, but unformulated, pattern present in the practice of some small group and not noted by any dictionary. I have focused on just the commonest variety of "established use."

How, then, if this phrase is understood as indicated, does the truth of a statement depend on the established uses of the expressions it contains? How, for instance, does the truth of the assertion "It's raining" depend on the customary use of its constituent terms? An initial, rough account that suggests itself is the following. A statement, assertion, claim, declaration, report, description, announcement, or the like is true if its component expressions are used in accordance with their established uses. Thus, if someone makes the statement "It's raining" when (a) water, (b) is descending, (c) in the form of drops, (d) from clouds, (e) in the immediate vicinity, and (f) at the moment of utterance, then the assertion is true. It is true because this particular use of the words corresponds, both word by word and overall, with the customary use of that verb, that tense, that combination. The verb requires drops of water falling from clouds; the tense requires simultaneous occurrence; and the combination of that verb with that tense and a dummy subject in the familiar phrase "It's raining" requires that the drops be falling round about. All these are established patterns with which the utterance, if true, conforms.

Add other words to the sentence, and the same analysis applies to them too. Suppose someone says, "It's raining hard." Whether as adjective or as adverb, *hard* belongs to a class of expressions that we might call "veiled comparatives."[6] If someone works, runs, hits, puffs, or gazes hard, he works, runs, hits, puffs, or gazes harder than is usual for that category of activity. Such is the use of this word in the language. So if it is raining harder than average as the words "It's raining hard" are uttered—that is, if more drops of water than usual are falling round about—the statement is true; otherwise not. Use-usage correspondence either holds or fails to hold.

Several basic traits of this correspondence can be noted prior to the refinements that will be added in later chapters. Generally speaking, the correspondence that characterizes true statements is *varied, complete, cumulative, indefinite, disparate,* and *interdependent.*

Varied. Since the established uses of expressions are varied, utterances may agree with them variously. "It rained hard" may agree with one standard use of *hard;* "The homework was hard" with a second; "The bread was hard" with a third. "It rained hard" may agree in one way with the standard use of *it,* in a second way with the standard use of *rained,* in a third way with the standard use of *hard*—though the sense of the word *agree,* as we shall see, need not vary from instance to instance.

Complete. To some extent even a false statement employs its expressions in keeping with their established uses, provided it is grammatical. If, in addition, the speaker uses the expressions in their standard senses, there is fuller agreement. Still, the conformity is not complete. To use the word *rain* for rain when it is not raining is like using a hammer "to drive nails" but missing one's aim and bending them over instead or like "singing the right note" but singing it flat or like using a dot on a map "to designate a city" when there is in fact no city at the spot marked. All these activities conform to some extent with standard practice, but not fully. Truth-correspondence is complete correspondence.

Cumulative. People drive nails in far more frequently than they bend them inadvertently, and they more frequently say it is raining when it is than when it isn't. Indeed, it is difficult to think of any instrument that is employed unsuccessfully more often than successfully or of any word that occurs more frequently in false statements than in true ones. Still, such a possibility is not logically excluded (think of harpoons or of talk about luminiferous "ether" a century ago). And conceivably the unsuccessful uses might reveal a recurring pattern (the harpoon might regularly fall short of its target, rather than beyond; the ether might mistakenly be said to exist, rather than be misdescribed). So might not the unsuccessful uses—missing the target, misdescribing the universe—conform as fully to standard behavior as the successful ones? Might not false statements satisfy the correspondence formula as perfectly as true statements?

One answer might advert to descriptive conventions, more general than those for an individual term, which would be contravened in such instances. Another could point out that even in such imaginary instances, although one constituent expression of the statements might perhaps conform to usage, others would not. In "Ether fills space," for example, even if we exonerated the subject expression *ether* (see below, *Interdependent*), the predicate would still be at fault. Its terms would not be used in keeping with their established uses (save in the partial sense of being idiomatic). This answer draws attention to a further feature of truth-correspondence: each and every word counts, and each aspect of each word.

An old saying asserts that the conformity of truth must be total, and that a single deviation suffices to falsify a statement. Our sample statement, "It's raining," bears this out. Were volcanic dust (not water) descending, it would not be raining; the statement would be false. Were water descending, but in flakes or pellets (not drops), the same verdict would result. Were the drops not falling from clouds but sprayed from a passing plane, or were they falling no longer or falling elsewhere, the statement would not qualify as true. A single such failure of correspondence would warrant the judgment "false."

Indefinite. *Rain* is a relatively well-defined concept; yet even it reveals some fuzziness at the edges. (How many drops establish that it is raining? At what consistency does rain become sleet, or vice versa?) Other concepts are fuzzier. So it is not always clear whether the use of an expression does or does not agree with the expression's established use. Furthermore, as we will see in chapters 6 and 7, truth-correspondence varies according to context, in specific yet imprecise ways, so that even if the established uses of expressions were sharply defined, truth-correspondence would not be. Just as no precise number of drops determines the difference between raining and not raining, so no precise amount of agreement between use and established use draws a well-defined line between truth and untruth.

Disparate. Some details of a statement's correspondence derive from the individual words and their specific uses, some from more general patterns in the language, and some from the overall configuration, verbal and nonverbal, of the utterance. Even so simple a declaration as "It's raining" illustrates all three modes of determination. The particular verb, *to rain,* determines the nature of the phenomenon required for truth: drops, of water, falling, from clouds. The particular tense, a feature of countless verbs and not just of *rain,* fixes the time. And it fixes it because such is the particular word combination within a specific type of setting.

Interdependent. Vary the combination or the setting, and the tense might not call for that time. Thus the present tense in the statement "It seldom rains in Arizona" requires no rain accompanying the utterance. Neither does the present tense in "When it rains, that curve is dangerous." Again, the identical set of words—"It's raining"—might be a true response to a question—for example, about what somebody said or about the meaning of a phrase in a foreign language—despite clear skies at the moment, or a false reply, despite abundant rainfall.

Fuller reflection reveals interdependence so complete that it invites comparison with the composition of forces in dynamics. In order to explain the overall trajectory of a projectile, for example, we must specify various factors: initial angle, acceleration, momentum, gravity, friction, and so forth. And to explain any single aspect of the projectile's flight at a given instant—its location, direction, or velocity—we must cite the same factors: initial angle, acceleration, momentum, gravity, friction, and so on. Each aspect is multiply determined. Similarly, to explain the correctness of a statement such as "It's raining," we must cite vocabulary, grammar, and context; and to account for any single aspect of the correctness—location, time, precipitation, form, source, composition—we must adduce the same factors: vocabulary, grammar, and context (for example, the verb, the tense, and the words just spoken).

To illustrate, consider the fact of precipitation. Why is that required to make the words "It's raining" true? Not solely because of the verb. Granted, *freezing* in place of *raining* would eliminate the requirement. But so would the addition of *not,* or the inclusion of "It's raining" in some longer sequence (for example, "If it's raining, the outing is off"). So would an antecedent query like "What is the shortened form of 'It is raining'?" or an antecedent request such as "Cite an English sentence that lacks the subject-predicate distinction."[7]

Here I am touching on extremely complex matters.[8] However, to grasp at least the general point and its validity, recall the comparison of words with tools. Suppose I observe a workman swinging a hammer. Does that activity agree with the standard employment of hammers? Well, is he hitting something with the hammer or making idle motions in the air or chasing away a wasp? If he is hitting something, is it a nail, a walnut, or his thumb? If he is hitting a nail, is he doing so in fury because it won't come out or calmly driving it in as part of building a bench? What is the overall setting, the total configuration? If I don't know that, I cannot judge correspondence comprehensively. The same holds for truth. It is not enough that the word *rain* be used grammatically. It is not enough that it be joined grammatically with familiar verbal companions, such as *is* and *falling.* It is not enough even that drops of water be descending at the moment one says "Rain is falling." What is the total context, the total speech act? Only from that can I judge total correspondence—that is, can I judge truth.

Truth *As* Correspondence

Correspondence might correlate regularly with truth (statements being true when and only when they achieve total correspondence) and nonetheless not be what we mean by *truth;* so equating the truth of statements with correspondence might be misleading. (It might be like equating our humanity with possession of a certain protein in the blood, on the ground that all human beings have it, and only human beings have it.) The question is: Do we call statements true not only *when* but also *because* such conformity obtains? Is the correlation between truth and correspondence a mere fact of nature, unknown to most speakers; or do the two coincide because correspondence is in fact the criterion of truth of statements, in the same defining, constitutive sense that "drops of water falling from clouds" is the criterion of rain, or "frozen flakes of water falling from clouds" is the criterion of snow?[9]

As a first response, notice that speakers of the language are typically familiar with all the key elements in the analysis just given. Nothing is hidden, nothing unknown. If, in our example, a person says that it is raining and another rightly terms the statement true, the second party typically knows both that drops of water are falling from nearby clouds and that the expression *raining* is routinely used for that phenomenon. When, on the other hand, a person calls an object "crimson" and another rightly terms the description false, the second party typically knows both the color of the object in question and the color that *crimson* designates; and knowing them both, he or she knows their disagreement. The present use clashes with usage.

I do not mean to suggest that these things we know are things we recollect or call to mind. When we call a dog *big*, we need not recall all the dogs we have ever seen or read about, calculate their average size, compare this dog's size with that average, recollect the use of *big* for larger-than-average sizes, then proceed to our predication. Yet these are all things we need to *know* to get the predication right. So, too, when we speak of truth or falsehood, we need not pass through any comparable rigmarole by noting the verbal and nonverbal aspects of the statement we are judging; recalling the established uses of its expressions; comparing the two, expression by expression and aspect by aspect; and recollecting the use of *true* and *false* for such correspondence or lack thereof. Yet these items, too, we need to *know* if we are to get the predication right.

Not only, then, are the items known to those who utter the verdict "True" or "False," but they guide the application of the terms. If speakers do not know either the established use of some expression in an utterance or the relevant particulars of its present use, or both, they are unable to apply the label *true* or *false*. If they think they know both sides of the equation—the established use and the present use—but are mistaken about either, they err correspondingly in their application of *true* and *false*. Thus, to start with usage, if a French-speaking person knows some English, but not the use of the word *sleet*, he cannot tell you whether the statement "It's sleeting," "Sleet is falling," or the like is true or false. And if he thinks the word is used for rain or snow, not sleet, he will misapply the words *true* and *false* accordingly. As for knowledge of the expression's use on this particular occasion, in all its relevant aspects, if a person supposes that water is still coming down when it isn't or is frozen when it isn't or is descending nearby when it isn't or is coming from clouds when it isn't, that too will adversely affect what he says about the truth of "It's sleeting." Linguistic correspondence is the criterion followed in predicating "True" and "False" of statements, claims, assertions, and the like.

To grasp this rather complex situation more clearly, consider the following parallel with traffic lights:

1. For the most part, cars cross on a green light and stop on a red one.
2. This correlation is no coincidence: the drivers *see* the lights and *know* their function, so follow them.
3. On some occasions, however, they see the red and cross anyway.
4. On others, they fail to notice the red, so fail to stop.
5. For both reasons, the correlation between green light and moving, red light and stopping, is imperfect. It just holds for the most part.
6. Both types of crossing on red—the knowing and the unknowing—are recognized as violations.

Similarly:

1. For the most part, when statements are termed true, linguistic correspondence holds between present use and established use; and when they are termed false, it does not.
2. This correlation, too, is no mere coincidence: speakers *note* the present use (for example, drops descending nearby) and *know* the established use of the expressions (for example, *raining*), and predicate "True" or "False" according as the particular use they note agrees or disagrees with the established use they know.
3. On some occasions, however, they note full correspondence, yet call the statement false; or note noncorresponding features, yet call the statement true. That is, they lie.
4. On other occasions they fail to note noncorresponding features and so call the statement true, or think they note noncorresponding features, when in fact there are none, so call it false. That is, they err.
5. For both these reasons (3 and 4), the correlation between linguistic correspondence and "true" and between linguistic noncorrespondence and "false" is imperfect.
6. Both these types of predication, the mendacious and the mistaken, are recognized as incorrect (as verbal violations).

The parallel points in this comparison are so numerous that, at first, it may appear more confusing than clarifying. However, the closeness of the parallel is not the comparison's sole merit. I have adduced familiar facts to illuminate others that are reflectively less familiar, and relatively simple phenomena to illumine more complex ones. A green light is far simpler than multiple, interdependent agreement between present uses of words and their established uses. Seeing a green light is simpler than noting the various aspects of an utterance. So once the point-by-point parallel is understood, the linguistic pattern may be more firmly grasped. The correspondence between present uses and established uses really does guide our use of *true,* in much the same way and to much the same extent that green lights guide our crossing of streets.

When I say "to much the same extent," I have in mind more than the exceptions just noted—lying or mistaken uses of *true,* knowing or unknowing violations of traffic lights. A reader of that initial account might ask: "Haven't you overlooked the many street corners where there are no lights to consult and we just look this way and that before crossing?" The answer is "No, this too is part of the parallel." As we will see in chapter 5 in assessing "redundancy," "performative," or "no-truth" accounts of truth, on numerous occasions we employ the term *true* without consulting any criterion. Insofar as there is a criterion, the one just sketched is it; but that criterion is not always operative.

A First Objection

Two kinds of objection may be raised against the preceding account of linguistic truth. First, it may be questioned whether the account is valid even for factual assertions like "It's raining." Second, it may be questioned whether it does justice to various other types of utterance (figurative, performative, evaluative, and so on). I shall consider difficulties of the first sort here and leave the others for later chapters. Part 2 has much to say about whether linguistic correspondence is a necessary, as well as a sufficient, condition of linguistic truth.

An objection of the first type arises from nonreferring statements like "The present king of France is bald." Here correspondence fails, yet we do not call the utterance either true or false.[10] From this it has sometimes been inferred that truth is a matter of descriptive correspondence only, not demonstrative correspondence, and that successful reference is a mere precondition of truth. Hence the correspondence formula, with its undiscriminating reference to established word "uses," looks too broad and too general.

This conclusion is unwarranted. Consider the analogous restrictions on the words *yes* and *no.* If (to cite another well-worn illustration) a man has not been beating his wife, then he cannot be said to have stopped beating her. Yet, if asked whether he has stopped beating his wife, he would not answer "No." To account for this, we need not reinterpret *no.* The correct explanation is evident and familiar. A negative reply would suggest that he was still beating his wife, not that he had not previously beaten her. For such is the more usual sense of the negative, and such the more usual situation. People seldom ask "Has it stopped raining?" when no rain has fallen or "Have you stopped smoking?" when the person has never smoked. Hence a negative reply generally signifies that the rain or the smoking has not ceased, not that it never began. And were the innocent husband to answer "No," this is how his answer would be understood. Though the reply would not be incorrect, it would be misleading.

Similarly, people seldom say "The king of France is bald" when there is no king of France or "Einstein's daughter was a chemist" when Einstein had no daughter. Descriptive failure is far commoner than denotative failure. Hence to call such statements false would suggest the wrong kind of failure, the wrong kind of disagreement with usage. It would suggest that the present king's head is hairy or that Einstein's daughter chose a different career, not that no such person exists or ever existed. There is no need, then, to modify the account of truth, even for these occasions. Still less need we infer that in all instances truth concerns only descriptive correspondence.[11] Another explanation is available.

The correspondence analysis does in fact apply without restriction to denotative aspects of speech, as well as to descriptive aspects. If, for example, a person does not know the denotative difference between the subject expression in "The lion is sleeping" and that in "The lion is a noble beast," he cannot judge the truth of either utterance—the particular or the general. And if he thinks he knows the difference but does not, he may reject the first assertion on the ground that some lions are not currently sleeping and the second on the ground that a two-week-old cub he is watching is making a fool of itself. To get "true" and "false" right, we must know both kinds of conventions, the denotative as well as the descriptive. Both kinds figure in the criterion by which we judge truth and falsehood.

What about the "Facts"?

It is accurate to say of viewpoints like those sketched in chapter 1: "*Correspondence* theories take the truth of a proposition to consist, not in its relations to other propositions, but in its relation to the world, its correspondence to the facts."[12] Yet no such description fits the account in this chapter. I have not paired off speech acts with the world, but speech acts with speech acts. The present use of expressions agrees with their established uses. That is what makes a statement true.

Not surprisingly, when people habituated to the traditional formulae first hear all this talk about "use" and "established uses" and the correspondence between them, they are wont to inquire: "But what about the *facts*? What about *reality*?" They are thinking, for instance, of the rain—the actual precipitation—that verifies "It's raining." The answer is that the Wittgensteinian account[13] just outlined embraces not only the present rain, but also innumerable previous showers for which people have used the same verb. It takes in far more rain than the traditional formula did.

It is this expanded coverage that elicits the objection and creates, paradoxically, an impression of narrowness. When people hear the expression "word use," they often think just of grammar or syntax. (It is as though, hearing talk of a hammer's use, they envisioned only idle movements in the air, without hands or nails or boards or end results.) So they have the impression that the "facts" have been left out, whereas they have been subsumed within a larger aggregate. The facts (for example, the rain) that formed one term of the correspondence in traditional accounts now figure as just one aspect of one term of the relationship. They belong to the words' use on a particular occasion, which agrees or disagrees with their established uses; and that use takes in the words' relations to one another (syntax), to speakers and recipients (pragmatics), and to the realities spoken of (semantics)—including, for example, the drops of water falling round about (which are as essential for the successful employment of *raining* as boards or nails are for the successful use of a hammer).

If, then, concern for the "facts" motivated correspondence theorists, their desires should be fully met by this new, linguistic account. *Linguistic* means broader, not narrower. The term *linguistic* is not synonymous with *syntactic* or *pragmatic;* neither is it equivalent to *semantic* or *factual.* Language embraces more than just sounds or people or things—much as chess embraces more than just pieces or players or boards. "Only in the stream of thought and life do words have meaning."[14]

Indeed, the linguistic account of truth is more fully "factual" than traditional explanations. In this account, "It's raining" goes right on being true or false regardless of what thoughts pass through the speaker's or the hearer's mind; it is the precipitation or the lack thereof that makes the statement true or false. As Wittgenstein remarked, with appropriate emphasis, "If I say falsely that something is *red,* then, for all that, it isn't *red.*"[15] It matters not at all what feelings, images, or mental representations accompany the words. It matters not at all whether I or anyone else has ever conjured up the full contents of the predicate (imagining, for instance, all possible shades of red, with the present shade included).

Furthermore, the correspondence is now fuller and less problematic than in previous accounts. A typical image is little better than a caricature of its referent, if indeed it copies it at all. And an isomorphic "concept," even if it faithfully mirrored some essence, would still be an abstract mental representation of reality. Raindrops, though, leave nothing to be desired as replicas of raindrops. The ones now falling as I say "It's raining" really do resemble those that have fallen on other occasions when people employed the same expression. Use-usage correspondence (in such cases as this) means reality-reality correspondence.

Word Use: Key to the Correspondence Puzzle

Because the system of signs that permits this verbal achievement is not present at any moment or anywhere laid out to view, it is easily overlooked, and various substitutes are sought, generally in "thought." The comparison with traffic lights goes far to explain this tendency. We have already noted that as we stop or start, the whole system of signs to which the lights belong remains, unthought of, in the background. We may add that the attempt to call the system to mind at each light and at each intersection would prove not only difficult, but also disadvantageous, even dangerous. Safe, effective driving requires that we attend to the present particulars of our situation. Similarly, effective use of *true*, or of words in general, requires that we attend to present circumstances and not to the complexities of syntax, pragmatics, and semantics. The linguistic system *needs* to remain in the background.

This comparison and these facts, as I say, go far to explain the mentalistic temptation to bundle the whole calculus into a single act. But they do not go far enough. After all, traffic lights occasion no deep puzzlement. No present-day Pilate has exclaimed, "What does obedience to traffic lights consist in?" If, then, people are perplexed about truth and fail to look to language for an explanation, why is that? Why do they experience special difficulty in this instance?

A chief reason is that statements, unlike traffic lights, are complex symbols, consisting of multiple constituent signs, and that, although the constituents' correspondence is what accounts for a statement's truth, it is statements, not their constituents, that are called true. It is this conceptual configuration, more than anything else, I suspect, that has veiled the nature of truth. To grasp clearly the configuration's power to perplex, consider the following two-stage argument, and note how apt it is to trip up the unwary (especially if it is never made explicit). Stage one:

1. Truth is a property of whole statements, not of individual words.
2. But truth is correspondence.
3. So truth is correspondence of whole statements, not of individual words.

Stage two takes this conclusion as a premise and continues:

3. Truth is correspondence of whole statements.
4. But a statement is generally an original creation, with no established use.

5. So truth cannot consist in correspondence between present use and
established use.

Hence recourse to linguistic correspondence seems excluded.

People really do reason this way. And it is not surprising that they do. Three
of the above statements are true, a fourth can be given an acceptable sense,
and the fifth (the final conclusion) cannot be seen to be false until the fallacy
of the whole concatenation is laid bare. Where, then, and how does error
slip in?

It is true that truth is a property of whole statements (1). It is true that
truth is correspondence (2). It is true, and important, that statements—
indeed, even sentences—are for the most part original creations, with no
established use (4). In this respect, a simple utterance like "It's raining" is
atypical. We cannot generally match statement with statement and note
their agreement. But it does not follow that truth cannot consist in correspondence between present and established uses (5). For the uses in question, which agree or disagree, may be those of individual expressions, not of
statements as wholes. Statements' correspondence may be composite. It
may derive in the manner we have seen, from the correspondence of their
parts.

"Philosophical problems," wrote Wittgenstein, "are like safe locks which
are opened by a certain word or a certain number, so that no force can open
the door until just that word is hit on, & once it is found, any child can open
it."[16] No forcing can provide a mental replica of "Hitler's invasion took
Russia by surprise" or "The cafeteria serves two thousand meals an hour."
No forcing can conjure up an established use in the language for the
sentence "My aunt mulches her begonias with cornflakes" or "A snowy owl
was spotted near Mobile." However, all these words—*mulch, begonia, cornflakes, owl, spotted,* and the rest—have familiar uses in the language. And
their uses in individual statements—even statements as novel as these—
may conform fully with their established uses. If they do, then and for that
reason the statements are true. "Word use" is the phrase that springs the
lock.

This solution is not precluded by assertion 3, rightly understood. To say
that truth is correspondence of whole statements, not of individual words, is
not to deny that individual words may be employed in accordance with
established uses, or that a statement's overall correspondence may be a
function of this piecemeal correspondence. After all, traditional correspondence accounts said something analogous. They recognized similarity already at the level of meaning, in the individual images or concepts, and saw
this as contributing to the global similarity of judgments that are "true."

Their error was to suppose that the whole content of a judgment expressed or expressible by a statement could be tucked into a mental representation.

Word Use: Key to the Problem of Reference

One problem for that previous conception concerned similarity: How could a mental act portray Switzerland or an entire clock or a rise in interest rates? Another problem concerned reference: How could an act in the mind pick out, unmistakably, the extra-mental referents of a thought or utterance: the country, the clock, the interest rates? The most perfect similarity, even if attainable, would not provide a solution, since it would leave no room for falsehood—that is, for the representation of a given referent *as it is not.* It remains to be seen, therefore, whether and how a linguistic explanation can account for reference, as well as for correspondence. Can it identify referents? Can it do so and still permit falsehood?

A simple, concrete example may illustrate both possibilities. Suppose I am in a jewelry store, examining watches, and in my hand I hold a watch that I am discussing with a salesperson. "The works were made in Switzerland," she remarks. Now, how is connection made with that watch's works and with the country named? The works are pinpointed as the referent of her remark by the total speech situation: by my holding one particular watch, by our looking at that one, by my words—for example, "This is an attractive one"—as I picked it up, by her reply—"Yes, and it's reliable: the works were made in Switzerland"—and so on. There is no need for a mythical act of the mind, intending that one object. Nor must mental feelers reach across the Atlantic and somehow make contact with the country mentioned. The name "Switzerland" does that. One country and one alone is caught in the verbal web woven by that name in its various forms: the name on *that* country's stamps, *its* borders, *its* documents, *its* buildings, *its* travel brochures, and not on others'; the name by which citizens, visitors, and others refer to it and not to other countries. It is held secure, Gulliver-wise, by a thousand Lilliputian strands. No mental act could weave such a complex pattern, but language can.

Notice, furthermore, that neither of these accounts—of the reference of "Switzerland" or of the reference of "the works"—relies on the works' being made in Switzerland, as asserted. The statement "The works were made in Switzerland" need not be true for the statement's double reference to succeed. The familiar use of "Switzerland" as the name of a specific country assures one reference; the verbal and nonverbal context of the statement in the store establishes the other.

Thus both aspects of speech—reference and correspondence—that appeared so problematic in isomorphic, mentalistic theories, look much less mysterious, though far more complex, in the linguistic perspective just roughed out in first approximation. No doubt the complexity of both the correspondence and the mode of reference helped to veil them from view.

Whether a linguistic approach will succeed equally well for mental truth—that is, for true judgments, beliefs, ideas, opinions, surmises, and the like—remains to be seen. As yet, we have considered only true utterances.

CHAPTER 4

THE PRIMACY OF LINGUISTIC TRUTH

Traditionalists may be slow to concede that chapter 3's new account of truth is an improvement on the old, as long as it covers only utterances. For, as Wittgenstein remarked (largely with his own earlier thinking in mind): "It seems that there are *certain definite* mental processes bound up with the working of language, processes through which alone language can function. I mean the processes of understanding and meaning. The signs of our language seem dead without these mental processes; and it might seem that the only function of the signs is to induce such processes, and that these are the things we ought really to be interested in."[1]

Mental Truth

The powerful influence of such thinking can be detected in theories of mental truth like those considered in chapters 1 and 2 (essentialist mirroring, empiricist imaging, atomist projecting). It can also be discerned in the primacy accorded mental truth (of judgments, beliefs, ideas, thoughts, and so on) over linguistic truth (of assertions, statements, descriptions, reports, and so forth) and the readiness with which the primacy is granted. Argumentation hardly seems necessary, and what arguments are suggested often cannot bear a moment's scrutiny.

Russell, for example, wrote in his *Philosophical Essays:* "The truth or falsehood of statements can be defined in terms of the truth or falsehood of beliefs. A statement is true when a person who believes it believes truly, and false when a person who believes it believes falsely. Thus in considering the nature of truth we may confine ourselves to the truth of beliefs, since the truth of statements is a notion derived from that of beliefs."[2]

Russell might just as well have argued: "The truth or falsehood of beliefs can be defined in terms of the truth or falsehood of statements. A belief is true when the statement that expresses it is true, and false when the statement that expresses it is false. Thus, in considering the nature of truth we may confine ourselves to the truth of statements, since the truth of beliefs is a notion derived from that of statements." The *non sequitur* would then have been manifest. Definition can go either way. True statements can be defined in terms of true beliefs, and true beliefs in terms of true statements. Hence, such an argument proves nothing concerning the primacy of one notion or the other.

However, most thinkers of the past have unhesitatingly assumed, as did Russell, that primacy belongs with the mental. Franz Brentano, for instance, wrote in like vein:

> It is with reference to the truth or falsity of judgement that the other things which bear these names may properly be said to be true or false: some things because they express a true or a false judgement, such as a false assertion, or a false utterance; some things because they produce a true or false judgement, as in the case of hallucination, or a slip in uttering or in writing a word, or a metal which is taken for gold because of similarity in colour; some things because they are intended to produce a true or false judgement, as for instance a true spirit or a false mannerism; and some things because one who considers them real judges truly or falsely—for example, a true god, or a true stone in contrast to one that is painted. Some concepts are called true or false with respect to that which coincides, or fails to coincide, with their content, since here a true or erroneous judgement turns upon a discovery about this content; thus we may speak of rectangular figure as not being the true notion of square, and so forth. . . . Truth and falsity in the strict or proper sense, therefore, are found in judgement.[3]

This game, too, can be played the other way round. Starting where Brentano did, we may define true judgments in terms of true assertions, rather than true assertions in terms of true judgments, and go on from there. In the next chapter we shall see Austin follow this route.[4] For isomorphists, however, only one solution seems conceivable. If beliefs, for instance, are not verbal, how can their truth be verbal? And if truth is correspondence, how can it be found in words? Our expressions do not resemble the things we speak about, but our thoughts resemble the things we think about. There, then, lies the key to understanding. Mental truth is the primary notion; linguistic truth is derivative.

Even James was an unwitting captive of this way of thinking. Ideas, he said, are what are true or false; so let us see what their truth consists in, and then we shall have the key to truth. For James, as for those he criticized, mental truth was the primary notion—indeed, the only one he considered. Thus the outcome of his critique in *Pragmatism* was not what he supposed. His objections did something to discredit the mentalistic type of explanation, but nothing to discredit the alternative, linguistic approach. So let us now look in that direction, as the preceding two chapters suggest, to see where primacy lies.

The most typical articulation of mental objects—whether those of hopes, fears, and regrets or of judgments and beliefs—is linguistic, not pictorial.[5] If a person hopes a settlement will be reached in the Middle East, fears the loss of a job, or regrets the invention of the atomic bomb, the object of that person's hope, fear, or regret may be illustrated, but is not fixed, by a mental representation. Words more likely do the job. Likewise, if someone believes that the recession will continue, judges that interest rates will rise, or surmises that life exists on other planets, the content of the belief, judgment, or surmise is typically fixed linguistically, by inner or outer words.[6] And in that case words are constitutive of the judgment or belief.

Here, then, is an initial answer to the first objection above: "If beliefs and judgments are not verbal, how can their truth be verbal?" One answer would be to point out the fallacy of such reasoning. Thoughts might be true, not intrinsically, but through their relation to true statements. However, a more persuasive argument than this mere possibility would be to indicate (as I have just done) that beliefs, judgments, thoughts, ideas, and the like are inherently more linguistic than isomorphists have generally supposed.

Furthermore, we are considering not simply thoughts in themselves, but the use of the word *true* and therefore the *discussion* of truth, whether mental or linguistic. And reflect how rare it is for the truth of a judgment or belief to be discussed without any mention of what judgment or belief it is. But to mention a judgment or belief is to identify it by words, and the handiest, commonest way to do that is to state it. So now the question is: If you state a thought, belief, or judgment, do you judge the truth of the statement by one standard and the truth of the thought by a second, distinct standard? Being distinct, do the two criteria sometimes conflict with each other? Do you find yourself saying, "The statement is true enough, but the belief it states is false"? Surely not. If the statement is true, the belief it expresses is true. And they are true by the same standard. But the criterion for the truth of statements, as we saw in chapter 3, is linguistic correspondence. That, then, is the key to truth: the key to linguistic truth *and* the key to mental truth. It is the primary notion and therefore the one I shall dwell on in sections and chapters to come.

To test the realism of this solution, imagine likely episodes or remember actual ones. Suppose, for instance, that two people are discussing college textbooks. "A college-text editor once told me," says one, "that they couldn't make money on a short book; it would have to be close to two hundred pages in length." "What a crazy idea," observes the other. "No, it's true," replies the first. He then goes on to explain; and the explanation he gives, in confirmation of the editor's "idea," is precisely the same as he would give for the editor's statement. Their truth is identically established. For the idea, as for the statement, he speaks of books and money and pages, since such were the terms of the statement, and cites possibilities and impossibilities, since the statement's key expression was "couldn't." Use-usage correspondence guides and grounds the vindication.

A Mentalistic Variant

Post-Wittgensteinian philosophy speaks little of mental processes or of isomorphic matchings in the mind, yet may tend in the same direction as the arguments just criticized. Thus, a viewpoint still current regards established word meanings as clues to what statements mean, and statements' meanings as clues to what speakers mean,[7] and speakers' meanings as the ultimate basis for judging truth and falsehood.[8] Linguistic correspondence drops from consideration.

For example, D. R. Cousin argues that "semantical conventions seem to me neither necessary nor sufficient for the purposes of a theory of truth. . . . I do not think they are absolutely necessary; for, if they were, a malapropism or a slip of the tongue, even if correctly interpreted, would make a statement false. And this, I think, we should not say."[9] To illustrate, suppose that someone observes, "The new program will cost at least ten billion dollars," and we know that he means "at least ten *million* dollars." And suppose the latter estimate looks accurate. We would not say, on the strength of his mere words, "You're wrong, that's false."

Neither, however, would we say, "That's true." Even if we "correctly interpreted" his assertion, in the sense of correctly surmising what he meant to say, we would at most remark, "What you mean is true." For what his words mean—what he actually said—is not. The program would not cost at least ten billion dollars.

So it appears that Cousin's objection can be answered satisfactorily by distinguishing between what a person means and what his words mean,[10] then recognizing that the same relationship holds for people's meanings as for their judgments, beliefs, ideas, and the like. A person's meaning is true, we might say, if the words that express it—for example, "The program will cost at least ten *million* dollars"—are true. The basic test of truth is still linguistic.

It might also be suggested, however, that *what* a person means is true or false, not his meaning it, and *what* the words mean is true or false, not the words themselves, save in a secondary sense. That is, *propositional* truth may be proposed as primary.

Propositional Truth

We have seen Russell's and Brentano's attempts to demonstrate that the truth of beliefs or judgments is the primary notion and that linguistic truth is a derivative, secondary one. Now, as Wilfrid Sellars notes, others have argued in parallel fashion that truth pertains primarily not to "forms of words such as would correctly be said to express propositions," but rather to "the propositions they would be said to express."

> The contention is the familiar one that, since no form of words can properly be said to be true or false unless it expresses a proposition and since one and the same proposition can be expressed by using different sentences in different languages, any theory of the truth of forms of words must presuppose a prior theory of the truth of propositions. The conclusion is drawn that, if a "semantic" theory of truth is a theory that claims that truth in a *primary* sense pertains to forms of words, then all "semantic" theories are based on a mistake.[11]

True applies primarily not to specific utterances, in these or those words, but to what the utterances assert—to their abstract propositional content, common to any utterances that say the same thing.

This inference is as evident a *non sequitur* as Russell's, for this argument too can be reversed. One might argue with equal legitimacy that since no proposition can properly be said to be true or false unless the words that state it are true, any theory that makes propositional truth the primary notion rests on a mistake. Definition, once again, can go in either direction. Hence, nothing follows concerning the primacy of either notion. Many thinkers, however, have unhesitatingly assumed that primacy belongs with propositions and their truth. "All truth and all error," wrote John Stuart Mill, "lie in propositions."[12] For Frank Ramsey, "Truth and falsity are ascribed primarily to propositions."[13] According to A. J. Ayer, "To say that a belief, or a statement, or a judgement, is true is always an elliptical way of ascribing truth to a proposition, which is believed, or stated, or judged."[14]

Accordingly, for thinkers like Ramsey and Ayer, truth is not a property of utterances any more than it is of thoughts. Indeed, it is not a property of anything. The word *true* in the statement "*p* is true" adds nothing to the statement "*p*." In the next chapter we shall consider further reasons for this view. Here it may be noted that the reasoning might have gone the other way, and reached the opposite conclusion; for Ayer himself points out that the "propositions" he speaks of are not ethereal entities distinct from their verbal renderings:

> Regarding classes as a species of logical constructions, we may define a proposition as a class of sentences which have the same intensional significance for anyone who understands them. Thus, the sentences, "I am ill," "Ich bin krank," "Je suis malade," are all elements of the proposition "I am ill." And what we have previously said about logical constructions should make it clear that we are not asserting that a proposition is a collection of sentences, but rather that to speak about a given proposition is a way of speaking about certain sentences, just as to speak about sentences, in this usage, is a way of speaking about particular signs.[15]

Accordingly, we can give the same solution as before. A proposition is true if its statement, in whatever idiom, is true. And the statement is true if its expressions are used in accordance with their established uses. Such, in fact, is the criterion we apply, for propositions as for assertions. Propositions typically get expressed, and their expression is assessed in the manner that is standard for expressions.

A lecturer, say, refers to Professor R's theory that learning involves no insight. "An interesting proposition," he remarks, "and important were it true; but it isn't." And he proceeds to cite instances of (what we call) learning involving (the kind of thing we call) insight, much as he might point to falling drops of water to refute the claim that it hasn't rained all day. Professor R's "proposition" is put to the same test as his assertion of it: the test of linguistic correspondence.[16]

Practical Primacy

G. E. Moore stated the definitional circle in terms, not of statements and beliefs or statements and propositions, but of beliefs and propositions: "An act of belief is true, if and only if the proposition believed in it is true; and it is false, if and only if the proposition believed in it is false. Or, putting the matter the other way, we may say: A proposition is true, if and only if any act of belief, which was a belief in it, would be a true act of belief; and a proposition is false, if and only if any act of belief, which was a belief in it, would be false."[17] Moore then added: "I do not pretend to say which of these two senses is the more fundamental; and it does not seem to me to matter much which is. What is quite certain is that they are two different senses, but *also* that each *can* be defined by reference to the other."

If definitions are a person's sole concern, such indifference is under-standable. Definition, in the sense of mere verbal matching, works just as well either way. But consider the comparison Brentano borrows from Aquinas and Aristotle:

> When we thus spell out the various uses of the expression "true" its ambiguity leaps to the eye. But it is equally obvious that these multifarious uses are all related to one use which is standard for all the others. A comparable case is provided by the expression "healthy," an expression we sometimes use in connection with a body, at other times in connection with a complexion, and then again in connection with food, medicine, a region, or a walk. It is the healthy body that is healthy in the strict or proper sense; other things are called healthy because they impart, enhance, or establish health.[18]

In this instance, too, definition can go either way: we might define bodily health as that fostered by healthy food, climate, and so on, or define healthy food, climate, or the like as that which fosters bodily health. Suppose, though, that a doctor is performing an annual checkup on someone. He does not determine the person's health by requesting a complete account of such causal antecedents as diet, recreation, stresses at work, and environment. A person who smokes may have no lung tumor; a person who does not smoke may. A person under pressure may have no ulcer; a person under no pressure may. And so forth. There is no alternative, then. To determine bodily health, you must examine a person's body; you can forget about health in the secondary sense. The reverse, however, does not hold. If you are checking a new drug or food for its healthiness, you *do* have to ascertain its likely bodily effects. You cannot simply examine the substance in your test tube, as you might examine a person in your office, and ignore the substance's potential for causing or destroying health in people. One sense really is more fundamental, both conceptually and practically, than the other. And doctors, researchers, and others have to know which one it is, at least unreflectively.

Now the same holds for *true*. To judge the truth of some assertion you read in a book or hear on TV, you need not know whether its author believes it; you need not surmise the contents of the writer's or speaker's consciousness and compare them with reality; you need not observe the effects on your own thinking as you read or hear the words. You need merely consider the statement itself and its correspondence or lack thereof (as described in chapter 3): Are the words used in conformity with their established uses? To judge the truth of a belief or a proposition, however, you must have some verbal expression of it and must assess the expression by the test of correspondence. Linguistic truth is the primary notion, and we need to know that it is.

Linguistic Priorities

The kinship just noted between *healthy* and *true* sets them off from most other words we might characterize as having primary and secondary meanings. Usually, a primary meaning is such in a temporal, causal, or statistical sense, but not in what has been termed a conceptual sense or in the functional sense just explained and illustrated. Generally, the primary meaning need play no part, or even be known, when the word is employed in its secondary sense.

A closer look at these various kinds of primacy—temporal, causal, statistical, conceptual, and functional—sheds further light on the concept *true*, and also on language in general, for primary-secondary pairings are extremely common. Peruse the thousand most-used words in the English language, and you will probably find that the majority have secondary as well as primary senses. Reflect a little further, and you may note that the meanings are primary and secondary in quite different ways, which do not always coincide. Set the term *true* against this background, and the special character of its primary-secondary pairings will stand out more sharply, by contrast, and still other respects will come to light in which the word's linguistic sense is primary and the mental and propositional senses are secondary. The concept will be clarified both intrinsically and extrinsically. Here, then, are some possibilities to consider:

Temporal primacy. One sense may come first chronologically in the development of a language, and another sense may follow it. Thus the word *vanilla* was used first for the plant or fruit and only later for the flavor. However, the sense that comes first chronologically in a language need not come first in the linguistic history of individual speakers. Thus, for contemporary speakers of the English language, acquaintance with *vanilla* as the name of a flavor usually precedes acquaintance with its use as the name of a plant. The temporal order is reversed. For many words, though, the personal sequence parallels the historical. Most people hear weather called sunny, windy, or stormy, for example, before they hear dispositions called sunny, orators called windy, or sessions called stormy.

Causal primacy. Frequently, though by no means always or necessarily,[19] where there is temporal priority, there is also causal dependence. The subsequent sense of *vanilla*, for example, resulted from the earlier sense; the flavor was called *vanilla* because the plant from which it came was thus called. So, too, when an individual speaker first applies the term *stormy*, say, to a debate or an interview or hears another person do so and understands the extension, this personal application or personal understanding stems from his acquaintance with the term's original sense as a description of weather.

Statistical primacy. Temporal primacy for the individual correlates closely with statistical primacy—that is, with greater frequency. *Vanilla* is now used much more commonly for the flavor than it is for the plant; so that is the use most people learn first. *Sunny, windy,* and *stormy* are used more frequently for weather than for dispositions, orators, or sessions; so those, again, are the senses with which most people start.

Conceptual primacy. The term *conceptual* here indicates a stronger type of dependence than that, for example, between the earlier sense of *sunny* and the later sense. There may in fact be a causal link between the first sense and the second, but there need not be. We might conceivably learn the meaning of "sunny disposition" before we learned the meaning of "sunny weather," as we do in fact learn the meaning of "vanilla flavor" before we learn the meaning of "vanilla plant" or "vanilla fruit." However, for some meaning-pairs, as Wittgenstein noted, "It is only if the word has the primary sense for you that you use it in the secondary sense"—or could so use it. For example, "Only if you have learnt to calculate—on paper or out loud—can you be made to grasp, by means of this concept, what calculating in the head is."[20] The one sense *must* precede the other.

Functional, or identificational, primacy. Sometimes the use which must be known for the word to be understood in its secondary sense must also be consulted for the word to be so applied.[21] Contrast *calculate* with *healthy* or *true*. When people report having calculated sums in their heads, they must be acquainted with the criteria for physical calculation but need not apply them. They need not write the calculation on paper, say, to determine whether the activity they performed was calculating and calculating that sum. That is, they need do nothing comparable to what a person must typically do in order to determine the healthiness of a climate or the truth of a belief. The climate's effect on *people's* health must be considered; the belief must be *expressed,* and its expression must be tested in the manner of any true-false utterance.[22]

From such dependence in both use and acquisition, we can infer that for the English language as a whole, as for individual speakers of English, the linguistic sense of *true* must have preceded the mental sense. We may not infer immediately, however, that the linguistic sense is more common; it just appears, in fact, to enjoy this primacy in addition to the others and to be first statistically, as well as temporally, causally, conceptually, and functionally. (Think, for instance, how often people discuss the truth of some assertion made in a conversation, column, article, book, or letter to the editor without regard for whether the known or unknown author of the assertion believed it; and how infrequently, by comparison, they raise that ulterior question, then appraise the belief for truth or falsehood.)

Nonlinguistic Priority

In this comparison of primary and secondary senses of *true,* I have been attending to the mental sense more than the propositional, because that has been the linguistic sense's chief, and usually successful, rival for prime rating. Its success is understandable. Mental, nonlinguistic truth has seemed to explain linguistic truth, and not vice versa. And mental truth has appeared more important than linguistic truth. The whole or principal purpose of language, it has often been said, is to communicate thoughts or beliefs. They are what is important; speech is just a means. The point of true statements is to beget true beliefs.[23]

It may sound fanciful to reverse this claim and suggest that a chief function of true beliefs is to generate true statements. And yet, as a Hegelian might say, objectified spirit is not purely instrumental. True statements are woven into the fabric of our culture. Our books, manuals, libraries, archives, and computers, as well as our minds, are stocked with them. Were there no informative use of language, there would be no Buddhism, Islam, or Christianity, with their scriptures, doctrines, and creeds; no history, philosophy, theology, mathematics, or modern science; hence no technology or its products—no trains, planes, telephones, cars, TVs, dynamos, dams, or harvesters; no clones, transplants, appendectomies, or genetic engineering. In short, there would be no Western civilization—indeed, no civilization at all, just a level of existence near that of brute animals. Creatures so deprived could not so much as say, or truthfully communicate, that they had a toothache, that the supply of arrows was running low, or that a boar had been sighted in the neighborhood.

Reflections like these help us to appreciate linguistic truth and all it has meant to humankind. No wonder *true* has been a prestigious term, and truth a constant concern. It may still appear, however, that primacy belongs to mental, noverbal truth as the source of verbal truth; that from this abundant reservoir these varied waters flow.

Were the source really nonverbal, though, linguistic waters would not flow from it. Any thoughts or mental acts that gave rise to physics, theology, dictionaries, computers, creeds, or universities would have to be verbal thoughts, not just nonverbal representations; words would be their chief medium, even in the mind. So too, any beliefs or cognitive dispositions that issued in such outcomes would likewise be linguistic; they would consist largely of propensities to verbal behavior—to the making of informative utterances concerning genes, binomials, stresses, Caesar's Gallic wars, and the like. Hence the inner source is a verbal source, and verbal truth is primary after all. It is present in the mind itself, as well as in the mind's products.

To grasp the point I am making, consider this contrast. Healthy foods and healthy climates would be unaffected were there no human beings. Carrots would contain just as much iron; Arizona skies would be just as clear, if not a good deal clearer. Without true statements, though, there would be no true beliefs of the kind that fill our minds. We would not be programmed the way we are, linguistically. Whereas bodily health may enter the definition of healthy food or climates but does not constitute them, verbal truth does largely constitute mental truth, as well as define it. True thoughts are largely verbal thoughts, verbally true; true beliefs are largely dispositions, word-induced and word-defined, to verbalize true utterances publicly or privately.

Backing for these assertions appears in chapter 2's critique of nonverbal representation (empiricist, essentialist, or atomist), and in chapter 3's solution to problems of reference and correspondence that mentalistic, isomorphic theories failed to clarify. Thus, those earlier discussions now reveal their full implications. The type of critique effected in chapter 2 calls in question not only the explanatory power of mental representation as the paradigm of truth, but also its relative importance. If there can be no mental picturing of a clock's works or of Switzerland, if there can be no mental mirroring of nonexistent essences, if there can be no mental feelers reaching out to logical atoms, then mental representation and mental, nonverbal truth count for that much less in the overall scheme of things.

In any case, primacy of value or importance should not be confused with explanatory primacy. What is most precious and most desirable need not be most enlightening. It is perfectly conceivable that true beliefs might be more important than true statements and that, nonetheless, the sense in which statements are true might contain the key to the sense in which beliefs are true. The present chapter has argued that such is indeed the direction in which to look for clarity. To escape from the merry-go-round of reciprocal definitions of truth, take the linguistic exit, not the mentalistic one.

So arguing, the chapter has justified its position after the chapter on verbal truth. Were linguistic truth just the more important variety, or were the linguistic sense of *true* just temporally and/or causally prior, in the language or for individual speakers, it might be treated second. But when the mental and propositional senses are parasitic on the linguistic sense for their acquisition, use, and reflective understanding, then no other order of explication is feasible: verbal truth must come first. And it has.

CHAPTER 5

PERFORMATIVES, AVOWALS, AND THE ASYMMETRY OF *TRUE*

I have suggested that the key to truth is linguistic correspondence. A statement, assertion, or the like is true if its use of expressions agrees with their established uses. Such is the criterion that regulates our use of *true* when we speak of the truth of utterances and, derivatively, when we speak of the truth of judgments or beliefs. Although this account is, I think, roughly accurate as far as it goes, it does not go far enough. It does not bring out, for example, that many times when we employ the word *true*, we apply no criterion at all. Linguistic correspondence may be the test of truth insofar as there is one; but that criterion is frequently inoperative. This is not a peculiarity of the word *true;* many other words reveal a similar duality. But the asymmetry of such words has been noted only recently, and the status of *true* as their next of kin has therefore passed unnoticed. Witness, for instance, the Austin-Strawson debate.

Austin versus Strawson

Inquiry into the nature of truth was enlivened in 1950 by a debate between Oxford philosophers John Austin and Peter Strawson, in which Austin espoused a view akin to that proposed in chapter 3,[1] while Strawson developed an antithetical position such as Ramsey and Ayer had previously advanced. Both men sought to elucidate the question of truth by examining the use of the word *true*. But they disagreed on two chief points: (1) what things, if any, we describe when we employ the word *true;* (2) how the word functions on those occasions.

Austin

1. In Austin's view, it is chiefly statements that we call true, and those in the sense of specific utterances on specific occasions. We also speak, for instance, of "true beliefs," "true descriptions," "true accounts," "true propositions," "true words," and "true sentences." But "true belief," to start with, is a secondary form of expression, whereas "true statement" is primary; the belief must pass the same test as the statement that expresses it.[2] As for "true descriptions" and "true accounts," they are "simply varieties of true statements or of collections of true statements, as are true answers and the like. The same applies to propositions too, in so far as they are genuinely said to be true (and not, as more commonly, sound, tenable and so on)."[3] Granted, philosophers sometimes employ the term *proposition* in another way, for "the meaning or sense of a sentence or family of sentences"; however, "whether we think a lot or a little of this usage, a proposition in this sense cannot, at any rate, be what we say is true or false. For we never say 'The meaning (or sense) of this sentence (or of these words) is true': what we do say is what the judge or jury says, namely that '*The words* taken in this sense, or if we assign to them such and such a meaning, or so interpreted or understood, *are true.*' "[4] Thus words, and sometimes sentences, are also said to be true (the former often, the latter rarely); we may, for example, say "His closing words were very true" or "The third sentence on page 5 of his speech is quite false." "But here 'words' and 'sentence' refer, as is shown by the demonstratives (possessive pronouns, temporal verbs, definite descriptions, etc.), which in this usage consistently accompany them, to the words or sentence *as used by a certain person on a certain occasion.* That is, they refer (as does 'Many a true word spoken in jest') to *statements.*"[5] They refer to specific speech acts.

2. Having determined *what* we call true, namely statements, Austin then asked *when* we call them true, and why. His answer resembled that in chapter 3: We call statements true when and because they conform to linguistic conventions. However, he described the conformity and the conventions somewhat differently. For a statement to be true, he suggested, there must be a stock of symbols ("words" in a broad sense) to communicate with and a world to communicate about, revealing both similarities and dissimilarities. In addition, there must be two sets of conventions:

> *Descriptive conventions* correlating the words (= sentences) with the *types* of situation, thing, event, etc., to be found in the world.

> *Demonstrative conventions* correlating the words (= statements) with the *historic* situations, etc., to be found in the world.[6]

For "The cat is on the mat," the historic state of affairs to which the statement refers may be the cat's position (Strawson's earlier interpretation)

or the state of the room at the moment of utterance (Warnock's reading).[7]
Given these preconditions, "A statement is said to be true when the historic
state of affairs to which it is correlated by the demonstrative conventions
(the one to which it 'refers') is of a type with which the sentence used in
making it is correlated by the descriptive conventions." The position of the
cat, for example, or the condition of the room containing the cat is of the
kind indicated by the descriptive conventions for "The cat is on the mat."

Such are the requirements for truth in statements, and such is the point
of calling them true. Others may deny that the adjective *true* is descriptive,
as Austin was aware. Yet "if it is admitted (*if*) that the rather boring yet
satisfactory relation between words and world which has here been discussed does genuinely occur, why should the phrase 'is true' not be our way
of describing it? And if it is not, what else is?"[8]

Strawson
Appraising what he termed Austin's "purified version of the correspondence theory of truth," Strawson observed:

> He describes the conditions which must obtain if we are correctly to declare a
> statement true. His detailed description of these conditions is, with reservations,
> correct as far as it goes, though in several respects too narrow. The central
> mistake is to suppose that in using the word "true" we are asserting such condi-
> tions to obtain. . . . What supremely confuses the issue is the failure to distinguish
> between the task of elucidating the nature of a certain type of communication
> (the empirically informative) from the problem of the actual functioning of the
> word "true" within the framework of that type of communication.[9]

In its actual employment, according to Strawson, the word *true* (1) does not
describe *anything*, and so (2) does not *describe*.

1. "My saying something," Strawson argued, "is certainly an episode.
What I say is not. It is the latter, not the former, we declare to be true." Thus
when, for instance,

> we say "His statement was received with thunderous applause" or "His vehement
> assertion was followed by a startled silence," we are certainly referring to, charac-
> terizing, a historic event, and placing it in the context of others. If I say that the
> same statement was first whispered by John and then bellowed by Peter, uttered
> first in French and repeated in English, I am plainly still making historical
> remarks about utterance-occasions; but the word "statement" has detached itself
> from reference to any particular speech-episode. The episodes I am talking about
> are the whisperings, bellowings, utterings, and repetitions. The statement is not
> something that figures in all these episodes. Nor, when I say that the statement is
> true, as opposed to saying that it was, in these various ways, made, am I talking
> indirectly about these episodes or any episodes at all.[10]

2. We are more likely, then, to spot the word's true functioning if we
change our paradigms. Granted, we sometimes call a statement true subse-

quent to hearing it made. And we may therefore think we are describing an episode. However,

> The occasion of my declaring a statement to be true may be not that someone has made the statement, but that I am envisaging the possibility of someone's making it. For instance, in discussing the merits of the Welfare State, I might say: "It is true that the general health of the community has improved (that *p*), but this is due only to the advance in medical science." It is not necessary that anyone should have said that *p*, in order for this to be a perfectly proper observation. In making it, I am not talking *about* an actual or possible speech-episode. I am myself asserting that *p*, in a certain way, with a certain purpose. I am anticipatorily conceding, in order to neutralize, a possible objection. I forestall someone's making the statement that *p* by making it myself, with additions. It is of prime importance to distinguish the fact that the use of "true" always glances backwards or forwards to the actual or envisaged making of a statement by someone, from the theory that it is used to characterize such (actual or possible) episodes.[11]

Strawson, then, denies that the adjective *true* is descriptive and views it as assertive. When I call *p* true, he says, I am asserting that *p;* I am not describing the assertion. Indeed, I am not describing anything. "The word 'statement' and the phrase 'What he said,' like the conjunction 'that' followed by a noun clause, are convenient, grammatically substantival, devices, which we employ, on certain occasions, for certain purposes."[12] But let us not be bewitched by their surface grammar. "To suppose that, whenever we use a singular substantive. we are, or ought to be, using it to refer to something, is an ancient, but no longer respectable, error."[13]

Neither, I would add, should we be bewitched by the single substantive *truth* or the single predicate *true* into supposing we must give a single account of truth, as Austin and Strawson did. It may be that the concept is two-sided, as many concepts are, and that each of these philosophers views it from only one side. And such, I believe, is the case. Sometimes *true* describes; sometimes it simply asserts. Hence, Austin's account works better on some occasions, whereas Strawson's does better on others. Each philosopher seems equally right and equally wrong concerning both the points at issue between them. To see that this is so, it is necessary to investigate the source of their contrasting views.

The Source of Disagreement

Once we acknowledge the asymmetry of *true,* the dispute may seem easily explained by the notorious proclivity of philosophers to generalize. Thus, aspiring to a single, unified theory and noting the descriptive use of *true,* Austin extended that use to all cases; whereas Strawson, noting the nondescriptive use, proposed a counter-generalization. From the asymmetrical concept arose their asymmetrical positions. There is probably some truth in this explanation. Yet how could two thinkers as astute as Austin and Strawson both have overlooked so basic a feature of the concept they examined? How could they have failed to notice its bipolarity? The explanation, I suggest, is a methodological failing shared by both men, a failing that I have allowed the reader to sample firsthand through lengthy quotations and one that characterizes much discussion of language and its concepts.

The failing has two components. First, linguistic analysts often fail to clarify sufficiently certain key expressions they employ (for example, "assert," "say," "declare to be," "talk about," "talk about indirectly"). Second, they frequently neglect the cognitive aspect of the expressions they discuss (for example, what a competent user needs to know, what a hearer typically learns). Either lack would be more surprising than it is were it not for the other deficiency. The neglect of cognitive functioning would be astonishing were it not for the assumption that such functioning is adequately indicated by noting what someone "says," "asserts," or "talks about" when he or she employs a given expression. This assumption, in turn, would be astonishing were it not for how little attention is usually paid to the cognitive aspect of expressions.

By way of illustration, consider the quotation above, in which Strawson states his principal objection to Austin's view. Austin's main mistake, he suggests, "is to suppose that in using the word 'true' we are *asserting* such conditions to obtain." "What supremely confuses the issue," he then explains, "is the failure to distinguish between the task of elucidating the nature of a certain type of communication (the empirically informative) from the problem of the *actual functioning* of the word 'true' within the framework of that type of communication." It would appear that Strawson views a claim concerning what is "asserted" as an elucidation of the word's "actual functioning." Yet, as he himself notes, the type of communication in question is informative; and it is far from clear that assessments of what is "asserted," "said," "talked about," or the like clarify an expression's informative functioning. Strawson does not so define the terms he employs. Nor does he—or Austin—otherwise allude to the knowledge typically required for, or imparted by, the correct employment of *true*.

Even simple samples show the need to be more specific. Suppose I tell someone "It's raining." The stuff called rain comes from clouds, not from planes or helicopters, and I know it does, and so does my hearer. If I thought the drops had a different source, I would not say "It's raining." But have I "referred to" the clouds? Have I "asserted" their presence? Have I "talked about" them, or talked about them "indirectly"?[14] Who can say? Without further specification, especially in speculative discourse, the sense of these expressions is too indeterminate to permit an answer.[15] What further precision, then, might we reasonably introduce so as to clarify the Austin-Strawson debate?

In a discussion of statements and of statements about statements and of the statements' actual "functioning," the facts to consider first of all are cognitive. What *knowledge* does a person typically need in order to employ a given expression correctly? What *knowledge* might another person thereby receive (provided he believed the speaker and did not possess the knowledge already)? In our example, a person who says "It's raining" needs to know that drops of water are falling, there, from clouds. And a hearer, if master of the same language, will acquire this same knowledge (provided, as I said, that he believes the speaker and does not possess the knowledge already). Regardless of what we may wish to say the speaker is "talking about," these are basic facts for this expression and its functioning. What, then, are the corresponding facts about *true* and *false*, first with regard to their bearer, then with regard to their role?

Speech Acts or Chimeras?

Let us begin with Austin's example: "The third sentence on page 5 of his speech is quite false."[16] To make this assertion, I clearly need to know details such as Austin mentions. In particular, I need to know that the specific sentence, as uttered in that speech, functions as a statement, not as a question, command, plea, or exhortation. And anyone who knows the English language and believes what I say will come to believe the same thing (provided, once again, that the person does not believe it already). Thanks to my utterance, such a hearer will know that the third sentence on page 5 makes an assertion.

The facts in this case favor Austin's first claim, concerning reference. Not that they sharpen its sense. But his thesis, if ill defined, at least is not misleading. It can readily, naturally, be given this cognitive purport. If to "refer to," "talk about," or the like means to observe, know, and convey information concerning, then what we talk about in such an instance as this is indeed "the words or sentence *as used by a certain person on a certain occasion*." Strawson's denial of this claim, on the other hand, must either receive a different sense, disconnected from cognitive functioning, or be wrong. And were his denial so defined, in terms of certain partial features of surface grammar, it would lose its interest. This, then, seems something he would not have said had he taken due note of the facts—in this type of case.[17]

Switch the example to the kind he favored, however, and the tables are reversed. His account then seems realistic, and Austin's looks far-fetched. For instance, in discussing the merits of nuclear deterrence, I might say: "It is true that we have gone forty years without another world war." Here, no statement has preceded mine, which I judge to be true. No utterance has occurred or has been perceived or identified as a statement, rather than a question or command. No competent speaker of the language, furthermore, will take me to be reporting a "historic event" or will come to that conclusion on the strength of my assertion. If, then, we adopt the same definition of "talking about" as before, then surely we are not talking about a speech episode when we say, as we often do, "It is true that . . . ."

Other sample sayings fall between these clear extremes. Take the assertion "That's true." To say this, I need to know that a statement has been made. I need to be reacting to some specific speech occurrence. But my hearer can hardly learn from me that his or her utterance was a statement.[18] Thus, if we define "talking about" in relation to just the speaker and what he or she needs to know, even here I may be talking about a speech episode and be calling it true. (Compare the pronouns *he* and *she,* which seldom actually inform anyone of the sex of the person just referred to, though the speaker needs to know it.) If, however, we define "talking about" in relation to the hearer and what he or she may learn, we reach a different verdict. These further observations make doubly clear how far our two authors were from providing adequate guidelines so as to clarify the issues for themselves and for their audience.

Functional Asymmetry: Performatives, Avowals, and *True*

Once we note the referential asymmetry of *true,* we can recognize its functional asymmetry. That is, once we become aware that sometimes when we employ the word *true,* we are, in a clear and realistic sense, talking about a speech episode, and sometimes we are not, we are in a position to recognize that the expression's function on those diverse occasions is likewise various. Sometimes, as Austin claimed, it describes; sometimes, as Strawson maintained, it asserts. In this duality it resembles two familiar types of expression, one brought to prominence by Austin, the other by Wittgenstein. In reaction to one-sided insistence on the fact-stating function of speech, Austin drew attention to the different role of certain expressions when they occur as "performatives," whereas Wittgenstein emphasized the nondescriptive function of psychological verbs when they appear in "avowals" (*Äusserungen*). Both these large classes of expressions, combining descriptive and nondescriptive uses, help to situate *true* on the map of language.

Performatives
Austin coined the term *performative* to pick out a familiar, straightforward type of utterance, such as "I warn you," "I forbid it," or "I accept your apology," which looks like a statement and no doubt would be classed as such, yet is not usually either true or false.[19] The person who makes such an utterance is not describing or reporting something (for example, an inward

act), but is doing something (for example, warning, forbidding, accepting an apology).

> Suppose, for example, that in the course of a marriage ceremony I say, as people will, "I do"—(sc. take this woman to be my lawful wedded wife). Or again, suppose that I tread on your toe and say "I apologize." Or again, suppose that I have the bottle of champagne in my hand and say "I name this ship the *Queen Elizabeth*." Or suppose I say "I bet you sixpence it will rain tomorrow." In all these cases it would be absurd to regard the thing that I say as a report of the performance of the action which is undoubtedly done—the action of betting, or christening, or apologizing. We should say rather that, in saying what I do, I actually perform the action. When I say "I name this ship the *Queen Elizabeth*" I do not describe the christening ceremony, I actually perform the christening; and when I say "I do" (sc. take this woman to be my lawful wedded wife), I am not reporting on a marriage, I am indulging in it.[20]

Here Austin does not classify *christen, apologize, pardon, forbid, bet,* and the like as performatives; for these verbs, which occur in performative utterances, may also be used to describe or report. Indeed, that is their typical function in other than the first person and other than the present tense when the utterance is a statement. "I apologized" reports an act I performed. "You apologized" and "She apologized" report the acts of others. "He apologizes profusely then proceeds as before" describes a third person's behavior.

Thus these verbs all play a double role. We might call them two-sided expressions; but that would not adequately suggest the intimate interplay between the two uses, the performative and the descriptive. A genuine act of pardoning, promising, ordering, christening, and the like, in order to function as such, must satisfy certain conditions, including—as an optional or mandatory feature—the performative utterance ("I pardon," "I promise," and so forth). The report or description, employing the same verb in other persons and/or tenses, takes these same conditions as the basis for its ascription. The qualifying criteria of the act, which make it a genuine, effective promise, christening, command, or the like, are at the same time the descriptive criteria for the report. Thus, each such concept forms a tightly knit whole.

Take promising. What counts as a promise and binds is what counts as a promise and gets reported as such; the criteria are identical. This does not mean, though, that they coincide within a single speech act. The person who says "I promise you" does not thereby both make and report a promise. The speaker does not observe and identify his own performance as it unfolds and describe what he is doing as he does it, by means of the selfsame words. But a recipient of his assurance does register the utterance and its setting when, for instance, he or she replies: "All right, remember: you've promised."

The reply "You've promised" does not inform the promiser of the promise just made, just as "That's true" does not inform the asserter of his or her assertion. Yet in each case the one who makes the rejoinder ("You've promised" or "That's true") needs to have observed (not reflected on) the speech act and its fulfillment of certain conditions as a promise or as a true statement. On other occasions, however, the word *promise* does inform. The same person who says "You've promised" may later say "He promised." And the hearer of this report now knows that the person mentioned performed a specific kind of action, probably with words. Similarly, if someone says, "The third sentence on page 5 is true," you know without looking on that page what type of linguistic act the sentence probably figures in. If it is true, it must be an assertion, not a question, a command, or an exhortation.

Thus a close analogy emerges. Just as the word *true* occurs in informative descriptions of assertions (for example, "The third sentence on page 5 of his speech is true"), in noninformative descriptions of assertions (for example, "That's true"), and in assertions (for example, "It is true that the general health of the community has improved"), so the word *promise* occurs in informative descriptions of promises (for example, "He promised to come"), in noninformative descriptions of promises (for example, "You've promised"), and in promises (for example, "I promise to come"). A similar parallel holds between *true* and verbs like *believe*, which appear in both reports and avowals.

Avowals
The word *avowal* serves as well as any to designate another type of utterance employing other familiar verbs (*hope, regret, fear, believe, expect,* and so on) in the first person singular indicative active. For example, "I *hope* interest rates fall soon," "I *regret* that you were inconvenienced," "I *fear* the worst is yet to come," "I *believe* his assurances," "I *expect* their reply will arrive within the next few days." In such assertions, the analogy with other verbs (*talk, see, buy, make,* and so on) and with other uses of the same verbs ("I hoped," "she will regret," "he fears," "we believe," "they wouldn't expect," and so forth) strongly suggests that we have observed our own sentiments or acts, have identified them, and now report them when we say, "I hope, regret, fear, believe, expect, ... *p*." However, this would be an illusion. In such utterances as these we do not typically report hope, regret, fear, belief, expectation, and the like, but express them.[21]

To use a concrete illustration, suppose a friend returns after a long absence, and I greet him or her at the airport. I may express my gladness with a smile, a warm handshake, or a "So glad you're back." Whatever the manner, nonverbal or verbal, no introspective scrutiny of my sentiments need precede my performance. By nature and by a particular training, a particular education, we are disposed to give spontaneous expression to joys, wishes, hopes, sorrows, beliefs, or expectations in certain circumstances.[22] The handshake and welcoming smile are such expressions, and so is the utterance "So glad you're back."

If the parallel between the verbal act and the others seems doubtful, consider this: even if I were aware of a certain gladness in my feelings as my friend appeared, how would I recognize it, introspectively, as being-glad-he (or she)-is-back? How, in our earlier illustrations, could I intuit within me the fear *that the worst is yet to come,* or the expectation *that their reply will arrive within the next few days?* As we saw in chapter 2, it is not possible to picture mentally the future, disjunctive content of such propositions as these. Indeed no isomorphic "concept" or combination of "concepts," no image or ensemble of images, no atomistic mental act, ever does or can depict as much as a statement declares. So no such content can be observed introspectively and reported by an avowal. The speech act *cannot* function that way.

The only place an expectation, for example, might perhaps be observed would be in its expression.[23] And a person who expresses an expectation does not both observe the verbal act under way and report on it in the selfsame words. "I expect interest rates to fall" does not simultaneously both express and report a person's expectation. Looking back, though, the same person may report, in the past tense, "I expected interest rates to fall." And others, having witnessed the verbal expression or other, nonverbal indications, may report in the third person: "He (or she) expects interest rates to fall."

Hence in the employment of these expressions, too—of *expect, wish, mean, believe, recall, marvel, understand,* and the like, as well as of *promise, predict, pardon,* and the rest—we note both reporting and nonreporting roles, yet a close link between them, so that they form in conjunction a single, bipolar concept (*expect, wish, mean,* and so on).[24] And for these expressions we detect the same range of possibilities as we did for performatives and the word *true,* namely: (1) uses that both report and inform ("He believes," "She expects," "I was convinced"); (2) uses that report without informing ("You believe that now, but . . ."); (3) uses that neither report nor (in that sense) inform ("I believe that . . . ," "I expect that . . .").

True
These comparisons exemplify a fact noted by Wittgenstein in discussing belief: "My own relation to my words is wholly different from other people's."[25] I do not listen to the sounds that issue from my mouth and thereby learn various things about myself—the same as others then recount about me.[26] I do not attend, for example, to the words "I believe *p*" and thereby discover that I believe, what I believe, or how firmly I believe it. But others

may and do. Again, I do not listen to my performative utterances and thereby learn that I am promising this, predicting that, or conceding something else. But others frequently do. Finally, if I say, "It is true that *p*," I do not discover from my words that I am making an assertion, namely of *p*, nor that its employment of expressions conforms to their established uses. Yet, once again, others may learn these things from my utterance and may then recount what they have learned.

The same expression that appears in the performative, avowal, or assertion sometimes reappears in the report, sometimes not. And the variation may occur at either end—that is, either in the report or in what it reports. "I believe *p*" may give rise to either "He believes *p*" or, for instance, "He's convinced that *p*," while "He believes *p*" may be based on "I believe *p*," "I think *p*," or simply "*p*." The sheer assertion does just as well as evidence of belief. Similarly, "I concede" may occasion "She concedes *p*" or "She grants *p*," while "She concedes *p*" may be based on the performative "I concede *p*," the performative "I grant *p*," or simply "*p*." The assertion "It is true that *p*" may be assessed as "true," but also as "accurate" or "correct". "What she said was true" may follow on her saying "It is true that *p*," "I assure you that *p*," or "*p*." Thus the connection between reporting and nonreporting uses of such bipolar terms (*believe, concede, true*) is not simple, evident, and invariant. The expressions might occasion fewer perplexities if it were.

The asymmetry of verbs like *believe* and *understand* has fostered disputes concerning the nature of so-called mental acts, much as the asymmetry of *true* begot the Austin-Strawson debate concerning the nature of truth. Let people assimilate "I believe" and "He believes," taking both as reports, and "I believe" (not based on external criteria) will then suggest an inner, private referent, whereas "He believes" (governed by behavioral criteria) will suggest a purely public referent. Isomorphists and introspectionists will defend the first position, behaviorists and physicalists the second. After all, both sides might insist, *believe* is not an equivocal expression; surely it means the same thing, regardless of person or tense. In like manner, let people suppose uniformity in the use of *true*, and it will appear either descriptive, because of samples such as Austin favored, or not descriptive, but assertive, by reason of samples such as Strawson stressed. The solution is to recognize diversity in the one word's employment. Combine these divergent samplings—Austin's and Strawson's—and another bipolar concept comes to light, comparable in important respects to the behavioral and psychological concepts that figure in performatives and avowals.

Conclusion

In this chapter I have underscored analogies between quite diverse expressions in order to establish and reinforce the point stated in the opening

paragraph. Chapter 3 was right, I said, when it identified linguistic correspondence as the key criterion of truth. The criteria of mental and propositional truth depend on the criterion of verbal truth; and the criterion of
verbal truth, insofar as there is one, is indeed agreement between the use
made of words and their established uses. Yet in numerous instances, *true*
ignores criteria. Statements of the form "It is true that p" follow no descriptive norm (other than that for p), but play a part in establishing a norm.
They figure among the assertions described as true or false.

We can now see that this situation is duplicated in countless other cases.
Insofar as there are criteria of promising, conceding, christening, declaring, pardoning, apologizing, and the like; insofar as there are criteria of
believing, hoping, expecting, meaning, wondering, and the rest, they are
behavioral. Yet often these verbs do not describe; no criteria guide their
appearance in performatives or avowals. Rather, such speech acts provide a
basis for descriptive applications of the same expressions that they employ
nondescriptively. They figure prominently among the criteria for promising, conceding, christening, pardoning, and the like, and for believing,
hoping, regretting, rejoicing, marveling, meaning, and the rest; they do not
themselves apply the criteria that they help to establish.

None of these verbs belongs to the large class of expressions considered
in the next chapter, however, whereas *true* does. Conversely, few, if any,
other members of that class besides *true* belong to the class of asymmetrical
expressions. The two groupings coincide at this one spot. In order to
pinpoint the concept *true* on the map of language, then, we shall now
examine its kinship with this further family of terms, "cognitive comparatives."

CHAPTER 6

COGNITIVE COMPARATIVES AND *TRUE*

One major obstacle to acceptance of an explanation of truth in terms of linguistic agreement is the common belief that the conscious activity of the mind is far more extensive than it actually is, with images or "concepts" or mental projections accompanying practically every word we hear or speak. Another major obstacle, paradoxically, is the realization that mental contents are in fact far skimpier than supposed. Once this is recognized, the rich, complex analysis I have suggested for *true* may appear unrealistic. Who ever thinks of all that correspondence—word by word and point by point—when he or she utters the word *true*? And if nobody thinks it, how can it be the word's meaning?

Cognitive Richness

One response is to revise the conception of meaning implicit in the objection and made explicit, for instance, in the famed Port Royal *Logic:* "To say that a written or spoken word means such and such is to say only that our minds entertain the meaning, that is, the idea connected with that word whenever we hear or see the word."[1] This account does not suit even the simplest terms. Supposedly, the truth-conditions for a word's application pertain to its meaning. Hence the meaning of *rain,* for example, includes rain's consisting of drops of water, falling, from clouds. Yet who thinks of clouds when he or she looks outside and says "It's raining"? Who, for that matter, thinks of the individual drops upon hearing someone say "It's raining"? Yet can there be rain without individual drops?

The truth-conditions of words are things we *know,* not things we generally think of as we use or hear words. When we say it is raining, we *know* that the drops must come from clouds if they are to count as rain, but we do not imagine the clouds and the distillation of drops and their falling from the clouds to the earth. When we hear someone say it is raining, we *know* that rain consists of falling drops of water, but we do not imagine the multiple, individual drops or their consisting of water, rather than of some sensibly similar substance such as alcohol. How could we? Nor, for that matter, do we conjure up any essence of clouds, drops, falling, or water.

It is necessary, then, to distinguish, more sharply than many thinkers have, between knowledge and thought. "It would be contradictory," declares the Port Royal *Logic,* "to maintain that I know what I say in pronouncing a word and that, nevertheless, I think of nothing in pronouncing it other than the very sound of the word."[2] There would be a contradiction only if knowing were synonymous with thinking, which it is not. Thinking, we might say summarily, is an act; knowing is not. My knowing the meaning of *rain,* for example, is not an action I have performed for the last fifty years or more.[3]

My concern here is not primarily to preserve the concepts *meaning* and *knowledge* from speculative misrepresentation. Such individual distortions, iceberg-wise, signal something more massive. They reflect and perpetuate a misconception of language and thought as a whole, stressing mental activity, rather than mental capacity. They obscure the *cognitive* richness of discourse.

Wittgenstein, we noted, spoke of the temptation to conceive language "as a permanent background to every sentence which we say, and to think that, although the sentence as written on a piece of paper or spoken stands isolated, in the mental act of thinking the calculus is there—all in a lump." The mistake is to suppose that the whole calculus or system is vicariously present in thought. Our *knowledge* of language, however, does indeed stand as such a background "to every sentence which we say."

Accordingly, there is nothing implausible about chapter 3's account of *true.* Granted, we do not call to mind the semantics, pragmatics, and syntax of each expression in a statement before declaring the statement true or false. But as competent speakers of the language, we do know these things about the expressions used, and we manifest this knowledge when we call a statement true or false. This point has already been spelled out in chapter 3. A second, related source of objections, however, remains to be considered at greater length.

Cognitive Comparatives

Predicates like *red, sweet, square,* and *sorrowful* are more complex than is often imagined; still, in comparison with many other terms, they are relatively simple. Hence they act as paradigms. We expect other words, though perhaps more complex and confusing, to function much as they do and may therefore grow skeptical if presented with some very different analysis. A rigmarole like that about use-usage correspondence, for example, may appear implausible. Switch the term of comparison, however, and such misgivings dissipate. Compare *true* with other paradigms—with its genuine next of kin—and the correspondence account appears quite natural.

As a first step in this direction, contrast a word like *red* with one like *big*. To correctly describe an object, say a truck, as red, I need to know two things: the color of the truck and the meaning of *red*. To correctly call the truck big, I need to know three things: the size of the truck, the meaning of *big*, and the size of trucks in general. For though a red truck is the same color (perhaps the same shade) as a red ant or a red planet, a big truck is not the same size as a big ant or a big planet—or anywhere near it.

Big is a veiled comparative. In most instances it means "bigger than the average"—the average ant, the average truck, the average planet, and so on—yet it does not spell out the comparison explicitly.[4] When we call an ant, a truck, or a planet big, no mention is made of the term of comparison or of the comparison. Nor does thought fill in what *big* fails to articulate. We simply *know* the rules for that word and *know*, for instance, the size of trucks; and on the basis of this knowledge, when we see a forty-footer, we call it a "big truck"—without necessarily adverting to anything but that one truck. Such expressions I shall therefore refer to as "*cognitive* comparatives."[5]

In contrast to the either-or character of classificatory concepts, these alternative types allow for more and less.[6] The characteristic on which a cognitive comparative focuses—size, weight, cost, correspondence—is typically one that admits of degrees. And the degrees can be expressed in explicitly comparative terms. We can say that things are large or small, but also that they are larger or smaller than others. We can say that statements are true or false, but also that they are truer or falser than others—that is, that they correspond more or less closely to the facts.[7]

However, not all cognitive comparatives, when spelled out, acquire the form "-er than" ("bigg*er than* average," "small*er than* most," and so on), since not all are adjectives, and not all express differences. Comparative scrutiny may reveal sameness, equality, or similarity (in size, speed, intelligence, use, and so forth), not difference; and in that case the meaning may be rendered by *same, equal,* or *similar,* not by "-er than." "Same size" and "just as big" are as comparative as "bigger than."

The configuration common to cognitive comparatives, therefore, and meriting the name, is the one just described, in which (1) three things are known, not two; (2) predication is based on the relation between the expressed and unexpressed terms of comparison; and (3) the relation is not verbally or mentally adverted to, but is nevertheless known. It is this configuration and not some particular instance of it, requiring some single formulation, that accounts for the label "cognitive comparative."

Hence *true*, also, is a cognitive comparative; this is the family to which it belongs. For although *true* differs from *big* in important ways, as we shall see, in the respects just noted it resembles *big*, rather than *red*. It too, we might say, is a three-pole, not a two-pole, concept. To correctly characterize a statement as true, we need to know three things (the meaning of *true*, the statement's use of words, and the words' established uses), not just two (the meaning of *true* and the statement's use of words). Calling a statement true is equivalent to saying that its use of words agrees with their established uses. This comparison, however, is not explicitly stated or explicitly thought. It suffices that we attend to the present object of description— that is, to the particular assertion and its use of words. We need not recall the words' established uses nor the rules for *true*, any more than we need to recall the average size of trucks and the rules for *big*. *True* is a *cognitive comparative*.

So are countless other words. Some are nouns, some verbs, some adverbs,[8] though most plentiful are the adjectives (*big, fast, deep, smart, thin, good, loud, easy*, and so on). Some occupy a continuum more densely (*miniscule, tiny, small, large, huge, enormous*), others less densely (*expensive* and *cheap, common* and *rare*). Some do double duty, now resembling *red*, now *big* (compare "three feet deep" and "deep ocean").[9] Some are simpler, others more complex. Some reveal one structure, some another, while retaining the general family resemblance.

Big and *true*, then, are by no means oddities. They and their kind are far outnumbered, however, by *red* and its kindred two-pole terms.[10] And these latter, being both simpler and more numerous than the three-poled cognitive comparatives, tend to shape our conceptions of how words work, so that we are ill prepared for such an apparent aberration as the concept *true*. For this reason, too, an analysis like that in chapter 3 may seem far-fetched.

One purpose of the present chapter is to counter this impression by further locating *true* on the conceptual map. Chapter 4 related it to other words with primary and secondary senses. Chapter 5 situated it with expressions used in performatives and avowals, which it resembles in having both descriptive and nondescriptive uses. The present chapter, centering on just the descriptive uses, places *true* within a different constellation of terms, that of cognitive comparatives.

A second aim of the chapter is to investigate in a preliminary way this little-explored area of language. Avowals, and especially performatives, though adverted to only recently, have already been subjected to close scrutiny. Cognitive comparatives, though if anything more numerous, have yet to receive comparable attention.

A thorough survey of cognitive comparatives would require a separate book. Here, guided by my focus on *true*, I shall make just a single, systematic foray into this unexplored territory. Starting with *big*, I shall work closer, step by step, to the spot occupied by *true*, in the expectation that, by locating this key concept in relation to its neighbors, I may be able to illumine both it and them.

Further Similarities with *Big*

The basic similarity between a word like *big* and the predicate *true* helps to dispel various prejudices and misconceptions. We have already noted how a mentalistic tendency, equating meaning with conscious representation, may work against acceptance of a more ample analysis. We do not *think* about linguistic correspondence, it may be objected, when we call a statement true. Neither, we might now add (with reasoning like Strawson's in mind), do we *talk about* the correspondence or *say* that it obtains when we utter or hear the word *true*. For this second reason, too, it may be inferred that such is not the meaning of the word. And once again *big* may furnish an antidote. The relationship that *big* expresses and that clearly belongs to its meaning is not something we typically "say" or "talk about" when we employ the term—not in the usual sense of "say" or "talk about."

When, for instance, we remark, "The big house on the corner burned down last night," we are not talking about all other houses, their size, and the relation between their size and the size of the house that burned down. We are talking about the house on the corner. Yet clearly we cannot articulate the meaning of *big* save in relational terms. We cannot spell out its meaning by means of inches or feet, as we might for the word *yard*, but must bring in much that we do not typically "talk about" when we say a thing is big.

What we "talk about" is the reference of our words, and the reference of words is not coextensive with their meaning. It is therefore fallacious to argue from restrictions on reference to like restrictions on meaning.[11] The meaning of *true* when we call a statement true reaches beyond the one statement to which we refer, just as the meaning of *big* when we call a house *big* reaches beyond the single house we "talk about."

Similar remarks apply to the expression "say that" and the objections it occasions. "When we call a statement true," it may be argued, "we do not say that its use of expressions corresponds with their established uses." Agreed; and when we call a house big we do not *say that* it is larger than most houses. Yet such is the meaning of *big*. *Big* is a veiled, implicit comparative, as *true* is; it does not spell out the comparison.

Hence a simple kindred term like *big*, by virtue of two traits it shares with *true*, helps to dissipate two different sorts of objection. It dissipates one type because, like *true*, it is comparative, yet not mental; it does not require or generally involve thinking out the comparison. It dispels another type because, again like *true*, it is comparative, yet not explicit; it does not mention or articulate the comparison. It does not talk about the comparative relationship or say that it obtains.

The kinship of *true* with *big* also helps to sort out the truth and the falsehood in remarks like the following:

> "True" and "false" have a constant meaning, whatever the synthetic statements or propositions to which they are applied happen to be; whereas the reasons—or the criteria—for their application vary with the particular synthetic statement or proposition, or kind of statement or proposition, involved. And the meaning of "true" and "false" can be learned or taught without reference to any *particular* criterion or set of criteria of truth and falsity.[12]

The opening assertion holds equally for *big*. Big clouds, for example, differ notably from big deficits; yet it does not follow that they are big in a different sense of the word. *Big* relates clouds to other clouds in the same way that it relates deficits to other deficits: it indicates that they are larger than average. Though the criteria of size differ from class to class, the sense of *big* does not. Or so we may reasonably assert. For notice how natural it was to say that in order correctly to label something "big," we need to know three things: the size of the thing in question, the size of things of that kind, and the meaning of *big*. We did not list the third item as "the meanings of *big*, one for each different kind of referent."

Similarly, when we recognize how greatly truth, like size, may vary from one class of utterances to another, we should hesitate to infer that the sense of *true* undergoes a like shift. For *true*, as we have seen, often functions as a cognitive comparative. And when it does, its sense may fluctuate no more than does that of *big* or *small*. From class to class it may indicate the same basic relationship—that of correspondence—between the various word uses it relates.[13]

This possibility must be kept in mind when it is claimed that factual statements, for example, are true in a different sense than logical or mathematical statements,[14] or that "the meaning of '*p* is true' needs revision when imported from ordinary into scientific domains," since "it is the inherent vagueness and indeterminacy of ordinary statements that is essential to their being true in the usual sense."[15] Granted, scientific terms and scientific language-games are typically more precise than nonscientific terms and language-games; but correspondence with precise uses is not a different kind of correspondence, in a different sense of the word, than correspondence with imprecise uses. Truth-as-correspondence does not alter; only the terms of correspondence do.

Yet there may be valid grounds for stressing the specificity of different varieties of truth. Suppose someone were to say: "Big is big. A big bang, a big debt, a big surprise—all are big in the same sense." Despite the common concept, one might suspect that important differences had been over-looked. A bang is not big in the same way as a debt is, or a debt in the same way as a surprise, or a surprise in the same way as a house. Bigness is not simply bigness, regardless of the referent. Indeed, in its various applications, even the sense of *big* may fluctuate somewhat.

Consider, for example, the bigness of books. More specifically, envisage a large medieval manuscript, with heavy binding, heavy parchment pages, and large illuminated letters. The pages may be relatively few and likewise the words, but if the volume measures twelve inches wide by fifteen inches long by two inches thick, it is a big book. The dimensions are what count. By contrast, consider a big crowd. Twenty people spread over an acre do not qualify as a big crowd, whereas five hundred people squeezed into a quarter of an acre may. Crowds are big numerically, not spatially. Books, on the contrary, are big spatially, not numerically. This is not something we could know simply by knowing about crowds and books plus the concept *big*. We need to know how *big* is used specifically for crowds and specifically for books—and specifically for worries, debts, explosions, surprises, cookies, candelabra, and the rest. The concept may not vary as much as its referents do, but it too fluctuates from case to case.

So does the concept *true*, in ways we could not predict if we knew only that the truth of statements consists in correspondence, plus the particular class of utterances to be judged. Coming chapters provide clear illustrations. Take performatives, whose truth will be discussed in chapter 9. "I swear that Sue did it" might be judged true provided the speaker did in fact swear and swear that Sue did it; or it might be termed true provided that Sue did it. Either convention is conceivable, and either would make truth a form of correspondence. But which convention we do in fact follow, and what form the correspondence does in fact take in this instance, only usage can reveal. Its verdict is that *true* connects differently to reportive and performative utterances. The truth of "I swear that p" does not resemble closely that of "I hear that p." The truth of p is decisive in the first case, not in the second. From this and similar contrasts it follows that it is not completely accurate to say, as in the second statement of the quotation above: "The meaning of 'true' or 'false' can be learned or taught without reference to any *particular* criterion or set of criteria of truth and falsity."

A further instructive likeness between *big* and *true* concerns the exactness of comparison between the spoken and unspoken terms of reference. A big dog, I said, is bigger than average. But how much bigger? A true statement, I said, uses words in accordance with their established uses. But how close must the correspondence be? One answer appears later in this chapter when I compare *true* with *accurate,* and another in chapters 7, 11, and 12 under the rubric "relative similarity." Here, already, a third, complementary reply emerges from a comparison with *big*.

An exact measure of bigness for dogs—say, five inches taller than average—could be applied only if we had an exact notion of the average size of dogs. That would require our knowing, first, just what animals, past or present, count as dogs, and, second, what size they are or were, so as to work out the average size. And even were such knowledge once acquired, we still might have to conduct a periodic survey, for the average size of dogs may change. Since similar difficulties arise for other classes of things—for big buildings, banks, books, trees, problems, expenditures, and so on—it is evident that *big* is not an exact measure.

Neither, for similar reasons, is *true* an exact measure of correspondence between a given statement's use of terms and their established uses. To the indefiniteness of *dog* there corresponds the indefiniteness of the concepts (*eat, speak, grass, dog,* and so on) that figure in statements. To the question concerning past generations of dogs and how far back we need to count, there corresponds the question of past word uses and how recent a use must be to count as an "established use" at the time of utterance. To the impossibility of knowing all dogs and their exact weights, there corresponds the impossibility of knowing all the speech acts that have employed the same terms as a given utterance and just how they employed them. A precise, comprehensive summation is as impossible in the one case as in the other, and a precise comparison is therefore as surely excluded. It is just not conceivable that *true,* given its cognitive structure, might indicate *precisely* how close the correspondence is between a statement's use of words and the established uses of those words.

A still more important parallel with comparatives like *big* concerns the objectivity of *true.* Told that truth depends on, indeed consists in, correspondence with established word uses, people may conclude that truth "is merely a matter of words." J. O. Wisdom writes: "The central idea here is that one theory may be exchanged for another one by altering the conventions to do with the meaning of basic terms. And here we have the central idea of 'truth as a convention,' not as recording something about the world."[16] One might as well conclude that *big* says nothing about things' size, since it relates their size to the average size, and the average size may change. A second error is linked with this first. Told that truth depends on word uses, people may feel that truth, if not a mere matter of words, is nonetheless rendered "relativistic." It may seem to rest on shifting sands and may therefore appear unreliable. Word uses vacillate; they vary from time to time and from context to context. However, so do sizes; and their variations affect our use of words like *big.* But that does not render our judgments of size unsure or make them "relativistic." Buildings in Manhattan, for example, are taller now than formerly. Hence some building once called "tall" or "large" may now be called neither. Yet there is nothing shaky or subjective about such ascriptions of size; and we should have no more misgivings about truth-assessments based on implicit comparisons with current word uses.

If anything, *true* is less relativistic than *big*. Suppose present-day Manhattanites were speaking about an earlier building. They would not call it large or tall if it had just four stories, even if four stories was tall for that period; whereas they would call an earlier statement true if its use of words conformed with the words' established uses at the time of utterance. It is for this reason that "Once true, always true" holds, whereas "Once large, always large" does not. The truth-value of a statement (I do not say "a sentence")[17] never alters.

Dissimilarities: Referent-Invariance and Complexity

Other parallels might perhaps be noted between *big* and *true*. But as a first important difference, notice that the same object may be characterized as large, small, or neither, depending on the noun used to designate the object, whereas no such reversal results from a switch in the noun modified by *true*. To illustrate: the selfsame object may be a large stone but a small boulder, a large house but a small mansion, a large animal but a small elephant, and so forth. The selfsame utterance, however, cannot be a true statement but a false declaration; the identical passage is not a true account but a false description; the same belief is not a true doctrine but a false conclusion. It is difficult to find matchings of *true* and *false* that resemble those for *large* and *small*. *True* and *false*, we might say, are more referent-invariant than *large* and *small*, or, for that matter, than most cognitive comparatives.

A further point of dissimilarity can be illustrated by means of *big* and *typical*. To apply *big* correctly, for instance to a car, we need to know just a single feature—the size of the car and of cars in general. To apply *typical* correctly, for instance again to a car, we need to know many features, both of the car in question and of cars in general.[18] Does the vehicle have four wheels or three? Does it run on gas or alcohol? Does it have a luggage compartment, an overhead rack, a back seat, a rumble seat, a supercharger, twin pipes? We need to know these and many other things in order to determine whether the car is indeed typical. Thus *typical* (or *usual, ordinary, standard,* and the like) is not only a cognitive comparative, like *big* and *true;* it is also a complex comparative, as *true* is, but *big* is not.

First, *typical* is a cognitive comparative. To apply the term correctly, one must know three things: the traits of the particular thing in question, the traits of things of that kind, and the meaning of *typical*. Suppose, for instance, that I know the meaning of *typical* and that I am thoroughly acquainted with my electric typewriter. I still cannot tell whether it is a typical electric typewriter unless I am familiar with other electric type-writers. These form the unspoken term of comparison for "typical electric typewriter," as dogs do for "big dog."

Second, this cognitive comparative is complex, in much the same way that *true* is. For one thing, it requires knowledge of multiple traits, as *true* does. For another, the traits vary in number, according as the object described is more or less complex (for example, a visit from grandmother versus a toothpick), much as the points of correspondence vary in number for *true*, according as an utterance is longer or shorter, simpler or more complex. In addition, the traits vary in kind from case to case, depending on the nature of the thing called typical, much as they do for statements called true, depending on the structure and constituent expressions of the statements. The relevant considerations for "Rain has been predicted" and "God is merciful" differ as radically as they do for typical toothpicks and typical religions.

From this comparison there emerges, finally, a parallel with what chapter 3 labeled the *cumulative* character of truth. A car may be typical in all other respects but if, for example, it has no hood or is painted in polka dots—if it departs in this one way from the majority of cars—it is not a typical car. No one would say it is. Similarly, a single aberration from established use suffices to make a statement false.

Minority and Nonminority Terms

The distinction between simple and complex comparatives permits consideration of a further difference between a term like *big* and the complex comparative *true*. *Big*, we might say, is a minority term; *true* is not.

To grasp the meaning of this contrast, consider the continuum of sizes, from tiny to huge, and the cognitive comparatives of size—*miniscule, tiny, small, big, large, huge, enormous, immense*—which partition the continuum into broader or narrower segments. *Tiny* picks out a narrow band at one end of the spectrum, *huge* a narrow band at the other end. *Small* covers a broader stretch than *tiny*, *large* a broader stretch than *huge*. And so forth.

A first thing to observe about this partitioning is that no term picks out the middle segment, between small and large. This is typical. Aside from compound expressions like *medium-sized*, I am aware of no cognitive comparative in the languages with which I am familiar that occupies the middle stretch of a continuum. None comes between *large* and *small*, *fast* and *slow*, *smart* and *stupid*, *strong* and *weak*, *cheap* and *costly*, *young* and *old*, and so forth. None indicates simply average size, average speed, average intelligence, average strength, average cost, average age, and so on (for the class of things in question). One or two such expressions may exist in English or kindred tongues; but if they do, they are exceptional.[19]

A second point to notice is that none of the specimens I have cited covers the larger part of a class or even half of it. Large birds are larger than average, fast cars faster than average, smart dogs smarter than average, strong odors stronger than average, expensive clothes more expensive than average, old houses older than average, and so forth; hence they are larger, faster, smarter, stronger, more expensive, and so on than most specimens of that kind. They are a minority.[20] And each of these terms is, in this sense, a minority term. So too are *small, slow, stupid, weak, cheap,* and the like, at the other end of the spectrum. A small tree is smaller than most, a slow pace slower than most, a weak floor weaker than most, a cheap fare cheaper than most, a stupid dog denser than most. And terms like *tiny, huge, awful, superb,* and *brilliant,* farther out toward the end of a continuum, are still more clearly minority expressions.

I know of no cognitive comparative that is a majority term in the same sense that *big* is a minority term.[21] Not one of which I am aware groups a referent with the majority of its kind (save perhaps on occasion and for some single class[22]). This does not mean, however, that all cognitive comparatives are minority expressions. Most complex cognitive comparatives are neither minority nor majority terms.

Consider again a word like *typical.* One atypical trait, I said, suffices to make a thing atypical. And an atypical trait is a minority trait. Most cars are not painted in polka dots. Most do not have just three wheels. Most do not have the engine exposed to view. Most do not have rumble seats. And so forth. Thus to call a car or anything else a typical member of its class is, in a sense, to class it with the majority—trait by individual trait.

It does not follow, however, that most cars are typical cars, or that most things of a given kind are typical things of that kind. If a majority of cars, say, are typical cars, that is a contingent fact and not a logical necessity. I am not sure that it is a fact, and yet I know the meaning of *typical.* To apply that word to a car I need know only whether most cars have four wheels, have engines, have them up front, have tires rather than tracks, and so forth. I need not know whether cars that vary somewhat from the norm—cars with tracks, fins, twin pipes, rumble seats, hoodless engines, polka dots, musical horns, and so forth—collectively constitute a minority or a majority of cars.[23]

A similar analysis, it seems, applies to the adjective *true.* If a majority of statements are true, that too appears to be a contingent fact, not determined by the meaning of *true* or *true statement.*[24] To correctly assess a statement's truth, I need know only whether its use of words agrees, word by word and trait by trait, with the words' established uses. I need not know whether a majority or minority of statements pass the same test.

Commendatory Comparatives

From this and earlier parallels it appears that *typical* bears a closer kinship to *true* than *big* does. It is a sibling, or at least a first cousin. In specific respects, however, other expressions resemble *true* still more closely than does *typical*. Terms like *healthy*, *legal*, and *good*, for instance, are not only complex cognitive comparatives like *typical* and *true;* they also have a positive connotation, as *true* does, but *typical* does not. They too are *plus* words. *Good* has received special attention, specifically in these three respects: as a cognitive comparative, as a complex cognitive comparative, and as a term of commendation.

First, *good* is often comparative, though not always. A good knife, for example, may be a knife that meets certain standards, without any implication that the majority of knives do not ("I kept all the good knives," someone remarks, "and threw the bent ones away").[25] However, a good knife may also be a better-than-average knife ("Hey, that's a good knife," a boy exclaims admiringly).[26] The type of appraisal shifts from setting to setting.

In either case, ascriptions of goodness are typically based on more than a single feature, and *good*, when used comparatively, may therefore be classed as a complex cognitive comparative. The criteria of goodness are multiple for individual classes of things and differ in number and kind from class to class.[27] A good apple, say, is called *good* for reasons (texture, taste, appearance, and so on) quite different from those for calling a car good (roominess, sturdiness, fuel efficiency, performance, looks, and so on). More specifically, the criteria for a good eating apple differ somewhat from those for a good cooking apple, and the criteria for a good family car differ from those for a good racing car.

Finally, *good* is not only a complex cognitive comparative, as *true* is, but also a term of commendation. Hence, given the versatility of *good*—its various senses, its applicability to the most varied things—one may wonder why the special term *true* exists in addition to *good* to commend statements and the like. Why not simply call utterances good, as one calls roads, concerts, homilies, or vacation spots good, when they satisfy the criteria for good things of their kind?

A plausible explanation is that statements may be good or bad in other ways, which are often more important than the statements' truth. Such utterances may be eloquent, persuasive, witty, appropriate, well-timed, prudent, effective, considerate, kind, moral, or the contrary. And truth does not determine which they are. Traitors have specialized in unethical truth-telling (concerning a friend's whereabouts, a company's secrets, a nation's defenses, and so forth). And the truths that gossips spread may cause as much damage as their falsehoods do.

For the most part, though, truth in statements is a desirable thing, and a halo of approbation therefore surrounds the word *true.* Accordingly, those authors who equate *true* with *affirmable, acceptable, warranted,* or the like are not entirely mistaken.[28] They just fail to indicate the specific type of value the word denotes; that it is a single, specific type; and that other types of value are sometimes more important. *Acceptable,* say, when applied to an utterance, is as broad and indefinite as *good.*

Species of Accuracy

As truth might be termed a variety of goodness, so also it might be termed a species of accuracy, correctness, or the like. Thus a closely related cluster of expressions are *accurate, correct,* and their kin. *Accurate,* for example, is a cognitive comparative, complex, and commendatory in much the same way that *true* is. Often it can simply replace *true,* as *good,* for instance, cannot. Yet *accurate* is not in general synonymous with *true.* Let us start with the points of similarity between this pair of terms, then pass to the differences.

First, *accurate* is a cognitive comparative. It, too, is a three-pole concept. To correctly describe a map, say, as accurate, we need to know three things: (a) the map's particular use of lines, dots, labels, colors, and so forth for the terrain it depicts; (b) the established use of such items on maps or maps of this kind or this particular map (for cartographers, like authors, may stipulate meanings for their symbols); (c) the meaning of *accurate.* To call a map accurate is to say, in effect, that its use of symbols agrees with their established uses. For a map cannot "agree with the facts" save in the sense that it portrays them in keeping with established modes of portrayal. These, too, we must know, in addition to geography, in order to know whether a given map is accurate.

Second, as this example suggests, *accurate* is a complex cognitive comparative. Maps, drawings, blueprints, descriptions, instructions, reports, and the like are accurate by virtue of their multiple details, and a single important deviation in any single feature renders them inaccurate. Let a street be wrongly named, for instance, or a river be misplaced, or a dot be too large for the town or city in question, and a map becomes inaccurate. Thus *accurate* resembles *typical, good,* and *true,* with their multiple points of comparison, rather than, for instance, *slow* and *tight,* which focus on just one such point.

Third, *accurate* resembles *true* as commendation. It is in general desirable for tables, maps, statistics, and descriptions to be accurate, as it is for statements to be true. Accuracy is usually a virtue, as truth is, and to say that something is accurate is generally to praise it, just as calling something true is. Furthermore, the praise is similarly focused; it does not require or suggest comprehensive goodness in the object or the act. A traitor's or a gossip's account may be perfectly accurate, just as it may be perfectly true, without being good overall.

In addition, *accurate* resembles *true* in three important ways that *typical*, for example, does not. First, the multiple traits that make something typical are for the most part logically independent of one another, whereas the traits that make something accurate or true are frequently interdependent, in the way pointed out in chapter 3 for *true*. Suppose someone says falsely, "It's raining." With "sunny" the tense might be right; with the past tense "raining" might be. But the verb is wrong, given that tense, and the tense is wrong, given that verb. Similarly, in a map that uses dots of different sizes for cities of different populations, an inaccurate dot is inaccurate not just because of its size or its location, but because of both together. As in the case of a statement's falsehood, the size is wrong because of where the dot is, and the location is wrong because of the size of the dot. A dot in that location would be accurate if it were a different size; a dot that size would be accurate were it placed somewhere else. By contrast, the traits of a baseball game, say, that make it atypical do so singly and independently. If the hour is three in the morning, or the place is a hangar, or the game lasts five hours, or forty runs are scored, then any one of these features, by itself and regardless of the others, suffices to make the game an atypical game of baseball. Thus *typical*, though complex, is less complex than *accurate* or *true;* its truth-conditions are multiple but are not interrelated as are those for truth or accuracy.

A second point of special kinship might be expressed by saying that *accurate*, like *true*, is doubly comparative. Think again of maps. A large, detailed map, say, fails to show a bend or two in the Mississippi and is therefore called inaccurate; a smaller, less detailed map omits the same bends and is not called inaccurate (just less exact or less detailed). Similarly, one person says that San Francisco is 3,001 miles from New York, and his detailed assertion is called false; whereas another person says San Francisco is three thousand miles from New York (give or take a few hundred) and no objection is made. In assessments of both these types, of accuracy as of truth, not only is the judgment based on correspondence or lack thereof, but the degree of correspondence expected and required is itself dictated by correspondence: closer in one case, looser in another, in keeping with familiar conventions.[29]

A further parallel surfaced already in chapter 3, with respect to the completeness of truth-correspondence. Even inaccurate cartography conforms somewhat to conventions (otherwise it would not be cartography), as do false statements (or they would not be statements). Cartographers use lines for borders, say, even when they draw the borders inaccurately, just as speakers use *rain* for rain and *snow* for snow and speak grammatically, even when they say falsely that it is raining or snowing. To signal complete correspondence with conventions is characteristic of *accurate* and *true*, but not of *typical*.

Accurate is so close a neighbor to *true* in the family of cognitive comparatives that it can generally replace it with little change of meaning: if a belief or assertion is true, then it is accurate; if it is accurate, then it is true. *True*, however, cannot substitute freely for *accurate*. Accurate maps, charts, blueprints, instructions, and the like are not called true.

Neither, for that matter, are individual words, on the one hand, or paragraphs, sections, chapters, or entire books, on the other. Statements—total, individual speech acts, in the middle range—are. Such is our use of *true*. *Accurate*, by contrast, we more readily apply at every level, whether the accuracy be verbal or nonverbal. Thus we term a whole map accurate, as we might a whole book or report; or a whole section of a map, as we might a chapter, section, or paragraph of a book; or an individual component of a map, as we might a single statement; or a single aspect of a component, as we might a single word. "This wiggle in the border is inaccurate," we might say, much as we might remark, "The tense is inaccurate." We would less readily say, "The tense is false."

Even apart from vagaries like "true north" and "accurate shot," then, *accurate* is not synonymous with *true*, despite their close kinship. They may be linguistic siblings, but they are far from identical twins.

Overview

From the samples considered above, we can sense why cognitive comparatives exist and why they exist in such numbers. They are so very handy, both verbally and practically. Think, first of all, how clumsy it would be, even in the case of a simple comparative like *large*, if we had to say "A dog larger than most dogs ran out," rather than "A large dog ran out," or "A larger tanker than average ran aground," rather than simply "A large tanker ran aground." The single word *large* is more convenient, verbally.

Reflect, furthermore, how often we wish to make such comparative assessments, and why. *Large*, for instance, may be equally handy when indicating the size of a dog, a tanker, a lake, a house, a deficit, a stadium, a problem, or an area of common interest. We might perhaps indicate the size of the lake by citing its measurements, the size of the stadium by saying how many it seats, the size of the house by giving the number of rooms—if we knew them. But repeatedly we do not possess such detailed information. A word like *large*—or *small, tiny, huge, enormous*—is therefore a handy tool of measurement, as well as a conveniently brief expression. Rather than relate the lake, stadium, or house to the markings on a ruler or the like, we can far more easily relate them to members of their class and their average size. The method is rough and ready, yet exceedingly convenient and useful.

Much the same analysis applies, point by point, to other simple cognitive comparatives—to *dangerous, slow, thin, costly, strong, efficient,* and the like; and it holds a fortiori for more complex comparatives such as some we have examined. Think of *true* and what it says so economically. The truth of statements, propositions, and beliefs is a matter of constant interest. And how handy it is to be able to remark, for example, "That's true," rather than, "Your use of those English expressions, in the circumstances, conforms with their established uses in the language." And how very much more convenient such a rough indication is than an itemized list of the multiple, interdependent points of correspondence! Such reflections as these instill new appreciation of an expression like *true.* It conveys a highly useful bundle of information with a minimum of fuss.

Yet these practical advantages are bought at an inevitable price. The complexity that makes brevity desirable makes clear vision difficult; and the brevity that makes communication easier makes clear vision still more difficult by veiling the complexity. Had we been in the custom of spelling out the good-making qualities of good things in relation to things of their class, fewer puzzles and confusions would have arisen concerning goodness. Had we more frequently taken the long way around and spelled out correspondence, less perplexity would have surrounded the concept *true.*

Even competent linguists, I have found, are sometimes unfamiliar with cognitive comparatives. Philosophers and others, often equally unaware, reflectively, of this large class of expressions, may fail to place *true* within it and may therefore miss the concept's most salient features. Hence, in this instance, at least, John Dewey's words seem apropos: "The immediate qualitative differences of things cannot be recognized without noting that things possessed of these qualitative traits fall into kinds, or families. That the family is more lasting, important, and real than any of its members; that the family confers upon its constituents their standing and character, so that those who have no family are outcasts and wanderers, represents a notable situation in most forms of human culture."[30] In Western thought, the concept *true* has had no recognized home and has therefore been an outcast and a wanderer. No one has known quite what to make of it. Once we meet its next of kin, as here and in the previous chapter, however, we can finally accept it for what it is. On the one hand, *true* is asymmetrical, as are the verbs that occur in performatives and avowals. On the other, it is also a cognitive comparative, as are the adjectives just examined; it is a member in good standing of this large and prosperous clan.

PART TWO

THE DOMAIN OF *TRUE*

As promised, part 1 portrayed the concept *true* "simultaneously in its full individuality (as a whole in itself), and in its subordinate position (as one element in a larger whole)." Inner scrutiny revealed that linguistic correspondence usually guides us when we call utterances true; that the mentalistic use of *true* relies on the linguistic; that the word operates sometimes descriptively, sometimes nondescriptively; and that it functions descriptively as a complex cognitive comparative. Outer comparison revealed kinship with countless other words that have primary and secondary senses, that are asymmetrical, and that operate as cognitive comparatives. More specifically, it revealed closer kinship with *healthy* than with *calculate, stormy,* or *vanilla,* and with *accurate* than with *good, typical,* or *big. True* was not merely located, but pinpointed, on the map of language.

Still, part 1's mapping remains only half complete. As yet, no attempt has been made to survey the borderline of truth, to ascertain what lies within and what lies without. Are metaphorical or figurative utterances true or false? Are performatives, questions, commands, moral and evaluative utterances, or trans-empirical extensions of terms? One aim of this second part will be to answer questions such as these. Another will be to determine how to choose from among alternative answers. By what test can it be decided that this or that utterance, or this or that class of utterances, counts as true-false? By the criterion of mere usage—is that the implication of equating truth with linguistic correspondence? Or does reflection force recognition that, although correspondence may be the content of the concept *true,* it does not provide an adequate or reliable norm of predication? And does it therefore turn out that the analyses of part 1, which articulate the concept, lack practical significance?

This latter line of inquiry, in particular, should allay the misgiving some may have felt, that "to worry only about the meaning of the English word 'true' is to trivialize the problem of truth."[1] One answer is that near-equivalents of *true* exist in other languages. Another is that analysis of the English concept casts light on basic facts common to many languages (correspondence, linguistic primacy, bipolarity, cognitive comparatives, and so forth, as well as others still to come). A third reply, soon to emerge, is that the norm implicit in the English concept *true* (as in non-English near-equivalents) holds for all speakers, thinkers, and inquirers, regardless of their tongue. The considerations that ground the norm's validity and demonstrate its importance are not confined to English.

CHAPTER 7

THE RELATIVITY OF LINGUISTIC TRUTH

In this chapter, two general queries initiate the scrutiny of truth's borderline. So far, I have not attended closely to the question of whether linguistic correspondence of the kind described in part 1 is a necessary, as well as a sufficient, condition of truth. Though the reply depends in part on verdicts still to come concerning specific classes of utterances, the issue is raised already by a second general query: How close must the correspondence be for a statement to be true? In answer to these related questions, this chapter acknowledges considerable flexibility, both in the use of *true* and of other terms. The next chapter then draws certain limits. With a balance thus struck between laxity and rigidity, subsequent chapters apply the lessons learned, first to the question of whether performatives are true-false, then to the question as to whether moral and evaluative utterances are true-false, and subsequently to disputes concerning the true-false status of empirical and trans-empirical utterances.

A Helpful Rule of Thumb

These discussions make repeated reference to what I here label the "principle of relative similarity"—PRS, for short.[1] This principle asserts, roughly, that *for a statement of fact, or informative utterance, to be true it suffices that its use of terms resemble more closely the established uses of those terms than it does those of rival, incompatible terms.*

To grasp the general drift of this prescription, consider a fairly typical specimen of speech.[2] When, at the tender age of two, a niece of mine first saw the Gulf of Mexico, she declared it to be a "big bathtub." Bathtubs she knew, and sinks, buckets, and the like, but neither oceans nor lakes nor ponds nor swimming pools. So of the terms she was acquainted with, *bathtub* came closest. She realized, of course, that this expanse of water and its receptacle differed notably from the familiar ones at home; the ones she now gazed on were enormous. Still, given the limited verbal means at her disposal, her choice of words was apt. The only trouble was that, unknown to her, English possesses a whole series of terms in successful competition with *bathtub*. *Pool* and *pond* come closer to what she saw, *lake* still closer, *ocean* and *bay* closer still, and *gulf* closest of all. Hence, despite the increasing similarity between their referents and the Gulf of Mexico, *bathtub, pool, pond, lake, ocean,* and *bay* do not qualify as true descriptions of that body of water, whereas *gulf* does. Only *gulf* satisfies the comparative criterion PRS.

Alternative conceptions of speech are often more rigid and exacting than PRS. It is common, for example, for the meaning of a statement to be construed as a function of the meanings of its constituent expressions,[3] and for the statement's truth to be judged by that composite meaning, with no other terms than the ones employed taken into account.[4] PRS's reference to *relative* similarity challenges this limited perspective, as well as the related notion that the similarity with standard applications must be close. How close the resemblance should be cannot be judged absolutely (by some norm applicable to individual terms or written into their individual meanings), but only comparatively, in view of the language's overall capabilities. It is not just the meaning of *bathtub* that makes "big bathtub" false, but for instance the presence of *gulf* in the language spoken.

Clarifications

If valid, PRS would be a notable refinement on the correspondence formula of chapter 3. However, the requirement it states is so flexible that one may wonder, on the one hand, whether it really does enunciate a sufficient condition of truth, and, on the other hand, whether any utterance which fails to satisfy it can be true. Perhaps it is a *necessary* condition of truth, not a *sufficient* condition. Before these questions can be addressed, PRS's key expressions must be clarified, so as to indicate more exactly what kind and degree of similarity are meant.

Statement of fact, informative utterance. Thus worded, PRS does not clearly embrace either the majority of performative utterances (which will be examined in chapter 9) or moral and evaluative utterances (to be considered in chapter 10). But neither does it exclude them; for it does not state a necessary condition of truth.

Its use of terms. The illustration "big bathtub," like most that come readily to mind, focuses attention on lexical aspects of use—that is, on individual terms (*big, bathtub, lake, gulf,* and so on) and their individual meanings. One might therefore be led to formulate PRS somewhat as Richard Swinburne does when he suggests that "an object is correctly called '*W*' even if it does not resemble the standard objects as much as they resemble each other, so long as it resembles them more than it resembles certain standard 'non-*W*' objects."[5] However, on other occasions, syntactic and contextual consider-ations are more pertinent, and the vaguer formulation I have chosen, with its noncommittal reference to the utterance's "use of terms," therefore seems preferable.[6]

A further clarification of the phrase "its use of terms" concerns sense and reference, intension and extension. Consider a case like the following:

> The word *artillery* originally signified "warlike munitions, implements of war; ammunition in the wide sense," and more especially "engines for discharging missiles, including catapults, slings, arbalests, bows, etc." . . . The invention of gunpowder led to the construction of engines of war of a new kind; nevertheless, the *function* being the same, the new machines were apprehended as belonging to the same category.[7]

Overall, these machines may have resembled other machines as closely as they did the earlier types of artillery; hence the word's new referents may not have resembled the old referents more than they did the referents of other nouns. However, the word's use, in the sense of its intension, did resemble the established use more nearly than it did that of any rival term. The word picked out varied referents precisely as instruments of war; and such is still its function in its new, extended application.

Resemble. Resemblance, or *similarity,* is not a sharp or uniform notion. Resemblance may be perfect or nearly perfect, as between one instance of yellow ochre and another. It may be extensive yet imperfect, as in the family resemblance between one kind of game and another. Other times the overlap may be minimal, as between a flying saucer and the table variety. Or there may be no overlap at all, as between one shade of blue or one sweet taste and another. Thus if all we know is that two things resemble each other, we cannot conclude any identity: they may share multiple traits, a single trait, or none.

These observations are necessary because so many thinkers, from Duns Scotus to Kai Nielsen, have equated similarity with total or partial identity.[8] "Logically," it may be alleged, "every similarity must involve a moment of identity, or else to speak of similarity is 'mere mystification.'"[9] Yet, quite commonly we speak of similarity where no such identity appears and where, perhaps, no single term exists to label the similarity or the features compared. Think, for instance, of two nameless, irregular figures, drawn on a board, whose contours are notably similar, yet which coincide in no segment. The figures are both formed by lines, it is true; but the line for one may be broad and fuzzy and white, while the line for the other may be narrow and sharp and green. So where, once again, is any "moment of identity" discernible?[10]

More closely. This phrase may appear to take sides on a debated issue but does not in fact do so. Some writers maintain, for example, that "religion can, and must, embrace 'paradoxes,' but if it embraces contradictions it is simply 'untrue.'"[11] Others, like Daya Krishan, contend that the law of contradiction does not hold for religious discourse: "Basically, the application of the law of contradiction presupposes a sharp, specific, and identifiable application of 'sameness,' and if this is not possible in a situation, it ceases to be relevant. The religious experience is concerned with that which is supposed to be beyond space, time, mass, and causality. There should be little wonder if it expresses itself in a conjunction of contradictory statements asserted as true."[12] PRS may seem to negate such reasoning as this and its conclusion. For contrary or contradictory terms may conform equally with established uses, but both terms cannot "come closer," so both cannot satisfy PRS. However, as formulated so far, PRS states a sufficient, but not a necessary, condition, and therefore does not exclude contrary or contradictory utterances. It does not yet deny that both may be true when expressions are stretched. Whether it should impose such a restriction will be considered in the discussion to come concerning possible tightening of the principle.

A second point worth mentioning with regard to the wording "more closely" can be illustrated by means of the expression "flying saucer." The alleged object referred to in this manner may resemble a saucer more than it does a bowl or a plate; but does the object as a whole resemble a saucer more than it does an airplane, say, or a rocket? And is *saucer,* therefore, the closest term available? The answer is that aspects of the object aside from its shape and its motion are shrouded in mystery. Hence the predication is focused, and within the intended focus *saucer* comes closer than *bowl* or *plate.*[13] As will be noted in a moment, diverse descriptions of a single referent, which pick out different aspects, do not count as rival terms.

A third observation stems from the heterogeneity of resemblance. The similarity of games or occupations, for example, involves overlapping traits; that of colors or pains, for example, does not. Nor can further overlap be discerned between many overlapping traits in concepts such as *game* or *occupation.* Problems therefore arise with regard to the phrase "more closely." Does multiple overlap automatically count as closer resemblance than the closest non-overlapping similarity—say, between one shade of blue and another? Does possession of more common properties automatically count as closer resemblance than possession of fewer such properties, even if the fewer are more nearly identical? If not, how are the respective claims of these different kinds of resemblance to be assessed?

No clear answer can be given to such questions, save by stipulation. The concept *similarity* is not sharp. This indeterminateness is no more of an objection to PRS than it is to the expression "similar" or "more similar."

Some things are clearly similar; some are not. Some things are clearly more similar than others; some are not. However, the problems I have cited suggest that the phrase "more closely" may cast doubt on PRS as a necessary condition of truth, if not as a sufficient condition. As merely a sufficient condition, it can safely prescind from a broad range of undecided cases, but not as a necessary condition.

The established uses. This phrase, the only one in common with the general correspondence formula of chapter 3, retains the sense spelled out there. For instance, it embraces semantic as well as syntactic features and stipulated uses as well as standard. Also, the uses in question, being uses of terms, are language-wide. Hence any particular application of the terms, no matter how common or how widely accepted, may fail the test of correspondence. ("Hitler is dead" or "God exists" may be false.)

Rival. Synonyms or near-synonyms do not count as rival expressions. Neither do terms at different levels of generality (a "flying *saucer*" may also be called an "unidentified flying *object*"). Nor do different descriptions of a single referent, focusing on different aspects (an artifact may also be called an invention; God may be termed both powerful and wise).

Contraries and contradictories do count as rival terms. So do "neighboring terms" such as Thomas Kuhn cites:

> A person who has watched chess, bridge, darts, tennis, and football, and who has also been told that each of them is a game, will have no trouble in recognizing that both backgammon and soccer are games as well. To establish reference in more puzzling cases—prize fights or fencing matches, for example—exposure is required also to members of neighboring families. Wars and gang rumbles, for example, share prominent characteristics with many games (in particular, they have sides and, potentially, a winner), but the term "game" does not apply to them.[14]

The boundaries of still closer neighbors are not only near but contiguous: *red* shares a border with *orange, bush* with *tree, book* with *booklet,* and so forth. Other borders overlap—*woman* with *worker, pony* with *pet,* and so on. That is, a woman may, but need not, qualify as a worker, and vice versa; a pony may, but need not, qualify as a pet, and vice versa. Hence these latter pairs with overlapping borders are not among those I count as rival terms. The former, non-overlapping ones are.

Terms. At an earlier stage in its formulation, PRS referred to "rival expressions," rather than "terms." But "expressions" include long, complex formulae (for instance, detailed definite descriptions) in addition to simpler, individual terms. And if understood so broadly, the principle would not conform to the everyday use of *true* and would be too restrictive. It is reasonable, for instance, for a person to say that he or she has played a game of chess by mail, even though the person might forego thus stretching the word *chess* and might, with considerable effort and hearer surprise, articulate what "chess by mail" merely suggests, spelling out the resemblances and differences between the behavior involved and that typically described as "playing chess." Not only are utterances like this convenient, effective, and therefore reasonable; they may also merit the label "true," despite their stretching of terms. In order, therefore, to exclude complex rivals such as a detailed description of chess by mail, the present formulation of PRS replaces the word *expressions* with *terms,* intending principally thereby the kind of expressions one finds in a dictionary (*iceberg, a priori, tour de force,* and so on), plus such sentence-elements as logical and mathematical symbols. The reasons, both descriptive and normative, for this specification of sense appear more fully toward the end of chapter 11.

Sufficient?

With the other terms of PRS now clarified (though still far from razor-sharp), we can attend to the word *suffices.* Does relative similarity, as just defined, really suffice for truth? Or is the principle perhaps too lenient? My response, as heretofore, will have regard for usage. Where usage is evident, I shall accept its verdict. Where lack of firm evidence renders the verdict of usage uncertain, I shall be tolerant. Where strong reasons suggest that its verdict is favorable, I shall incline to acceptance of an utterance as true.

With regard to "It's raining" or "There is water on the floor," the verdict of usage is not in doubt. If such utterances achieve at least relative similarity, that suffices; despite peripheral imperfections in the correspondence, of a kind I shall note in chapter 11, they are true. It is with respect to extended uses of words that doubts may arise. Had there been no other term available, my niece's calling the Gulf of Mexico a big bathtub might perhaps have been a meaningful, legitimate, effective use of speech; but would her utterance have been *true?* Would we say it was? Should we? (The more likely it seems that we should, the more likely it is that we would.)

In this imaginary case, what was described as a bathtub would resemble an ordinary bathtub less than an ordinary bathtub resembles a bucket, a sink, or a casserole. It would just come closer to a bathtub than to any other item for which there was a name. In trans-empirical utterances the same configuration might commonly occur and be countenanced by PRS. God, for instance, might be termed wise even if he resembled wise human beings less than wise human beings resemble foolish; it would suffice that the resemblance between God and the wise be closer than the resemblance between God and the foolish (or infants, imbeciles, computers, and so on). For anyone inclined to think in terms of absolute, not relative, similarity (that is, without regard for other words and their conceptual boundaries), such leniency may seem excessive. The question is whether we should, or typically do, think in such absolute terms.

I have already noted (in chapter 2) that many a borderline instance of a concept resembles a borderline instance of a neighboring concept more closely than it does distant members of its own class. In this common situation, we do not go by similarity alone. To do so would lead to false predications—to ones we would all label false—and to much linguistic confusion. Noting, for example, that a pamphlet of thirty pages comes closer to a book of a hundred pages than the latter does to a thousand-page tome, we would call the pamphlet a book. And if the pamphlet counted as a book, so too, by like reasoning, would a two-page flier. After all, it differs from the hundred-page book by only ninety-eight pages, whereas the latter differs from the thousand-page tome by nine hundred pages. Hence the flier, too, would merit the name "book," were sheer similarity our norm. But of course no such rule guides us, either in applying terms like *booklet, book,* and *flier,* or in applying *true.*

It is clear, furthermore, that we do readily extend terms in accordance with the principle of relative similarity. Consider an example already cited. Some years ago, putative objects in the sky got referred to as "flying saucers," even though they resembled saucers in the cupboard less than those saucers resembled bowls or plates. They just resembled saucers more than they did bowls or plates, and "saucer," accordingly, was the term adopted. Given the modifier "flying" and the context of utterance, no one supposed that the objects referred to closely resembled typical saucers (in their construction, contents, weight, size, and so forth); the referral proceeded without a hitch. For the linguistic proclivities of most hearers, as of most speakers, resemble those of my niece. If we lack a term for the thing in question and wish to describe or refer to it, we use the nearest terms available.[15] The question with regard to PRS, then, is not whether we do or should employ expressions in the way it describes, but whether when we do so employ them, the resulting predications are called true, or should be. (Once again, reasons for what we should say may suggest what we do say; a priori evidence may supplement a posteriori evidence.)

Concerning extensions which have grown familiar, there can be little doubt. If, for instance, someone now claims to have sighted a flying saucer, his assertion is judged no differently than the claim to have formed a mental "picture," to have had an organ "transplant," or to have played "chess" with a computer. Our language is full of extended uses that have become standard uses and therefore occasion little puzzlement or hesitation. We know that the computer is not being credited with hands or the organ with roots, that the picture cannot be measured in inches or feet, that the purported flying object was not an everyday saucer. And we therefore assess the statement's truth by the correspondence between its use of the term and the term's currently well-established (though extended) use.

Only concerning the initial occurrence of such extensions might we feel misgivings. Perhaps we imagine ourselves, forty years ago, hearing a person declare without preamble: "I could hardly believe my eyes; off toward the horizon, a huge saucer was hurtling across the sky." Our assessment would probably be not merely that the statement was false, but that the speaker was mad. Huge saucers in the sky are the stuff of fairy tales or *delirium tremens.* However, such a linguistic scenario is hardly realistic. It is unlikely that when the expression "flying saucer" was first uttered, anyone who read or heard it supposed that the saucer in question was of the table variety.

If, then, "flying saucer" and countless kindred expressions are typically as effective the first or tenth time as the thousandth, it seems questionable whether we do or should treat them differently at the start than we do later and should withhold the label "true." Granted, in the fuzzy border that surrounds most concepts, including the concept *true,* dissimilarities may be cited, as well as similarities. In first-time extensions, for example, there is no correspondence with *established* word uses—unless relative similarity, as defined by PRS, is considered, along with syntax and the like, as another standard feature with which word use may conform. But why not? The person who first spoke aptly of inventing a flying machine or sighting a flying saucer conformed to this customary manner of reporting or describing new realities.

Since the manner is familiar, we might reasonably articulate the sense of such extensions in terms of PRS; and once they were so interpreted, no doubt would remain concerning their truth. Thus, if the inventor of video games said, "I have invented a new kind of game," we might take this as roughly equivalent to: "I have invented an activity which resembles the activities called games more than it does the activities called by any other, incompatible name." And this statement would be true.

In confirmation we may ask why, even with time and growing familiarity, statements like "I invented a new kind of game" count as truths and not as familiar errors or familiar nonsense. One answer might be that what they now state is what they stated originally, and that what they stated originally is what makes them true, even now. This answer looks especially plausible with regard to trans-empirical utterances, for instance, in metaphysics and theology.

Such utterances occasion many misgivings but not, I believe, with regard to PRS. On the whole, in discussing trans-empirical matters (God, the unconscious, things-in-themselves, the ultimate constituents of matter, and so on), whoever supposes a basis as firm as relative similarity is ready to make use of the expression for which it holds and to judge the resulting predication "true," while those who challenge the predication's truth typically do so for reasons which imply no contrary norm. If the latter recognized the assertion as alleging relative similarity, they would accept it as meaningful; if they believed that the purported similarity was in fact realized, they would accept the assertion as true. I shall return to these points in chapter 12.

Possible Countercases

In keeping with PRS, we extend the word *calculate* from calculating on paper to calculating "in the head." With further stretching, relative similarity may no longer hold. The phenomena, as Wittgenstein put it, may "gravitate towards another paradigm."[16] This comparison with gravitation suggests a difficulty for PRS. Something new that arrives on the scene and needs to be indicated—whether a flying saucer or a newly invented pastime—is drawn, I suggested, to the nearest concept. However, as nearness alone does not determine the force of gravity (some bodies attract more strongly than others, by virtue of their mass), so similarity alone may not determine the strength of conceptual attraction. Some similarities may count for more than others.[17]

Thus, in one recent theory, " 'water' rigidly designates H_2O, regardless of what superficial properties the H_2O may or may not have."[18] If this is an accurate account of how we do and should employ *water* and kindred terms, then it appears that at least in some instances relative similarity does not suffice as a condition of truth. A new substance might look, feel, taste, and smell like water (that is, be equally odorless); but if it had a different chemical composition, we would not and should not call it water. The single dissimilarity would count for more than the numerous similarities.

The word *superficial* suggests a reply to this objection. Look, taste, odor, and smell are deemed superficial, and microstructure basic, largely for physical reasons. The structure affects the freezing point, the boiling point, the point of maximum density, and many other properties. Hence a substance that differed from water in its chemical composition would doubtless differ from it extensively and not just in some single feature. And until we knew in what respects it differed, in what manner, and how notably, we could not know whether it "gravitated towards some other paradigm."[19] If, however, despite its different composition, it resembled water more than any other substance with a name, we might do as we have done in similar cases and label it "false water." *Water* would name the substance, and *false* would signal the difference, as *fool's* does in "fool's gold." Were the stuff to become common, doubtless we would find a new name for it, as we did for the kinds of things first labeled "flying machines" or "horseless carriages."

Some concepts may resist this line of solution. According to Putnam, if we encountered an illness whose symptoms differed from those of multiple sclerosis but whose cause was the same, we would call it multiple sclerosis; if, on the contrary, we encountered an illness whose symptoms resembled those of multiple sclerosis but whose cause was different, we would not call it multiple sclerosis.[20] For such concepts as this, causal similarity, not overall similarity, is decisive. Hence they appear to contradict PRS. However, to the extent that this analysis is correct, it demonstrates the causal focus or intension of the concepts in question; if symptoms can indeed vary at will without affecting the term's application, they form no part of the established use of which PRS speaks. (See the second clarification under "established use," above.)

Another possible source of discontent with PRS even as a sufficient condition of truth is suggested by Mary Hesse's remark: "It is possible that the primary recognition of, for example, a whale as being sufficiently similar to some fish to justify its inclusion in the class of fish may be explicitly overridden in the interests of preserving a particular set of laws."[21] Here it makes a difference, I would say, whether the inclusion or exclusion in question takes the form of stipulation of meaning or of dogmatic declaration concerning what whales "really are." Only the former is an acceptable alternative (see the next chapter); and it poses no problem for PRS. Stipulations of meaning do not figure among the speech acts to which the principle applies. It concerns only statements of fact.

A further objection may arise from the fact that extended uses of the kind I have cited often get classed as "analogies" or "metaphors," and that analogies and metaphors are not generally called "true," but rather, "apt" or "good."[22] This difficulty does not seem serious. It is true that metaphors, for example, when characterized as metaphors, are not likely to be labeled true or false. But utterances that employ the metaphors are commonly so described. Thus it may be that "when the bud of a potato is called an 'eye,' the designation is a metaphor,"[23] and that this metaphor is neither true nor false; but when someone says "I removed all the eyes" or "The potatoes have more eyes than usual this year," the statement may be true or false.

More problematic are cases like the following. A stone, we would doubtless say, is neither dead nor alive. Yet PRS might seem to give a different verdict; for does not *dead* come closer than *living* or any rival term? In reply it may be suggested that *dead*, as defined by usage, is equivalent to "no longer living" and therefore conflicts with a term like *inorganic*. This reading of usage rests on the distinction between extending a term to phenomena long familiar from which it has been withheld and extending it to new ones. In the first case usage has drawn a line; in the second it has not. So it is reasonable to define *dead* in a way that excludes stones, but not reasonable to define *game* in a way that excludes video games or *chess* in a way that excludes playing with computers or *machine* in a way that excludes the Wright brothers' invention.

This distinction is pertinent to subsequent discussions concerning the borderline of *true*. Other types of utterance besides statements reveal extensive correspondence, both syntactic and pragmatic, with established uses. So if *true* indicates linguistic correspondence, may it not be extended to these other speech acts—to commands, say—on the strength of PRS? Granted, the correspondence of commands differs from that of statements. But whereas we have a term for statements' correspondence, we have no terms except *reasonable, legitimate, grammatical,* and the like for commands' correspondence; and these are not rival, incompatible expressions. A statement may be reasonable, legitimate, and/or grammatical, as well as true. The answer, here too, is to note the limitation drawn by usage. As stones are long-familiar items and are not called dead, so commands are long-familiar utterances and are not called true. Hence, just as *dead* conflicts with *stone* and *inorganic*, so *true* conflicts with *command* and *imperative*. It has successful rivals in the language.

Necessary?

When the bounds of truth are so loosely drawn that talk of "flying saucers," "mental pictures," and the like may qualify as true, it may appear that any further leniency would be laxity, and that relative similarity should therefore be viewed as a necessary condition of truth and not just a sufficient condition. However, a variety of utterances might thereby be excluded whose claims to truth deserve consideration.

In some, the term employed does not seem to be the nearest, yet communication proceeds unimpeded. As S. I. Hayakawa notes, "Statements of the kind: 'I've been waiting *ages* for you—you're an hour overdue!' 'He's got *tons* of money!' 'I'm so tired I'm simply *dead!*'—which are nonsensical if interpreted literally—nevertheless 'make sense.' "[24] For of course they are not interpreted literally. They are understood to mean, for example, "I've been waiting a long time for you," "He has lots of money," and "I'm extremely tired." And these assertions may be true. So if the hyperbolic variants are equivalent in sense, may not they too be true? Wouldn't typical speakers say they are? Hearing "He's got tons of money" or "She waited ages for a reply," wouldn't they readily respond "That's true," undeterred by the terms *tons* and *ages*?

Perhaps they would, but the truth of such figuratively worded versions may be granted without rejecting relative similarity as a necessary condition of truth. "Relative similarity" is similarity relative to rival terms; and synonyms or near-synonyms, I said, do not count as rival terms. Hence, both figurative and nonfigurative equivalents may satisfy the norm, the first in accordance with figurative conventions of speech, the second in accordance with nonfigurative conventions. In their own ways, both may agree equally with usage, and may agree with it more nearly than does any *rival* term. Neither is in competition with the other.[25]

An earlier discussion poses a second, similar challenge to greater similarity as a necessary condition of truth. This is not the first time I have asked how close correspondence must be to merit the verdict "True"; nor is PRS the first answer I have suggested. According to chapter 6, "Not only is the judgment based on correspondence or lack thereof, but the degree of correspondence expected and required is itself dictated by correspondence: closer in one case, looser in another, in keeping with familiar conventions." If we ignored these conventions, we might suppose, for example, that in stating the distance to San Francisco, one must provide the most precise measurements possible and that any other estimates are false. "Three thousand miles" will not do, if "three thousand and one" is available and states the distance more exactly. However, "three thousand" may conform as perfectly with rough conventions as "three thousand and one" does with precise conventions. And what standards apply depends on the particular utterance and its context. So it appears once again that rival predications may both be true, even though neither conforms more closely to usage than the other.

In response it may be questioned whether an expression like "a thousand and one" should count as a rival *term* (since it is composite and is not found in any dictionary), and, especially, whether it should count as a *rival* term. If in one setting "three thousand" means "*roughly* three thousand," and in another setting "three thousand and one" means "three thousand and one, *to the nearest whole number*," these expressions differ but do not conflict.

A third challenge comes from the alleged acceptability of contradictory utterances. As we saw, for Krishan, the law of contradiction does not hold in religious discourse. Others would question its relevance more broadly—for instance, with regard to mystical utterances, whether religious or nonreligious. "Stace regards it as certain, and I regard it as possible," writes one author, "that the contradictory statements of the mystics, far from being meaningless, far even from being false, may be said in some sense to be true: in the sense, namely, that as much about the experience as can be said within that conceptual system, has been said."[26] R. C. Zaehner, who doubtless would concur, offers this illustration:

> When Mr. Huxley speaks of being a "Not-self in the Not-self which was a chair," I know that, as far as the normal, rational consciousness is concerned, he is talking horrid gibberish, but I equally know that I have myself experienced precisely this and the joy experienced as a result of this uncontrollable and inexplicable expansion of the personality is not to be brushed aside as mere illusion. On the

contrary: beside it the ordinary world of sense experience seems pathetically unreal.[27]

Closely comparable, at least linguistically, are certain experiences analyzed by Wittgenstein. When, for instance, we see the picture of a galloping horse, we do not merely *know* that this is the kind of movement that is meant. We may express our experience by saying we *see* the horse galloping.[28] And yet we would acknowledge that, in the ordinary sense of the terms, no galloping occurs, nor is any seen.

A problem therefore arises for acceptance of relative similarity as a necessary condition of truth. "Gallops" and "doesn't gallop," "sees" and "doesn't see," "self" and "not-self" may perhaps be equally correct and incorrect; but both members of each pair cannot approximate more closely the words' established uses. And if they only come equally close, they fail to meet the requirement of greater similarity. Yet is it not meaningful and true to say, for example, both that the horse is not galloping and that I see it galloping?

Such apparent contradictions may generally be resolved in the manner made familiar by traditional theology. In the Scholastics' "three ways," divine traits are first affirmed, then denied, then affirmed in a higher, "eminent" sense. The point of this exercise is to retain the affirmations, while guarding against a too literal understanding of them. And each denial may therefore be read as meaning "not in the usual sense of the word." God is not wise, for example, in the ordinary sense of *wise*, as applied to human beings. Similarly, Huxley is not a "Not-self," nor does the viewer "see" the horse galloping in the ordinary sense of these expressions. Accordingly, since the words in such affirmations do not have their usual senses, the supposedly contradictory expressions are not in fact contradictory or even incompatible. Neither, therefore, do they rate as rival terms, whose equal validity might show PRS to be unduly rigid if worded as a necessary condition.[29]

More serious is the challenge from extensions based on causation, not resemblance. Verbal transfers from effect to cause (for example, of *healthy* from people to climates, diets, and the like) are relatively rare and cannot be freely multiplied (for example, by calling chimney sweeps clean or mosquitoes feverish). However, even a rarity may invalidate a universal claim. And extensions in the other direction, from cause to effect, rather than effect to cause, are common and freely made. We speak, for instance, of intelligent questions, thoughtful answers, clever inventions, prudent actions, sad looks, angry accusations, and so forth, as well as of intelligent, thoughtful, clever, prudent, sad, or angry people. The answers, questions, actions, accusations, and the like do not resemble the people; yet we use the same terms—*smart, prudent, angry,* and so on—for both. It seems arbitrary to decree, a priori, that such extensions by causality can give rise to true predications only when the extensions have become well-established uses, to which current applications of the terms may conform and thereby qualify as true.

A further challenge to the proposed restriction on truth is implicit in Wittgenstein's critique of similarity as the sole basis of verbal stretching. A concept, he observes, sometimes forces itself on us without our noting any similarity.[30] For example,

> Let us ask the question "What is the similarity between looking for a word in your memory and looking for my friend in the park?" What would be the answer to such a question? . . .
>   One might be inclined to say "Surely a similarity must strike us, or we shouldn't be moved to use the same word." . . . But why shouldn't what we call "the similarity striking us" consist partially or wholly . . . in our being prompted to use the same phrase?[31]

Do we call thoughts "deep" because they resemble deep wells or answers "sharp" because they resemble needles or notes "high" because they resemble mountains?[32] And is it only now, when they are standard, that such turns of phrase may be used to make true assertions? Are they automatically false or meaningless the first few times, and do they only gradually become capable of truth as they get better established? Relative similarity looks too stringent if taken as a necessary condition of truth.

It is sometimes suggested that at least the impression made on us, for instance by deep sorrows and deep seas, is similar, and that this explains the common term. However,

> does a high roof also make the same impression on us as a high C? And when we see a sharp curve in the road, does our reaction resemble a sharp pain? And as for deep sorrow, does our feeling as we gaze into a deep pool resemble our grief at the loss of a friend? Of course not. We would never venture such hypotheses were we not inclined to think that there *must* be something common to account for the common word—if not an essence, then at least some perceptible link. But if we look instead of thinking, we often find nothing of the kind.[33]

James Ross's characterization of such verbal stretching seems felicitous. Citing similar samples, he speaks of "meaning differentiation, not by a speaker's design, deliberation or intent, but by semantic contagion."[34] Such contagion takes many forms. Recalling various figures of speech—"the apple of my eye," "pretty pickle," "black soul," "soul of charity," "property of the Crown," "set sail," and the like—or reflecting on the very expression "figure of speech," we may sense how dogmatic it would be to insist on relative similarity as a necessary condition of truth.

The considerations that favor the truth of apt extensions by contagion are at least as weighty as those that tell against it. For one thing, *true* commends or endorses, and such extensions are often commendable. In addition, they conform to customary modes of extension and in this sense correspond with the words' established uses. Though brought about by contagion, not resemblance, they resemble other extensions by contagion. Finally, although commands and questions, for example, may also be commendable and may conform to established uses yet are not true, the utterances under consideration here serve to describe or report, as do the utterances typically termed *true,* whereas questions and commands do not. "He's *deeply* depressed" is as factual as "He's *very* depressed," and the latter is as factual as "He's very *sad.*"

Conclusion

In chapter 3 it was suggested that a statement is true if its use of words agrees with their established uses, but how close the agreement is or should be was not specified. Chapter 6 shed some light on this question by noting the relevance of wording and context but could not answer the question satisfactorily without adverting as well to the alternative expressions available in the language. This missing dimension has now been added. Truth is achieved, the present discussion has suggested, if an informative utterance's employment of terms corresponds more closely to the terms' established uses than it does to those of rival terms. The same stipulation looks too strict, however, if stated as a necessary condition of truth.

Implicit in this verdict is a challenge to the original analysis of truth in chapter 3. The data that tell against greater similarity as a necessary condition of truth tell against any similarity, hence against linguistic correspondence, as a necessary condition of truth. At their first appearance, extensions by causality or by contagion do not resemble or correspond with the established uses of the expressions they employ, at least not in the full, typical manner suggested by the analyses in chapter 3 (for example, of "It's raining"). And to equate linguistic truth with linguistic correspondence may therefore appear mistaken or misleading.

A first reply might expand and emphasize a point just noted. "It is not possible," writes Hesse, "to make a distinction between literal and metaphoric descriptions merely by asserting that literal use consists in the following of linguistic rules. Intelligible metaphor also implies the existence of rules of metaphoric use."[35] So too, causal extensions resemble other causal extensions; extensions by contagion resemble other extensions by contagion. They may be first-time extensions of a given term, but they are not first-time utterances of their kind.

A second reply might be that these first-time occurrences, with their lesser correspondence, are a marginal phenomenon in comparison with more typical instances of truth. The vast majority of true statements are statements whose employment of words corresponds with the words' established uses in the fuller manner exemplified by "It's raining" and are recognized as true on this basis. Accordingly, the equation of linguistic truth with linguistic correspondence suffices as a summary characterization. It is roughly accurate.

Furthermore, the equation most clearly suffices in those areas and types of discourse where the question of truth is most likely to arise and where the guidance of correspondence is most needed. Poets need not speak as scientists, historians, or philosophers do; scientists, historians, or philosophers should not speak as poets do. The vagaries I shall document in chapters 8, 9, and 10 cannot be justified as poetic innovations. Where intelligibility and verifiability matter, so does correspondence, within the bounds of PRS. A poet may declare that a bird is not a bird or that all life is but a dream; a philosopher had better show more sober concern for the everyday use of words.

Finally, and most significantly, in refusing a restriction on truth, I have not accepted the contrary expansion. I have not said that original, non-resembling extensions of terms are sometimes true; I have just said that it would be dogmatic to claim that they never are or can be. It might be equally dogmatic, however, to claim that such extensions are true, in the absence of any firm supporting evidence from usage. For though certain similarities might be noted in favor of calling them true, relevant dissimilarities might also be cited in support of the opposite verdict. After all, even for first-time extensions that satisfy PRS, the verdict is debatable; and those extensions resemble paradigm instances of truth more closely than do the innovative sayings here in question.

Doubts like these are to be expected. Practically any concept, including the concept *true*, permits borderline cases which neither clearly merit nor clearly fail to merit the appellation. In such instances, usage's verdict is "Undecided." If the similarities and dissimilarities all pointed one way, there would be no uncertainty, and the cases would not be borderline. It is precisely the mix of similarity and dissimilarity with standard paradigms that occasions the characterization "borderline cases." And the attempt to eliminate the uncertainty by a pro or con pronouncement would merely shift the uncertainty to some new borderline. No border can be made razor-sharp.

For reasons that will become more apparent later on, I have preferred to report the concept *true*, rather than revise it. Chapter 3 gave an overall impression; subsequent chapters, including the present one, have added details. This procedure may be compared to viewing an impressionistic painting (say a Monet) first from a distance, where contours are clear, then up close, where they appear as mere dots and dabs. Both types of viewing contribute to understanding the painting, just as both kinds of reporting contribute to understanding a concept. It is helpful to know a concept's overall contours; it is helpful to know that they are not definite but dissolve into myriad, heterogenous details. As usual, when examined closely, the borderline looks blurred.

Such an outcome for the chapter and the way it was reached may occasion misgivings. In accepting relative similarity as sufficient but refusing to require it, I have wished to abide by the common employment of *true* and to show reasonable tolerance towards effective modes of speech. However, what I view as reasonable tolerance may strike others as intolerable license. ("Does just anything go?") And the usage I accept as a guide, others may dismiss as irrelevant. ("Is philosophy mere lexicography?") Both these misgivings I shall now address, as I turn more fully and explicitly from descriptive to normative considerations.

CHAPTER 8

THE CONCEPT *TRUE* AS NORM

Norms and guidelines cannot be inferred from mere concepts and definitions.[1] From the mere meaning of a word, we cannot deduce what course of action to follow—not even when the word is a practical term like *reasoning,* an ethical expression like *justice,* or an honorific label like *truth.* Thus the equation of truth with correspondence, for example, does not indicate automatically that truth, so defined, is something to strive for, still less that it should serve as a primary goal of inquiry or principal test of what to think and say.

Correspondence-theorists have seldom been troubled by such considerations, since correspondence, as they conceived it, seemed so obviously desirable. Accurate mental representation appeared as necessary for successful living as accurate blueprints are for successful construction or accurate maps for successful navigation; and accurate translation of these mental contents into spoken or written symbols appeared to be the chief way to transfer true representations from one mind to another. As for the sheer contemplative value of truth-by-correspondence—well, who has ever conceived or found a market for an *impressionistic* camera or an *impressionistic* television set? People want to know how things really are.

Had the mental medium of cognition appeared as arbitrary as the linguistic medium was often said to be, more misgivings might have been experienced. But it appeared that images or concepts were nature's gifts, not man's invention, and were no more to be questioned than one's limbs or inner organs. Different peoples might drape their legs differently—with togas, pants, or kilts—but all of them used their legs for walking. Different peoples might have different diets, but all digested with their stomachs. So, too,

Romans, Greeks, and Germans might utter different sounds, but they all spoke the same inner language of the mind. Concerning correspondence there, in that medium, no doubt could arise. Legs were made to walk with, stomachs to digest with, and minds to mirror reality with, in the only way available to human beings.

Once abandon this conception, however—once replace the language of the mind with the language of the marketplace and mental mirroring with mere conformity to stipulated or conventional meanings—and the spell is broken. The value question surfaces, distinct from the factual or the conceptual question, and has to be faced squarely: If *this* is what truth consists in, does it really deserve our obeisance? May we not be better advised to pursue some other goal and adopt some other norm?

The chances are good that the contents of such a prestigious concept, when brought to light, will turn out to have some practical significance. If the truth that analysis reveals and that people have generally sought is, basically, linguistic correspondence, then doubtless such correspondence has some value. It appears unlikely that so widespread a quest has been totally deluded. It might be, however, that a concept which serves well enough in everyday affairs has less relevance in theoretical inquiries. Perhaps correspondence should be our main concern when we assess such assertions as "It snowed last night," "I left the key in the lock," or "Oak burns longer than pine," but should concern us less in semantics, ethics, sociology, physics, metaphysics, or theology. Perhaps other criteria should take priority when we assess statements like "Performatives are true and false," "All actions should maximize happiness," "Energy and mass are interchangeable," "Nonsensible objects are isomorphic with their sensible effects," or "God is good."

I believe, on the contrary, that truth-as-correspondence, understood in the light of the last chapter, merits general acceptance, both as an account of usage and as a norm. The various types of truth to be examined in chapters 9–12—performative, moral, empirical, and trans-empirical—reveal variations in the pattern of correspondence but require no revision in the general formula of chapter 3. I believe, furthermore, that such correspondence typically embodies important values, that these values explain the traditional prestige of truth, and that the everyday concept of truth does indeed reveal a norm we should follow in every type of discourse, and specifically in theoretical discussion—for instance, here, in the discussion of truth itself. The uses of words not only do, as a matter of fact, repeatedly conform to their established uses, but they should consistently do so, in every area of inquiry.

However, neither the general accuracy of the correspondence analysis nor the general validity of the norm it suggests is self-evident. Both require demonstration; and both will receive demonstration here, starting with the norm's validity. This issue, so momentous in itself, has relevance for all sections of the present study. On its solution depend both the practical significance of chapters 1–7, which raised the issue, and the guidelines to be followed in the remaining chapters.

The Norm's Validity

It is understandable that a pragmatist like James should identify the truth of ideas with their utility; for true ideas and the true statements that beget or express them do indeed "lead prosperously." Whether in science, history, philosophy, theology, or everyday affairs, truth is advantageous on the whole. However, as many have noted, prosperous leading is not identical with truth but is its consequence. Truth is correspondence. That is what explains its advantages.

To illustrate, suppose your neighbor Mrs. Smith tells you the ice is thick. You believe her and go skating. If she has spoken truly—if her use of *thick*, for example, agrees with its customary use—the ice holds, and you enjoy yourself. If she has spoken falsely—if her use of *thick* does not agree with normal usage—you do not succeed in skating nor do you enjoy yourself. You may not even survive.

In such a simple paradigm the need for correspondence is fairly evident. Thick ice will hold you, thin ice will not. *Thick* is used for the first condition, *thin* for the second. And you are familiar with this usage. So Mrs. Smith should not take such liberties but should stay with the word's established use.

This example may appear too jejune to have much significance for speech as a whole. However, I agree with Wittgenstein's remark: "If we want to study the problems of truth and falsehood, of the agreement and disagreement of propositions with reality, . . . we shall with great advantage look at primitive forms of language in which these forms of thinking appear without the confusing background of highly complicated processes of thought."[2] For the simple forms are not separated by a break from the more complicated ones. The same sort of advantages that recommend correspondence in "The ice is thick" recommend it in weather predictions, estimates of tensile strength, budget reports, doctors' diagnoses, market analyses, hypotheses concerning the greenhouse effect, and so forth. Correspondence pays.[3]

Its utility can be sensed from a comparison with constancy in nature. To judge the future, we must consult experience, and in going by experience, we must suppose that the future will resemble the past. If we make the supposition that it will be different, no grounds in experience are left—in fact, no grounds at all by which to judge the likely course of events. And if, when we looked to the past, we found no regularity—if we discovered, for example, that the sun did now one thing, now another, in identical circum-stances—once again we would be without guidance. For which of the several things that the sun did in the past would it do next time? Accord-ingly, for us to make any judgments at all about the future, we must not only consult the past, but must consult its recurring patterns. There is no conceivable alternative.

In the world of symbolism, correspondence is similarly basic. If words and other signs were used now one way, now another, without rhyme or reason—if their present uses did not conform with uses somehow estab-lished in the past, through familiar practice or stipulation—we could not go by them; and if we could not go by them, they would cease to function. So also, to a large extent, would we. The linguistic regularity of "The ice is thick," of weather predictions, estimates of tensile strength, budget reports, doctors' diagnoses, market analyses, scientific hypotheses, and the rest is as vital for our welfare as the regularity of the ice, the weather, the materials, the markets, the diseases, and the various other phenomena described, reported, or explained.

In history, theoretical physics, cosmology, metaphysics, theology, and the like, where interest centers more on knowledge itself than on its conse-quences, the practical advantages of correspondence are less immediately evident than in the samples so far considered, and its advantages for inquiry itself come into prominence. These advantages are chiefly two: first, com-munication; second, verification. Correspondence grounds understand-ing; understanding permits us to confirm or disconfirm, through argument and evidence.

Think again of our simple example. Were the word *thick* used now for thick, now for thin, now for in between, or now for thick, now for white, now for rough or slippery, there would be no telling what anybody meant by the utterance "The ice is thick." Effective communication would cease, and so would verification. Verbal constancy, on the other hand—that is, conformity at least in intention, hence frequently in fact, with established word uses—permits both understanding and testing. And the greater the constancy, the surer the understanding and the testing. Knowing, for example, that by *thick* a person really means thick, I also know what evidence to consider and cite for or against the person's claim that the ice is thick. Fruitful inquiry and discussion are made possible.

Whether practically or cognitively, the significance of correspondence can hardly be exaggerated. *Homo sapiens,* it has been said, is most adequately characterized as *animal symbolicum,* not just *animal rationale.* Linguistic sym-bolism, especially, is second nature to us, not only in the sense that it pervades our whole existence, even our private ruminations and solilo-quies, nor merely in the sense that we live and perform in this medium with unreflective ease, but in the further sense that just as there would be no nature without laws of nature, but a chaos in which no living being could survive, so without symbolic regularity, there would be no symbolism, no world of language in which *animal symbolicum* could survive. The most crucial type of symbolic regularity, without which government, science, literature, business, education, medicine, technology, mass media, and indeed our whole society and culture would vanish, is the particular variety and degree of regularity called "truth." Without it, humankind as we know it would not exist.

I may appear to be overdramatizing, but emphasis seems warranted. For Wittgenstein was right. Familiarity may easily blind us to "the aspects of things that are most important for us." Thus blinded, we may "fail to be struck by what, once seen, is most striking and most powerful."[4] Failing to see and be struck by it, we may fail to take it into account and may suffer the consequences. In the present instance, we may fail to note the importance of correspondence and may therefore pay little heed to it, either in our own linguistic practice or in our assessment of the practice of others. As we shall see, such has often been the case. Indeed, many thinkers, when they weigh the pros and cons of a way of speaking, consider anything *but* its agreement or disagreement with established patterns of speech.[5]

Three main misunderstandings, it seems, block acceptance of correspondence as a norm, and three clarifications are therefore needed: first, of the difference between usage and established uses; second, of the difference between established uses and established opinions; third, of the senses in which established uses are—and especially are not—theory-laden. Once these clarifications have been made, in the present chapter, it will be possible to grasp why and in what sense linguistic correspondence merits adoption as a general criterion of what to say. Subsequent chapters will then illustrate the norm and its utility, by means of sample debates concerning truth.

Usage and Established Uses

The term *usage* refers to customary, widespread practice—to "use in the language," not for instance to personal definitions. Yet the latter too, as noted in chapter 3, can give rise to "established word uses" by which the truth of statements can be assessed. If a writer or a speaker stipulates a meaning for some expression, we keep that meaning in mind when we judge the truth of that person's assertions.

Thus the sense of the recommended rule should be noted. It does not enjoin that we never depart from "ordinary language." It suggests merely that we take *some* established uses, common or uncommon, as our guide. Whether we leave the language as it is or stipulate new meanings, we should recognize the need to adopt one procedure or the other and to abide thereafter by the decision. The uses established by usage or stipulation should at least codetermine (and in certain types of utterance totally determine) what we say. Within the ample limits loosely traced in the last chapter (relative similarity accepted; hyperbole, causal connection, contagion, and figurative speech not excluded), our use of words should conform to their established uses.

Thus generously defined, the norm I am proposing may seem trivial. Yet it is in fact far from trite. For one thing, as just noted, the stakes are high. For a second, the norm is widely ignored. For a third, it is disregarded not only through inadvertence, but largely through conviction. Serious reasons are thought to tell against it. Let me linger a moment on each of these three points—the stakes, the deviations, the reasons alleged—before examining the third at greater length.

First, when the norm is thus broadly understood—in terms of established uses and not just of usage—the values at stake are nothing less than the possibility of communication and verification. Without word meanings distinct from the assertions that employ them, the assertions could not be understood, nor could they be checked for accuracy. But word meanings arise through patterned speech or explicit stipulation and continue to serve their purposes of communication and verification only if we honor the meanings thus established—that is, only if we accept them as normative. If we stipulate a sense for a term, we cannot then disregard that sense when we employ the term in assertions; if the assertions are challenged, we cannot dismiss the stipulated sense as irrelevant to the assertions' validity—not if we wish to be understood or to further the inquiry at hand. Neither, if we have stipulated no sense of our own, can we dismiss the existing sense or senses—the one(s) provided by usage—as irrelevant. Either way, we would be rejecting correspondence as our norm, and in rejecting it, we would be abandoning the only basis for fruitful discussion and inquiry.[6]

Second, even if the word *correspondence* be conceived elastically, as I have recommended, it still seems true to say that disregard for correspondence is extremely widespread. The disregard takes two principal forms. First, there are speakers and writers who simply ignore existing meanings and stipulate none of their own, with the result that their assertions constantly depart from usage and, if judged by its standard, would have to be labeled false. Second, there are those who advert to existing meanings, object to being bound by them, but provide no alternative meanings of their own by which their claims might be understood and assessed. In either case, communication and verification are effectively blocked. Thus, not only does the norm of correspondence represent important values, but those values are widely subverted by disregard for the norm.

By way of concrete illustration, consider certain startling claims repeatedly advanced by Bertrand Russell. Citing the discoveries of modern science, Russell declared that nobody has ever seen another person, touched a table, heard a nightingale sing, and the like. True, common sense and naive realism suppose the contrary; they suppose, for example, that we see physical objects. But science knows better.[7] Physical objects originate impulses, which reach our eyes, stimulate our nerves, and finally reach our brains. The end results, there in the brain, are all we actually see. Thus, "To say that you see Jones is no more correct than it would be, if a ball bounced off a wall in your garden and hit you, to say that the wall had hit you. Indeed, the two cases are closely analogous. We do not, therefore, ever see what we think we see."[8]

For Russell, verbs like *see* and *hear* express direct, unmediated awareness. To say that one sees a horse or hears a train is therefore to assert such a direct relationship with the horse or the train. The animal or the machine is immediately present to the mind. But this, he insists, is a mistake. We are never related in this way to the things we say we perceive, but only to the contents of our minds, resulting from the things' activity. Hence, all our usual assertions about hearing, seeing, touching, feeling, tasting, and the like are erroneous. They betray a naive, prescientific viewpoint.

When I say that for Russell verbs of sensation express immediate awareness, I do not mean that such was his estimate of usage or the outcome of his linguistic inquiries. Reflection on the actual functioning of such verbs could hardly have yielded such a result.[9] After all, most people, like Russell, are acquainted with the basic facts of physics and physiology. Yet most people, like Russell in his everyday use of words,[10] speak of watching parades, observing cloud formations, feeling the earth tremble, hearing an explosion, and so forth. And it is inconceivable that on all such occasions they state deliberate falsehoods. No, Russell simply did not attend to established word uses, for he prided himself on being a philosopher, not a mere lexicographer.

Such departures from established uses, in the name of theoretical advance, are more the rule than the exception in much speculative writing. Just as Russell denied that we see or hear physical objects, so others, in similar fashion and for similar reasons, have denied that lights flash;[11] that objects are red or yellow,[12] hot or cold;[13] that we hear anything but sounds;[14] that adults were once children;[15] that anything has value;[16] that light rays are colored;[17] that we ever step twice into the same stream;[18] that people take an interest in their activities;[19] that tables and the like are solid objects;[20] that the sun rises or sets;[21] that people are buried;[22] that they are agreeable or useful;[23] that they love one another;[24] that they feel pain in their extremities[25] or pleasure in their sexual organs;[26] that anything ever changes, comes to be, or passes away;[27] that we see automobiles or hear music;[28] that animals act[29] or feel pain;[30] that unjust laws are laws;[31] that sentences have meaning;[32] that what we call "life" is really life;[33] that individual people ever think;[34] and so on, endlessly.[35]

When I say that these denials resemble Russell's, I mean that they contest familiar sayings, by virtue of supposedly superior knowledge or insight; that the denials result from or embody new uses of familiar words; that their authors do not advert to this fact or see their claims in this light, since they do not attend to the established uses of words or see any need to. Correspondence between their use of words and the words' established uses, standard or stipulative, is not an acknowledged or operative principle for them.

And yet it clearly should be. What holds for "The ice is thick" holds for "I saw her yesterday," "I hear a train coming," "He grew up in North Dakota," and the like. Clarity and concord are not served by insisting that nobody ever *sees* another person; that nobody ever *hears* anything outside the mind; that nobody has ever existed, identically the same, even ten months in a row, much less for ten years, and hence that no single person has ever *grown up* anywhere; and so forth. When the actual senses of words are thus ignored and abandoned, communication breaks down, futile debate ensues, and effective discussion and inquiry sputter to a standstill.[36]

The numerous pronouncements I have cited, starting with Russell's, illustrate both the first and the second reasons for stressing the rule of correspondence: they attest the rule's practical importance, and they attest how widely it is disregarded. Hence, to urge its acceptance is not a superfluous suggestion; it is not like advising people to walk with their legs, hear with their ears, or breathe with their lungs.

A third reason for stressing the norm and its validity is the fact that, besides being disregarded in practice, it is also resisted in theory. Some deviations result from mere oversight: a word's established use has simply not been noted, but if the discrepancy with that use were recognized, it would be corrected. More often, however, this is not the case. Either the relevance of word uses, as distinct from the assertions they appear in, would be questioned; or this distinction itself would be challenged. For further confusions besides the one just considered remain to be dealt with. Still more consequential is the common conflation of established word uses and established beliefs.

Established Uses and Established Opinions

Any believer in correspondence, even flexibly conceived, knows how often in discussion he must question or contest some statement, since it conflicts with standard usage, and no alternate sense has been suggested. He knows, too, how frequently this appeal to usage will be rejected, and why. Usage is equated with common sense, and ordinary language with ordinary opinions.

Although it may be too harsh to call this equation an "enormous howler,"[37] it does seem seriously mistaken. One person, employing familiar words, meanings, and modes of speech, may make the most extraordinary assertions—may claim to have lived five hundred years, to recall his existence within the womb, or to have read in an ancient manuscript about the structure of DNA. Another person, employing unfamiliar words, meanings, or forms of speech, may utter nothing but truisms—may, for instance, claim that no one steps into the same stream twice, and by this statement mean merely that no one, stepping twice into the same stream, plunges his foot both times into identical water.[38]

Despite this evident contrast, the confusion between everyday forms of speech and everyday opinions appears as commonly in theoretical literature as it does in theoretical conversation.[39] Its presence can be sensed, for example, when one reads: "If we philosophers want to get beyond the cake of 'common sense' and make any fresh discoveries or win any new perspectives, I am afraid this cult of 'ordinary language' will never do."[40] "It is a philosophic task to criticize the categories found in the ordinary use of language, and it is inevitable that as a result of the criticism they should be clarified and modified. If they were not, there would be no such thing as intellectual advancement."[41]

Copernicus, it would seem, had to redefine *Earth* or *orbit;* Harvey had to redefine *heart* or *blood;* Watson and Crick had to redefine *helix, heredity,* or *DNA* if they were to make any advance in understanding. Likewise, when, in the course of this study, I adverted to the linguistic dimension ignored by isomorphists and pragmatists, I supposedly had to create new senses for *language, linguistic, words,* and the like. How else could the fly be freed from the bottle? And when Wittgenstein spoke of "assembling reminders for a particular purpose,"[42] he cannot have had in view anything so jejune as simply calling to mind familiar, unnoted facts—even if those facts, when once adverted to, appear "most striking and most powerful." Concepts would have to be altered.[43]

Such claims appear plausible only if, for example, the word *concept* is used indiscriminately both for concepts in the sense of word meanings and for concepts in the sense of theories. And so it repeatedly is. In a work aimed at conceptual clarification one can read: "Suppose we consider, first, our current ideas about the historical evolution of human knowledge and understanding—i.e. the *growth* of concepts—and, secondly, those about the development of such understanding within the lifespan of human individuals—i.e. the *grasp* of concepts—what can we then learn about the *worth* of concepts—i.e. the foundations on which their intellectual authority rests, and the standards against which it is to be appraised?"[44] When the evolution of human knowledge and understanding is thus equated with the growth of concepts, one must suppose that the development of new theories, beliefs, or views of reality is at least part of what is meant; and when the word *concepts* is employed throughout, one must suppose, in the absence of any contrary clarification, that word meanings are also part of what is intended. Yet neither here nor earlier in the same work, or elsewhere in many comparable writings, is this distinction drawn, between concepts as word meanings and concepts as theories. The distinction is either not noted or is deemed unimportant or is, perhaps, opposed as mistaken or misleading.

The same conflation takes many forms and can be stated in many ways. The instrument is conflated with the act. The medium is confused with the message. A system of communication such as the English language is equated with acts of communication. Concepts are taken for conceptions.[45] "Ideas" or "notions" are thought of indiscriminately as contents of individual words or contents of entire propositions. Or, to return to where I started, someone suggests that words be used in their customary senses, and the suggestion is taken as an appeal to common sense. Ordinary meanings are confounded with ordinary beliefs. No wonder the appeal is rejected.

The conflation of meanings with opinions reverses the presumption in favor of familiar meanings. It is evident that as a medium of communication a language known to all is preferable to one known only to the speaker. It is equally evident, on the other hand, that popular assumptions or theories are more likely to be mistaken than those of experts. Hence, once meanings are confused with theories, and everyday meanings with everyday opinions, the skepticism which the opinions often merit is transferred to the meanings, with disastrous results. Babel and bedlam ensue.

Various factors help to explain the prevalence of this confusion between meanings and opinions. These include, for example, the surface similarity between statements of fact and statements of meaning, the confusion of referents with meanings and of new referents with new meanings, the practice of many thinkers in whose writings and discussions the distinction between concepts as word meanings and concepts as theories does indeed disappear,[46] and the fact that the linguistic medium of communication does not exist apart from acts of communication (like pigments on a palette waiting to be used). Still more effective in obscuring the distinction between meaning and theory, perhaps, is the fact that theories significantly affect meanings, in ways that I shall discuss in a moment. Theories, when accepted, enrich the cognitive content of terms and lengthen dictionary entries. The chemical analysis of water, for example, when once diffused among the populace, adds to the dictionary definition of *water* and to the information the word imparts.[47] It is easy to overlook the fact that a word is not a proposition and that its meaning is not a theory, or the fact that when, in the course of discussion, a theory is questioned or contested, the corresponding theoretical content generally drops from a word's meaning for the duration of the debate and does not count as defining.[48]

Thus meanings shift from context to context. In one setting a theoretical trait counts as defining; in another it does not. Accordingly, whoever views meanings globally, without regard for context, as people often do, may recognize no distinction between defining and nondefining traits, and hence none between concepts and theories. In the language as a whole, for a given theoretical trait, there may indeed be no such distinction. The chemical analysis H_2O, for example, which dictionaries cite for *water*, can be taken either as an empirical hypothesis or as a defining property, depending on the context.[49]

Senses in which a Language is and is not Theory-laden

Directly or indirectly, the common conviction that languages and their concepts are theory-laden generates resistance to the rule of correspondence.[50] In a sense, languages and their concepts *are* theory-laden, but in just what sense needs to be examined more closely. Otherwise the distinction between concepts and theories may appear to break down, and it may appear naive to suggest that nonneutral assertions be checked against supposedly neutral meanings.

A language is theory-laden in the sense that its individual words are theory-laden, and its words are theory-laden in the sense that their content, or power to inform, is determined by the theories to which people subscribe. The message which words convey is conditioned by the recipients' convictions.[51]

Suppose, for example, that a woman says she saw a man struck by a car. A typical twentieth-century hearer of this assertion would suppose that light rays had traveled from the man and the car, had entered her eye and struck the retina at the rear, causing electrical impulses to travel along the optical nerve to the brain. To be sure, neither the speaker nor the hearer would think about these things; nor would they infer them; nor would the speaker mention or talk about them; but for a typical, present-day hearer of the word *saw*, they would be the automatic content of what was said. Widely held theories of optics and physiology would work this *cognitive* effect. Ask the recipient of the report, and this is the kind of thing he or she would tell you.

Practically no common term of the language has failed to acquire some such content, and practically no commonly held theory has failed to affect the content of some familiar term(s). Optics loads our color words with theory; physiology, our words for bodily actions; physics and chemistry, our words for physical objects and occurrences; biology, our words for living things and their activities; astronomy, our words for heavenly bodies and events; economics, our words for business transactions; and so forth.

And science takes up where prescientific thinking leaves off. We now believe that the woman who spoke and the man she saw are composed of cells, molecules, atoms, and subatomic particles. Such is the current content of words like *I, man,* and *car.* But these theoretical entities of physics, chemistry, and biology, inferred from sensible phenomena, are continuations of our belief in bodies—the woman, the man, the car that struck him—distinct from the stimuli to which we believe they give rise, and existing before and after we or anyone else observes them. Such popular metaphysics also gives content to our words.[52]

Speakers, however, though endowed with the same theoretical beliefs as hearers, are seldom guided by them in their use of words. The beliefs generally play no role when we are young; and they generally play no role when we are older and our heads are full of theory. The woman, for example, does not first check to see whether light rays did in fact traverse the space between her and the accident, impinge on her retinas, and generate impulses along her optic nerves, then, on the basis of this evidence, declare: "I saw a man struck by a car." Nor does a child who utters the same words first check to see whether physical objects, distinct from his or her visual impressions and existing before and after them, did in fact give rise to the impressions. In both instances such checking is out of the question.

Words can still function effectively at this pre-theoretical level on those relatively rare occasions when somebody challenges, questions, or discusses the truth of an accepted theory. When some scientist challenges the organic origin of petroleum, for example, communication continues without a hitch, despite the fact that most of us, if asked to define *petroleum,* might mention an organic origin. Similarly, when Berkeley and contemporary phenomenalists deny the extrasensory existence of bodies, we can understand the denial and discuss it, thanks to the basic empirical content of the physical concepts employed.

Reflecting on this contrast between operative, nontheoretical criteria and the rich cognitive content conveyed by our terms, we see that not only do we generally not consult, check, or think about the theory or theoretical content, or need to, when we use the terms; we do not even need to know or accept it.[53] For example, to use the word *petroleum* correctly, we generally do not need to know or believe that petroleum did or did not have an organic origin. To use the word *see* correctly, we need not know anything about optics or physiology. To use the words *man, woman, car,* and the like correctly, we need not get our metaphysics right. Even when we state the origin of petroleum mistakenly or describe the process of sight mistakenly or explain the extrasensory source of sensations mistakenly, we do not

misapply the word *petroleum, see, man, woman,* or *car.* Even in these utterances, we use the terms correctly to pick out referents that, by means of
other terms, we then describe or explain inaccurately. The identification is
accurate; the description or explanation is not.

These reflections suggest what is right and what is wrong in the type of
critique often directed against "ordinary-language philosophy." Consider,
for example, these remarks of Brand Blanshard:

> It is surely untrue that "any philosophical statement which violates ordinary
> language is false." When the plain man says "grass is green," he means, I suppose,
> that it is green whether anyone sees it or not. But is Berkeley really answered by
> pointing out this fact? That is far too short and easy a way to escape him. For he
> was not proposing a new usage; indeed he was quite ready to speak with the
> vulgar if he could think with the learned; he was maintaining that the plain man,
> in supposing grass to be green when no one saw it, was universally mistaken in the
> plain sense of "mistaken," and about one of his plainer meanings. I think that in
> this he was probably right.[54]

I shall not debate the soundness of Berkeley's or Blanshard's metaphysics.
Nor shall I defend the dictum that Blanshard rightly contests, for it ignores
the possibility of stipulated meanings. However, the preceding analysis
suggests how cautious we should be about equating "ordinary language"
with the opinions of even the majority of speakers. Someone who questions
or disputes the organic origin of petroleum does not "violate ordinary
language." Neither does someone who, like Berkeley, contests the popular
metaphysics of most speakers. For whatever people's beliefs may be, it is not
metaphysics that guides them when they say, for instance, "The grass in my
lawn is green." And even were they explicitly to debate the nature of grass
and greenness, they would not define *grass* and *green* in terms of their
respective theories. The common empirical criteria operative in everyday
speech would permit communication and debate.

Thus Blanshard may be right when he asserts that Berkeley continued to
"speak with the vulgar." However, he cannot have it both ways. He cannot
consistently maintain both that Berkeley's metaphysics violated ordinary
language and that he continued to speak with the vulgar. If the latter claim
is correct, then the simple truth, plainly put, would seem to be that his
metaphysics disagreed with popular modes of thought, but his use of words
agreed with popular modes of speech. He did not suppose, though he
might have done so with more justice than Russell, that familiar words like
grass and *green* were so infected with error that he had to deny the existence
of any such thing as grass or any such thing as greenness whenever no one
was looking. As Blanshard himself says, Berkeley *spoke* with the vulgar and
thought with the learned.

Blanshard's critique makes better sense, then, if we take it as directed, not
against ordinary language or ordinary-language philosophers in general,

but against the type of ordinary-language philosopher soon to be considered, who, confusing concepts with beliefs, requires us, for example, to accept the beliefs of the Azande if we wish to use their concepts or speak their language. Blanshard is right. To speak with the vulgar, the primitive, the naive, the mistaken, *in their language,* we need not *think* as they do, in the sense of sharing their convictions. The frequency with which this distinction is blurred or overlooked by ordinary-language philosophers and their critics highlights its importance.

The Neutrality of a Language and its Meanings

I could expand and vary the preceding sampling of cases and texts, so as to document more fully how widespread is resistance, in theory and in practice, to the norm of correspondence. But I will not do so. Instead, I shall now counter in a more systematic, positive fashion the underlying notion that the words of a language and their established uses are somehow loaded with theory in a sense which precludes acceptance of the norm. In all respects that are pertinent for the norm's validity, a language and its meanings are theory-neutral. For example:

Though "theory-laden," word meanings are not themselves theories, opinions, or propositions. This distinction is denied implicitly more often than it is explicitly. We read, for instance: "Human beings have used the word 'love' for a very long time. In the Western World, particularly through the vehicle of the Christian tradition, the word has perhaps been more frequently used or, at least, thought, than in any other culture area—more frequently and in more senses. Yet how many persons in our culture have understood the *true* meaning of this word?"[55] "Only Jesus Christ," another author writes, "has fully revealed to us what love is, what the word 'love' really means, but we can make some preliminary observations at a natural or common sense level."[56] Remarks like these suggest that the meanings of words—or at least, their "true meanings"—are hidden truths to be discovered by means of insight or revelation, not by reflection on the words' familiar uses. Yet words have the meanings we speakers of the language give them, and the meanings we give them are not theories.

In this connection it should be noted that what I have termed the "theoretical contents" of words are not theories, but the fallout of theories. They are what the words impart to those who hold the theories. When, for example, a person claims to have seen an object and we believe the report, we believe that light traveled from the object to the speaker's eye(s), struck his retina(s), stimulated the optic nerve(s), and so forth. This theoretical content results from various theories that typical hearers hold, but it is not itself the theories that account for it. The verb *see* in "I see it now" or "Owls see better at night" does not convey any general explanation of either light or sight. Not even when it occurs in a general explanatory statement does the single word by itself convey the whole theory expressed by the statement.

Word meanings are not true or false, accurate or inaccurate. This follows, in part, from the preceding. And it is not negated by the identification of words' meanings with their standard or stipulated uses. For the uses may be exemplified in and by specific sayings, but they are not the sayings, any more than the colors or shapes we note in varied objects are identical with any or all of the objects. It is the sayings and the views they express that are true or false, accurate or inaccurate, not the individual words or meanings exemplified in them.

Employing words in their established senses does not by itself guarantee truth. A person may use the right English words for what he or she wishes to say, but the resulting statement may be false. The person may, for instance, think that it is raining and use the verb *rain* to say so, in its customary sense of drops of water falling from clouds; yet the statement may be false, since no such drops are coming down. This essential ingredient needed for full correspondence (see chapter 3) may be lacking.

Employing words in their established senses, everyone may be mistaken in some single theory or assertion. For instance, even if all speakers of English were to affirm that the earth is the center of the planetary system, in the standard sense of *center,* their assertion would nonetheless—indeed, for this very reason—be false; for the earth's actual position is not of the kind standardly indicated by the word *center* in countless sayings about cities, circles, yards, gardens, rooms, and so forth. Similarly, as Stuart Brown has observed, "It used to be believed in medieval England that weasels gave birth to their young through their ears. But we are under no compunction to say that this belief was true relative to anything—though of course it was *thought* to be true."[57] For, once again, the majority assertion clashed with majority usage, of *weasel, ear, through,* and the rest. The animals called "weasels" do not perform the action called "giving birth" in any such location as that suggested by the phrase "through their ears."

Words can be used with identical senses to assert or deny the same theory.[58] Thus it may be true, as Thomas Kuhn remarks, that "the moon belonged to the family of planets before Copernicus, not afterwards; the Earth to the family of planets afterwards, but not before."[59] Yet, during their great debate, Copernicans and Ptolemaists did not defend their conflicting views as true by definition. They could and did employ terms like *Earth* and *moon* and *planet* in basically similar senses, with disputed points removed from the terms' definitions for the duration of the discussion.

This observation extends to the regions of theory something that we experience every day. When one person affirms and another denies that deficits fuel inflation, they are not talking at cross-purposes. They do not give different senses to the words they use. Again, when one party asserts and another denies that cigarettes cause cancer, they do not mean different things by *cigarettes, cause,* or *cancer.* The meanings of the words do not shift from speaker to speaker; hence their assertions are not mere tautologies. Deficits are not inflationary or cigarettes carcinogenic by definition for one side and noninflationary or noncarcinogenic by definition for the other.

Even linguistic theorists may overlook these simple facts of linguistic life. Thus, a specialist in language and its relation to thought has written: "It would be startling indeed if the word 'justice,' for example, were to have the same meaning to the nine justices of the United States Supreme Court; we should get nothing but unanimous decisions."[60] Rather, it is such an assertion that is startling. Suppose the justices all equated justice with "equal treatment before the law" or "giving each person his or her due"; would that assure unanimous verdicts? Or suppose, more concretely, that they accepted a utilitarian criterion of justice and aimed at maximum happiness for all; would they invariably agree on what maximizes happiness?

It appears that the author of this comment has confused what a word means in a given assertion with what the whole statement means or asserts. He has conflated a given verdict with the meaning of some single word used to express it and has not noticed that words can be used with identical senses to express conflicting verdicts. In this respect, too, word·meanings are neutral.

A person may understand a theory perfectly, by means of shared word meanings, yet reject the theory. He may understand the theory of luminiferous ether yet deny the existence of such ether. He may understand belief in God yet deny the existence of God. He may understand claims made for ESP yet deny the existence of ESP. Thus a statement like the following must be read with care: "In the case of the wavicles there is virtually no significant separation; our coming to understand what the objects are *is* for the most part just our mastery of what the theory says about them. We do not learn first what to talk about and then what to say about it."[61] Here, learning "what to say" means learning the idiom, not embracing the doctrine. We may grasp and aptly express a theory that we nonetheless reject.

This possibility appears to have been overlooked when another writer observes: "I would be inclined, for example, to say that what it makes sense to utter often depends on the regularities found in nature. Thus it no longer makes sense, in one way, to talk about the 'ether' as classically construed, although it is obviously possible to discuss that term intelligibly."[62] On the contrary, it still makes sense, if it ever did, to talk about ether (not just the term) and to assert or deny its existence. For "talk about" is not synonymous with "assert" or "deny." And the denial of ether is as intelligible as the assertion of it, thanks to the same shared meaning. Indeed, it is the common, classical sense of the word *ether* that makes the assertion false and the denial true, just as it is the common, classical sense of *witch* or *ghost* that makes the assertion of witches or ghosts false and the denial true. In some other senses of the terms, the truth-values might be reversed.[63]

Established word meanings—indeed, standard, nonstipulated meanings—can be used to express any debatable theory. Stipulated senses may sometimes be more convenient than familiar ones, but they are not indispensable for understanding. For stipulations rely on preexisting meanings, and these meanings may be used to say the same thing.

> Thus it would be possible to express all that is intelligible in Kant, using everyday German (or English), or all that is intelligible in Bradley, using everyday English (or German), and so for James, Bergson, Descartes, or St. Thomas. Words would have to be stretched, and creatively exploited, as usual, but in continuity with everyday usage. For, after all, that is how philosophers themselves have introduced their readers into their personal conceptual systems (in so far as they succeeded in doing so); they used familiar words with familiar meanings. So it must be possible to reverse the process and get their thoughts back into the mother tongue, eliminating all radical shifts in meaning such as I have already illustrated in the case of "see," and such as Wittgenstein had in mind when he recommended that we return terms to the language-game which is their home (*Investigations*, §116).[64]

If, however, a theory cannot be expressed with the aid of established meanings—even allowing for stretching like that discussed in the last chapter—then the theory, if such it can be called, is not expressible or debatable. It will have to be kept to oneself.

Word meanings seldom commit a speaker to any disputed theory. This eighth point is related to the first and second but does not follow from them. And it merits special mention, since so many people, when invited to speak English as it is spoken, suppose that they are being urged to say and believe what other speakers of English say and believe. And those who issue the invitation may elicit resistance by falling into a similar confusion. Thus, Max Black recounts hearing

> a philosopher of neo-Wittgensteinian persuasion argue that the language of the Azande, who believe in the prevalence and efficacy of witchcraft, must simply be "accepted" because "that language game is played." He proceeded to assert that there was (could be?) "nothing wrong with their language"—indeed that questions of right and wrong "simply could not arise." To speak the language of the Azande is already to be committed, by the rules of that language, to belief in witches: so, if we wish to persuade them by rational means, that is to say by using the only language they understand, we ourselves must believe—or at least speak as if we believed—in witchcraft.[65]

Here the answer is simple. Doubtless we could say in Azande as we could in English when belief in witchcraft still prevailed, "There are no witches." This possibility indicates the sense in which a language, though it may be more or less practical for various purposes, is neither right nor wrong.[66] The Azande are no more committed by their common language to belief in witches than speakers of English are committed by the language they speak to belief in witches, ghosts, Adam, Atlantis, unicorns, ether, or phlogiston—or ever were.[67]

Suppose, though, that somebody skeptically questions the existence of any pains other than his own. Is he questioning whether others have groaned, screamed, writhed, or exclaimed "Ouch"? No, not just that. Yet, if it is pains that he is questioning and not just pain behavior, how did the word acquire that extra, nonbehavioral content save through the existence of other people's pains—and lots of them—at least in the past? Sensations which he alone has felt cannot have given meaning to a common word in the language. Thus it would appear that his use of the word *pain* does, in a sense, commit him to belief in the existence of others' pains.[68] As Wittgenstein remarked, "Scepticism is *not* irrefutable, but *obvious nonsense* if it tries to doubt where no question can be asked."[69] "If you are not certain of any fact, you cannot be certain of the meaning of your words either."[70]

Some would contest even the type of exception I am admitting;[71] but I see no need to insist that word meanings never commit a speaker to any theory, in any sense of *commit* and any sense of *theory*. For the type of antiskeptical argument that I have just developed with regard to pains has limited application. And debate seldom descends to the level at which it applies. And even when it does, the norm of correspondence retains its validity.[72]

Let me elaborate on these points, starting with the first. People seldom debate the existence of others' pains, but they do dispute the existence of God, evolution, ether, phlogiston, witches, neutrons, ESP, human freedom, rational life elsewhere in the universe, and the like. And none of these words—*God, evolution, ether, phlogiston,* and so forth—requires for its sense the existence of the thing or things debated. Such meanings are acquired differently, through implicit or explicit definition. Hence there is no contradiction, I would say, in denying the existence of God. Nor is there any incoherence in questioning human freedom when, as is generally the case, what is questioned is nothing experienced or experienceable.[73]

Even on the rare occasions when doubts are voiced concerning the existence of bodies, for example, or of other people's pains, the norm of correspondence still applies: words should still be employed in keeping with established uses. If there is no way to express the skeptical hypothesis save by using words and meanings that invalidate it, this is not an arbitrary restriction imposed by the norm. As far as the rule of correspondence is concerned, we are free to stipulate other meanings if we can, then abide by them. If, for instance, a private ostensive definition like that envisaged in paragraph 258 of Wittgenstein's *Philosophical Investigations* really did establish a connection between the sign "S" and a private sensation, it might perhaps be possible to use the sign in that newly established sense and to ruminate privately regarding whether other people also experience Ss. And "S" would then be the sign to use in converse with ourselves to state whatever conclusion we reached, whether skeptical or nonskeptical. The rule of correspondence would still hold.

The errors a language or an idiom suggests to unwary thinkers are not errors of the language or the idiom, nor do they warrant its rejection. The course of Wittgenstein's thinking is instructive in this regard. Impressed by the power of surface linguistic analogies to deceive,[74] Wittgenstein at first envisaged an ideal language whose structure would mirror the structure of reality: verbal objects would represent nonverbal objects; verbal relations would represent nonverbal relations (for example, spatial relations between written names might represent temporal relations between objects, or temporal relations between spoken names might represent spatial relations). Later he came to realize that such an "ideal" notation is neither practical nor possible. And even if it were, it too would not be free from potentially misleading analogies. A temporal relation for a spatial relation, or vice versa, would be as open to misconstrual as anything in current usage. Generally speaking, therefore, the remedy for language-induced misconceptions is not removal of the source, but removal of the misconceptions.

It may be that some currently familiar form of speech is more deceptive than an alternative mode of expression would be, and should therefore be replaced. However, such a case for revision would be difficult to substantiate. Three major obstacles stand in the way.

First, in order to demonstrate the need for change, it does not suffice to show that the current idiom deceives in a given manner, whereas its rival would not; their varied, overall power to deceive must be compared. This is seldom done. The complaint has been voiced, for example, that "nouns and adjectives symbolize states; they can represent only the static. But if reality is not static, as Bergson holds it is not, nouns and adjectives can only misrepresent and distort reality."[75] Accordingly, "we must try to remould our language so as to talk wholly in verbs, and if we cannot talk intelligibly in that fashion—as indeed Whitehead shows we cannot on almost every page of his book—we must constantly remember that we are speaking falsely."[76] To this typical grievance I would reply that some nouns and adjectives (for example, *hard, circular, silicon*) symbolize static states, whereas others (for example, *action, active, speedy*) do not; and if some thinkers are so hoodwinked by mere surface analogies as to imagine that all nouns symbolize what only some nouns do, the remedy is, not to express dynamic reality by means of verbs alone, but to disabuse these thinkers of their error. For even if verbs were somehow syntactically more suggestive of the dynamic (and this is a very big *if*), a language consisting entirely of verbs would contain analogies as deceptive as those it avoided. Verbs for boulders would resemble verbs for whirlwinds; static, written verbs would represent things in flux; visible signs would stand for sounds; and so forth.

Furthermore, even if we could come up with a substitute mode of expression that was less speculatively misleading overall, it might not be more practical than the existing mode and therefore might not be preferable. Chapter 6 provides a full illustration. Cognitive comparatives "are so very handy," it explains, "both verbally and practically. . . . Yet these practical advantages are bought at an inevitable price." Duped by surface similarities, philosophers have construed three-pole terms like *true* on the model of two-pole terms like *red* and have thereby incurred deep perplexity. However, language is not intended solely or principally for philosophers, and the philosophical price is worth paying. Other remedies are available for speculative puzzlement.

Finally, even if a substitute mode of expression were both practically and speculatively preferable, revision might still not be warranted. For, as Kurt Baier has noted, "We must keep in mind the difference between the question 'what would be the best use?' and 'would it be better to go on having the old, misleading use or to try to introduce the new use?' "[77] This distinction is pertinent in any area of contemplated innovation, Baier suggests, but with regard to the use of words "there is a much better case for conservatism than elsewhere. For one thing, it is very difficult to unlearn the ordinary use of words. The ways in which we use words become second nature to us." Furthermore, "the implications of the uses of words are very far-reaching and not all immediately obvious. Yet, if changes are not carried through for all the implications, the new use will be extremely confused." More serious still, "to change one's own use of a word does not bring about a change in other people's use of a word. One is likely to be misunderstood if one uses words in one's own private way. But even if one could persuade others to make the same changes, they would themselves be exposed to the same dangers and difficulties [as oneself]. . . . And if one managed to persuade a large number of people, but could not persuade all, the result would most likely be confusion and misunderstanding."[78]

In summary, three reasons ground the assertion that the errors which a language or an idiom suggests to unwary thinkers do not justify rejection of the language or the idiom. It is difficult to conceive any such innovation which would (1) be less misleading overall than the mode of expression it replaced, (2) be equally practical, and (3) not be more troublesome to introduce than its prospective advantages merited.[79] A substitute idiom or language might satisfy one or two of these conditions, but rarely, if ever, would it satisfy all three. And even if it did, it would still pose no challenge to the norm of correspondence. The advantages of revision would warrant a new mode of expression, introduced as such, not new predications, ignoring existing usage.

Implications

In this chapter I have suggested that three main misunderstandings block acceptance of correspondence as a norm. First, established uses may be equated with standard usage, with the result that the rule appears too restrictive. Second, they may be confused with established opinions, and their validity may therefore be contested. Third, they may appear too loaded with fallible theory to serve as safe guides of what to say or how to say it. Now that these difficulties have been dealt with—at least in preliminary fashion—it becomes possible to discern more precisely in what sense linguistic correspondence merits recognition as a general norm.

First of all, there is no need to adhere willy-nilly to accepted meanings or forms of speech. Linguistic innovation is often reasonable. Often it is practically automatic; new situations, conceptions, or discoveries elicit new meanings or modifications of old, as a matter of course.[80] In any case, however, there need to be meanings distinct from the claims that are made by their means. And, other things being equal, better-known meanings should be preferred, precisely because they are better known (just as familiar languages should be preferred, because they are familiar). If special benefits appear to outweigh the advantage of familiarity, new meanings may be introduced—provided that they are clearly indicated, that their advantages are plausibly argued, and hence that existing meanings are both noted and realistically assessed in comparison with the new ones.[81] If these recommendations appear platitudinous, recall how many authors have disregarded them.

Second, when I speak of preferring familiar meanings or forms of speech, I do not mean familiar sayings or opinions. And when I speak of announcing and justifying linguistic innovations, I do not mean that everyone who advances a new theory or viewpoint must justify his or her use of words. Galileo, for example, did not need to; nor did Darwin or Mendel. Their theories may have altered or enriched the cognitive content of the words they employed—*sun, earth, planet, species, heredity, pea,* and so forth; but they did not require or entail any departure from the words' familiar meanings. Those who contested or denied the new viewpoints could use the same words in the same senses as the innovative thinkers they opposed.[82]

The cumulative lessons I have mentioned—the preference for familiar terms and meanings, the care to distinguish new meanings from new theories, the concern for correspondence with established meanings, old or new—point to a style of discussion at variance with that favored in much contemporary literature. It is widely supposed that scientific rigor and speculative freedom legitimize a more "theoretical" approach. This viewpoint is so deeply, firmly rooted that no remarks of mine are likely to dislodge it. However, lest truth as correspondence lose by default, I can at least present more fully than I have seen attempted elsewhere the considerations that commend familiar forms of speech and, more broadly, the rule of correspondence. Subsequent chapters carry forward this endeavor.

CHAPTER 9

A PARADIGM INQUIRY: ARE PERFORMATIVES TRUE-FALSE?

In everyday life, discussing everyday matters, we regularly take usage as our guide. If one person says it is raining and another, observing more closely, says it is sleeting, they do not get embroiled in theoretical debate about the matter. The first person does not challenge the second's "thesis," and the second then cite the standard application of the words *sleet* and *rain,* only to have this evidence rejected as irrelevant. Nor does the rain-theorist thereupon propose an argument to the effect that sleet, too, is really a species of rain. He or she does not insist on the close similarity between rain and sleet or deride as "purely arbitrary" the borderline drawn by usage or propose a simplification for the sake of more accurate understanding or stress the underlying unity (both sleet and rain are H_2O) allegedly overlooked by unreflective users of the language.

In speculative discourse, however, analogous moves are common. Usage is widely spurned. Familiar meanings are abandoned, and no substitute meanings replace them. Meaning and theory tend to merge indiscriminately. Hence theories proliferate, uncontrollably. In the last chapter I outlined reasons why such developments are unfortunate. In this chapter and the next I shall spell out these reasons more fully and document their relevance more concretely, by means of sample debates about truth culled from recent literature.

The specific debates to be considered have been chosen for their relevance to the stage now reached in this inquiry. Part 1 focused on evident instances of truth and obvious uses of *true.* But just how far, we may ask, does the concept *true* extend? What varieties of speech act does it encompass, and which, accordingly, would the correspondence account have to cover in order to be valid generally? Some utterances are either clearly true or clearly false, or at least clearly one or the other. Other utterances—cheers, jeers, greetings, imprecations, and the like—are clearly neither true nor false. Between these extremes lie various forms of speech whose status is less obvious. Are performatives true or false? Are avowals? What of meaningless assertions, counterfactuals, hypotheticals, statements about the future, descriptions of nonexistent entities, undecidable hypotheses in mathematics? The account of linguistic truth so far given, in chapters 3–7, has said next to nothing on questions like these.

However, chapters 3–7 have provided, and chapter 8 has confirmed, a clue to their solution. In order to be judged both reasonable and true, statements, including those about truth and falsehood, should conform to the established uses of the words or other signs they employ. If objects are of a kind called geraniums and not of a kind called tulips, then that is what they should be called; they are geraniums, not tulips. If their flowers are of a hue called red and not of a hue called green, then they are red, not green. The words' established uses so determine. Similarly, if utterances are of a kind competent speakers term true or false, then they are true or false; otherwise they are neither. And if usage yields no verdict, there is no verdict. The concepts *true* and *false,* like most others, have a broad, indefinite borderline; and linguistic acts that fall on or within that border rather than on one side or the other cannot truly be described as being or not being true or false. The assertion or denial would lack linguistic backing.

This reasoning may appear circular. It may seem to base its assertions about truth on a preceding analysis of truth, antecedently accepted as valid. However, the answer to this objection should be clear from the last chapter, where descriptive considerations yielded to normative ones. What accredits verbal correspondence as a standard, here and elsewhere, is not its being labeled "truth," but the basic values it subserves. Its advantages for fruitful discourse and inquiry will now be demonstrated more fully, specifically with regard to the borderline of truth.

In the discussion of truth, as in that of other matters, the role of established word uses as arbiters of what to say is frequently contested and frequently ignored in ways that might be largely remedied by closer acquaintance with the concept *true* and with the values it represents. To confirm and illustrate this judgment, I shall examine instances in which the relevance of usage (the usual source of established word uses) is contested and others in which it is ignored, with the consequence that the bounds of truth are either unduly broadened or unduly narrowed. As a first illustration, I shall consider the truth or falsehood of performatives, which, like other types of utterance I shall note, lie largely beyond the borderline drawn by usage (that is, by the usage of *true* and *false*), yet which many theorists contend are true or false. In the next chapter I shall turn to moral and evaluative utterances, which usage labels true and false, yet which theorists often treat as "masqueraders" unworthy of such labeling. In one case the concept *true* is stretched; in the other it is tightened; in neither is usage heeded. It would be better, I shall argue, to leave the concept *true* alone and simply to understand it. Such tugging of words, this way and that, seldom furthers understanding; it merely diverts attention from substantive issues.

At the start, the double focus of these two chapters, on truth both as an object of inquiry and as a norm guiding inquiry, may appear confusing. However, I see no alternative. If I were to choose other paradigm debates and insert chapters on the nature of community, the essence of sacrifice, the definition of time, the limits of life, or the like, in order to illustrate the virtues of truth-as-correspondence, I might focus the methodological issue more sharply; but the intrusion of such totally alien topics within an essay on truth might prove equally confusing. And the perimeters of truth would still have to be determined, including or excluding various types of utterance, in accordance or not with established uses of *true* and *false*. And arguments would therefore have to be considered for and against the norm of correspondence, precisely as it bore on these inclusions or exclusions. The double focus cannot be avoided. So I have chosen to wing two birds with a single stone and to conduct the two inquiries—the substantive and the normative—simultaneously, within the compass of two chapters, rather than three or four.

Graham on Performatives

Keith Graham's study of J. L. Austin bears the revealing subtitle "A Critique of Ordinary Language Philosophy."[1] In criticizing Austin, Graham wishes to criticize a whole movement or tendency of which Austin is a leading representative, a tendency characterized by what Graham considers excessive reliance on and deference to "ordinary language." Since Graham's criticisms are themselves typical, his discussion has a double interest. For the concept of truth and its extension, his views on performatives have special relevance; for the norm of truth, the reasons backing his views have equal relevance. I shall therefore dwell on both—the underlying reasons as well as the resulting verdicts.

Austin, notes Graham, regarded it as too obvious to need demonstration that explicit performatives are neither true nor false.[2]

> He does argue specifically against the idea that a performative like "I promise . . ." is a true or false description *of an inner spiritual act,* and he points out that when someone utters these or similar words but fails to perform the action in question—say, because another concomitant condition is absent—we do not speak of a false bet or promise. But the first point does not show that the words are

not a true or false report of *anything*, and the second point is an exceedingly weak reason for Austin's conclusion, representing one of his few lapses into ordinary language philosophy while discussing language as a subject. We may have many reasons, good or bad, for saying or not saying something, and it is our reasons, rather than our not saying something, which are of paramount importance.[3]

Graham declares that his own reason for calling performatives true or false is simply that there is no reason not to.[4] Imagine, he suggests, that on some occasion I make the assertion "I am saying something" or "I am speaking in English." Wouldn't the utterance be true? And wouldn't the words themselves make it true? So why not construe a performative like "I promise" similarly, as a true account of itself?[5] Granted, it is not just a report or a description: it makes a promise. Granted too, that for it to be a promise, it must have an appropriate setting. I cannot, for example, make a promise when alone, whereas I can truthfully say "I am speaking" when alone. But why should these peculiarities count against a promise's truth or falsehood? Hence, performatives being comparable in various respects to true-false assertions, Graham proposes to "take as obvious the reverse of what Austin takes as obvious."[6]

Now, who is right? Well, if Austin's use of words conforms with their established uses, what he says is true; if Graham's use of words conforms with their established uses, what he says is true. It makes no difference that they are talking about truth and falsehood, rather than about the weather or the price of avocados. The same rule holds. Thus, if competent speakers of English call falling drops of water, but not falling flakes, "rain," then falling flakes are not rain. It is no use arguing that both come from clouds, that both have the same chemical analysis, that the flakes may melt the moment they touch the ground, and so forth. They are not rain. Similarly, it is no use stressing the similarities of performatives with other assertions, as Graham does, and ignoring their dissimilarities; there is no point in arguing that performatives can fail or succeed as other assertions can, that they may inform or misinform as other assertions can, and so forth. If usage draws a line between "I hear you" and "I warn you," as Austin thought it does, then the first utterance is true or false and the second is not.

Of course, word meanings may arise through stipulation as well as through usage; the phrase "established uses" in the correspondence formula acknowledges both sources. It is not dogmatic or narrow. Graham, however, stipulates for his terms no personal meanings that might make his assertions true; and he dismisses usage as irrelevant. Let us see why.

Usage Dismissed

According to Graham, philosophy is concerned with analytic, borderline, and comprehensive questions, and usage will not help even with the analytic kind. For when we attempt to delimit a concept (for example, *knowledge* or *causation*) more precisely, we not only observe current applications of the term but imagine unusual cases never before considered or discussed.

> A consideration of actual cases will provide us with the limits of application where this means the range of cases over which we do apply the concept in question, but not where "limits" is taken to mean the range over which we might, could or would be prepared to apply the concept. There are reasons for thinking that it will be useful to know the limits in the latter sense, and not just the former, if the rationale of a concept is to be given. As we pare away from the hypothetical situation more and more of the features normally present where the concept applies, then if we are still prepared to apply the concept we shall come nearer to finding out what, in the situation, actually gives the grounds for the concept's application, as opposed to being merely accidentally present features wherever it applies. In this way, a consideration of fantastic cases may serve as an aid to the better understanding of actual cases.[7]

One need not imagine fantastic cases to see how this method might work. Take the concept *chess.* Normally, people play chess face to face. Yet when they play by mail, we do not hesitate to call the game "chess." When they play in their heads, with perhaps only an imagined board and imagined pieces, we apply the same term with equal readiness. When a computer replaces one person, and not even an imagined board and imagined pieces figure in the playing, we still call the game "chess." And if we envision both human contestants thus dispensed with and one computer matched against another, then, too, we may be prepared to say that the computers are playing a game of "chess."

Now, after paring away the board, the pieces, the rules for moving them, even the human beings who usually play the game, do we thus arrive at "what actually gives the grounds for the concept's application"? Not in the least. For as new, different situations arise, we are ready to spin fibre on fibre, as Wittgenstein put it, till finally there may be no overlap at all between the beginning and the end of the series. The final application may share no single feature with the initial, more typical examples.

In suggestions like Graham's, we sense the lingering presence of essentialism. For him, too, it is "as if the sense were an atmosphere accompanying the word, which it carried with it into every kind of application."[8] So we are invited once again, it appears, to engage in a hunt like the one Wittgenstein described so memorably:

> In case (162) the meaning of the word "to derive" stood out clearly. But we told ourselves that this was only a quite special case of deriving; deriving in a quite special garb, which had to be stripped from it if we wanted to see the essence of deriving. So we stripped those particular coverings off; but then deriving itself disappeared.—In order to find the real artichoke, we divested it of its leaves. For certainly (162) was a special case of deriving; what is essential to deriving,

however, was not hidden beneath the surface of this case, but this "surface" was one case out of the family of cases of deriving.[9]

If, then, usage is to be disregarded in conceptual inquiries, it will have to be for different, better reasons than Graham here suggests. What we might or would or should say in unusual circumstances is no sure guide to the meanings that our expressions have in more familiar settings.[10]

Imaginary applications of a word may be as distantly related to its customary uses as word roots are to present meanings. Indeed, Graham's method closely resembles the once popular tactic of consulting etymologies in order to elucidate the meanings of words. Both approaches ignore usage. Both assume it may be wrong. Both suppose an underlying, mysterious identity, impervious to time and circumstance, in one case between a word's current sense and its source, in the other between its sense and imagined applications. And neither guide is reliable or helpful. The identity or nonidentity of present meanings with past or prospective meanings could be ascertained only if we already knew the present meanings, by some other means than imagining unreal cases or tracing etymologies.

Negative Grounds for Revision

In his general critique of Austin, Graham complains of "his ingrained *conservatism.*" "The tendency is always to preserve from change those descriptions of the world which happen to be the current ones, in the belief that they would not be current if they were not worth preserving."[11] In advancing this critique, Graham does not distinguish between descriptions and forms of description, hence does not differentiate between conservatism in what Austin says and conservatism in how he says it. Such distinctions are not operative in his thinking.[12]

Accordingly, he goes on to observe: "In the absence of any valid general argument in favour of such conceptual conservatism, it will be necessary to give some justification for any piece of current usage on its own account—something which Austin rarely does."[13] Evidently, Graham does not count either intelligibility or verifiability, by virtue of shared meanings, as a general argument in favor of "conceptual conservatism." With meaning and theory fused as they are in his thinking, shared meanings would mean shared theories; and thinkers can hardly be required to agree theoretically as a precondition for theoretical discussion and inquiry. Mere familiarity is hardly an argument in favor of a *theory*. So Graham never cites it as a reason for abiding by established terms or meanings.[14]

Not surprisingly, with the most evident advantages of conceptual conformity lost to view, Graham inclines toward innovation. After all, he would doubtless say, familiar concepts are popular concepts and so are likely to suffer from various defects, whereas the concepts reflectively crafted by theoreticians are likely to prove superior in numerous respects. Thus Graham lists both negative and positive reasons for conceptual revision.

Negatively, he warns that "matters may come to light in the course of seeking an analysis which give reason for abandoning a concept (the conditions for applying it may turn out to be irremediably confused, the concept may turn out to apply vacuously to all situations, it may express something inconsistent, and so on)."[15] Here, as previously, for each sample indictment it is necessary to distinguish between concepts as words or word meanings and concepts as theories.

In the first of Graham's three reasons for abandoning a concept, the phrase "conditions for applying it" suggests the application of a word, not the statement of a theory. Hence, illustrative examples might include the words *essence, form,* and *substance* as defined by hylemorphic theory,[16] or *object* as operative in Wittgenstein's *Tractatus.* By his own later admission (for example, in §49 of the *Philosophical Investigations*), the criteria for applying the term *object,* in its technical Tractarian sense, were hopelessly confused. In such a situation, the concept is not even useful for purposes of negation. If we denied *Tractatus* objects, we would not know what we were denying.

Abandoning hylemorphic or Tractarian theories, we would also abandon the concepts used to state them. However, the familiar, nontheoretical uses of the same terms—of *essence, form, substance,* and *object*—would remain. We could go right on speaking of "forms of life," "sticky substances," "large objects," and the like. For it is not readily conceivable that familiar, everyday meanings would be similarly flawed. To merit like rejection, they would have to be associated with some one doctrine, and the doctrine would have to be confused, and the confusion would have to have escaped general notice. Even Russell, critical though he was of standard usage, did not suppose that the everyday use of *see* or *hear* is confused; he thought the word's meaning results in false statements, not empty nonsense.

When Graham speaks, in second place, of concepts that turn out "to apply vacuously to all situations," he may have in mind examples like *Piltdown man* and *phlogiston.*[17] For these terms, as we now know, lack reference. However, such samples do not bear out his assumption that we should therefore abandon the concepts. The expressions "Piltdown man," "witch," "luminiferous ether," "phlogiston," and the like, with the meanings that account for their lack of reference, are still the best ones with which to express the mistaken theories that begot the terms, the reasons for and against the theories, the experiments that disproved them, and so forth. The concepts—the words and their meanings—need not be abandoned; only the theories need be—not, however, because they "apply vacuously to all situations," but simply because they are mistaken.

Suppose, though, that the vacuity resulted from inconsistency in the criteria of application and that the concepts therefore "expressed something inconsistent" (the third reason in Graham's list). Suppose, for example, that *see* did not mean merely "be directly aware of" (as Russell imagined) but "be aware of and not aware of": wouldn't that be sufficient reason to jettison the concept? Doubtless it would, but what word has such a meaning, and how could it? What theory, for that matter (if such is the meaning of *concept* in this instance), says that we are aware of things we are not aware of?

A likelier illustration of "inconsistency," to make sense of Graham's suggestion, would be the sort of confusion I had in mind when I cited hylemorphic concepts such as *essence* and *form*. It seems to me that when we seek to understand these concepts, one indicator points one way and another points another way, so that no genuine understanding results. We do not see clearly that the word has a meaning as contradictory as "awareness without awareness," "square circle," or "married bachelor"; rather, we remain perplexed as to which reading to prefer. For example, in interpreting "substantial form," should we put more stress on Aristotle's comparison with shape or on arguments that suggest kinship with efficient causality? In interpreting "essence," should we give more weight to the implicit verbal reference in the naming of the class or to the frequent insistence that essential definition is not concerned with words? When such quandaries prove insoluble, they may justify our dropping a concept; but they seldom arise with regard to everyday concepts like *see, hear, touch*—or *true*.

Yet *true* may be the kind of concept Graham had in mind, for it often occasions talk of "inconsistency."[18] The everyday concept *true*, it is thought, leads to semantic paradoxes. If, for instance, someone says "The statement I am making is false," then his statement, if true, is false, and if false, is true. However, what lands us in this dilemma is not the common concept *true* but our insistence on applying it to anything and everything that looks like a statement of fact (for example, "The statement I am making is false"). And this is a mistake. To cite one counter-instance from among many: "The chair is dirty," uttered in the absence of chairs or in the presence of chairs without indicating which one, is neither true nor false.

It is often supposed that if we think up odd examples like the Liar's saying and thereupon find ourselves in logical difficulties, everyday concepts account for the difficulties, and improvements on the concepts will free us from them. I would suggest, as others have,[19] that improved understanding of existing concepts may resolve the difficulties. For it is not readily conceivable that a noncontradictory concept (for example, *square* or *circle*) would dictate contradictory verdicts (for example, "The square is circular," "The circle is square," or "The figure is both circular and square"). Neither is it readily imaginable how, in real life, either usage or stipulation would give rise to a contradictory concept (for example, combining the traits of *circle* and *square*).[20]

I shall return to semantic paradoxes in chapter 13. At this point let me sum up by saying that once the distinction between theory and meaning is adverted to, none of Graham's three reasons appears a likely ground for revising an everyday concept like *true*. The current use of *true* and *false* for statements but not, for example, for christenings or invitations is neither confused nor vacuous nor inconsistent. Were christenings, say, just like the utterances we call true and false, it might be inconsistent to exclude them; but they are not just like other, true-false utterances. Hence there is no inconsistency. And the concept is far from "applying vacuously to all situations."

Positive Grounds for Revision

Perhaps in this instance Graham would not allege any confusion, vacuity, or inconsistency. He further advises, however: "In the absence of an analysis which gives compelling grounds for using or not using a given concept, we shall have to base our decision on many other considerations: whether the concept allows a sufficiently sophisticated view of, or response to, the world, whether it allows adequate explanation of the data to which it applies, whether it fits in well with other concepts we employ and see good reason to employ and so on."[21]

Again, these remarks make no mention of familiarity as a strong reason for retaining a given meaning. And they make readier sense for conceptions or theories than they do for concepts in the sense of word meanings. Russell, who thought in similar fashion, might claim that it is more sophisticated—more scientifically up to date—to say that we see our brains than to say that we see the seashore or the hills. Yet his use of the word *see* in the sense of direct awareness would not yield a more sophisticated concept; if anything, the everyday sense of *see* is more sophisticated, especially nowadays. As was explained earlier, for contemporary speakers and hearers the word is heavily freighted with physical and physiological theory, as it was not, and perhaps could not be, in Russell's usage.

As for the concept *true* and the extension Graham urges, I cannot imagine how labeling performatives true and false might allow a more sophisticated view of the world or permit a more adequate explanation of the data or fit better with other concepts we employ. I can sense, though, how Graham might believe it does. Having defined performatives in terms of truth and falsehood, he then "explains" performatives by means of this definition. *"A statement-act S is performative,"* he writes, *"if and only if it brings about the truth of the content it expresses as a consequence of people's so regarding it.* When it is taken in conjunction with my earlier discussion I suggest that this definition provides an adequate analysis, insofar as it shows in a clear and non-obvious way how performatives work."[22] Graham might just as well have suggested, however, that a statement is performative if and only if it realizes the content it expresses (that is, is indeed a promise, donation, appointment, or what have you) as a consequence of people's so regarding it. Use of the word *truth* adds nothing to his explanation. The only non-obvious thing about Graham's account (aside from its generality) is its terminology.

It is not obvious that performatives should be called true or false. Nor is it obvious that just explicit performatives, which name the action performed, should be classed as performatives. Austin broadened the term *performative*, because of the basic similarity between, for instance, "I order you to be there" and "You will be there!" Both these utterances issue an order, yet neither is cast in imperative form ("Be there!"). So the latter, too, may be termed a performative. Graham, however, resists this extension and uses the same definition as before to demonstrate the superiority of his position. The "important and distinguishing feature of performatives," he argues, is their "becoming true as a result of being uttered, or being used to create their own truth."[23] And "You will be there!" does not satisfy this criterion, whereas "I order you to be there" (in his account) does.

Were it written in some Platonic heaven that only explicit performatives are genuine performatives, the virtues of Graham's terminology and consequent refutation might be more evident, at least to heavenly observers of the debate. As it is, Graham recognizes how bizarre his position may appear. Does not Austin have a right to his own term? Graham replies that though Austin may have introduced the word *performative*, by way of certain examples, "The fact that it is Austin who first singles out these examples gives no special prerogative to the account which he then proceeds to give of what is peculiar about them. And in fact I argued that there were various deficiencies in the elucidation of the nature of performatives which he gives by considering his four original examples as paradigms, in particular his suggestion that they cannot be true or false."[24] This reference to the "nature of performatives" gives the impression once again that the class is somehow defined independently of how anyone uses the word *performative*, and that Graham has discovered this true nature, thanks to his related intuition that, regardless of how anyone employs the words *true* and *false*, performatives are in fact true and false.

Doubtless this interdependence of the concept *performative* and the concept *true* can be seen as an instance of what Graham means when he speaks of one concept "fitting in well" with another. For him, the extended concept *true* fits very nicely with the restricted concept *performative*. It allows him to specify the "nature" of performatives, and it allows him to settle disputes. "When we come to the borderline problems which Austin raises about performatives, many can be resolved by means of our analysis."[25] For example, "To say 'I apologise' in the appropriate circumstances *is* to apologise; and to say 'I am sorry' in those circumstances is equally to apologise. This is the common feature of the two utterances, and this is what might tempt us to say that 'I am sorry' is also a performative. But this would be a mistake, and for the same reason as in our earlier case. The statement-act 'I am sorry' does *not* create the truth of its own content as does 'I apologise.' "[26]

It may appear dogmatic to thus roundly declare Austin wrong on the basis of one's double redefinition of *performative* and *true*. But Graham does not regard his definitions as mere stipulations of sense. They are theoretical moves, backed by theoretical considerations. They permit a more sophisticated representation of reality, a more adequate explanation of phenomena. Here, for example, they mark off performatives (as Graham defines them) from nonperformatives.

Once more, however, this alleged advantage is illusory. The same demarcation could be effected, and often has been, without restricting the concept *performative* or extending the concept *true*. People could continue to speak of "explicit performatives" (for example, "I apologize") and "nonexplicit performatives" (for example, "I am sorry") for the same reasons as before. In explicit performatives the act is named; in nonexplicit performatives it is not. There is no need to add: "And therefore in the first case the utterance *verifies* itself whereas in the second it does not."

Arguments from Similarity/Dissimilarity

Discussing truth, Graham stresses the similarities between performatives and true-false utterances; discussing performatives, he stresses the dissimilarities between explicit and nonexplicit performatives. Thus his mode of argumentation suggests an underlying rationale of the kind stated by H. P. Rickman:

> We analyse concepts to discover their meaning, arguments to decide on their validity and situations in order to describe them adequately, but these are only preliminary stages. Having, through analysis, understood how concepts have been used in common speech or technical discussions and considered the facts to which they refer, we need not go on using them if they obscure similarities and differences. We must construct new patterns by re-defining these concepts, coining new ones, or even by creating a whole new scheme of related concepts.[27]

Thus, Graham might argue that the present borderline of *true* and *false*, excluding performatives, obscures their similarities with true-false utterances. Others, however, might urge with equal plausibility that the extended border he proposes would obscure the dissimilarities between performative and nonperformative utterances. It might give the impression, say, that the principal point of a performative is to inform the hearer about itself.[28] So the question inevitably arises, here and in countless kindred instances: What if similarities or dissimilarities are obscured whichever choice we make? Won't the conflicting arguments cancel out? And won't the independent virtue of familiarity therefore cast a deciding vote in favor of existing terminology?

In simpler illustration, suppose it were argued that pink so closely resembles nearby reds that it too should be labeled "red." Opponents might counter that extending the term *red* to cover pink would obscure the difference between that color and even the closest shades of red. Since the similarity and dissimilarity are equal, an impasse would result were similarity alone considered relevant. However, the existing concept *pink* enjoys the decisive edge of being familiar and therefore being more readily understood. Whatever the sociological or psychological basis of the concept's present borderline, honoring it has practical advantages.

Such a simple illustration may appear naively irrelevant to the theoretical concerns of authors like Rickman and Graham. But such is not the case. For one thing, appeals to similarity or dissimilarity are perhaps the commonest type of argument for broadening or narrowing a concept. And, as in this instance, a given demarcation can seldom be accused of obscuring both "similarities *and* differences," as Rickman puts it;[29] each competing option generally obscures one or the other, not both (if, indeed, the term *obscures* is warranted in either case). What one highlights, the other veils; what one veils, the other highlights.[30] Hence mere similarity or dissimilarity carries no more weight than in this simple instance. The only relevance of the greater complexity in typical real-life altercations is the stricter obligation it imposes of making clear just what alleged advantage warrants sacrificing the benefits of familiarity and ready understanding. In more complex cases, the desirability of conceptual revision, one way or the other, is likely to be far from self-evident. Yet promissory notes are more common than hard cash—mere allusions and surmises are more frequent than actual demonstrations—when the benefits of conceptual revision are alleged.[31]

In answer to demands for explicit justification, appeal is sometimes made to the common, innocent phenomenon of nontheoretical extension by similarity. When computers were invented, they were called "machines," on the strength of evident similarities with existing members of the class and despite their evident difference in other respects. Again, by virtue of certain similarities with persons, and despite still more evident dissimilarities, they were said to "think," "calculate," or give "answers" to "questions" when "asked." The process of conceptual stretching by resemblance is continual, natural, and reasonable. So why object when a theorist like Graham invokes equally strong and obvious similarities as a ground for stretching the concept *true?*

Because performatives are not some new invention or discovery requiring a new name. We have names for these speech acts—for example, *welcome, warn, apologize, christen, command*—and familiar ways to describe them. And the description "true" or "false" is not, typically, among those ways. To call a baptism true, on the strength of its resemblance to an assertion of fact, would be as confusing, misleading, and unreasonable as to call a carrot a turnip or a table a chair, on the strength of equal or still greater similarity.

The Resulting Morass

Confusing, misleading, unreasonable—such, generally, is the verdict implicit in J. Houston's survey of the dispute in which Graham and others have engaged. One side cites affinities, the other disaffinities. "But what makes an affinity an important one? Surely this depends very much on one's interests and purposes. It remains to be discussed which affinities are important, as it remains to be discussed which analogies should be noted. It is not clear to me how, if at all, the discussion should proceed from here."[32] Apparently the possibility does not occur to Houston—or if it does, does not merit mention—that in the absence of any clear advantage one way or another we might just as well leave the word *true* alone and allow usage to decide, as we normally do in nontheoretical discussion. Let red things be called "red" and true things be called "true." The outcome of the alternative approach is clear from Houston's own words: "In this paper I have been able to find no reason to side with such as Austin or Harrison, or to side with such as Lemmon. It has been one of my purposes to bring out the inconclusive state of this debate about explicit performatives—even as I have tried to advance it a little. But further, it is of interest that we may see much of the difficulty as arising from uncertainty and unclarity over what it is to be truth-values anyhow."[33]
    Houston's assessment looks accurate and does indeed have interest, as claimed. We seldom find people perplexed as to what it is to be red or what it is to be snow. They may inquire into the causes of redness, the constituents of snow, or the like; but no argument ensues as to whether pink is red or sleet is snow or noodles are really spaghetti. Why is that? The main reason, it seems, is that the inquirers are not philosophers. Were philosophers to turn their attention from performatives and truth to redness, snow, and spaghetti and treat them in like manner, similar disputes and uncertainties might be expected to arise. For once any consideration *but* usage is regarded as relevant, affinities clash with disaffinities and analogies with disanalogies in puzzling alternation. Cut loose from familiar meanings and left with mere sounds, discussion drifts on uncharted waters.[34]
    Elsewhere, using the debate about abortion and the "personhood" or

"humanity" of the unborn as an illustration, I have documented more fully and concretely the chaos that results when words' established meanings are ignored.[35] In this controversy the terms *person* and *human being* have acquired a score or more of different meanings, according as each argument has required. The outcome is babel, or something worse than babel; for at least when languages proliferate, speakers recognize the difference; whereas when meanings proliferate and sounds and marks remain the same, the interlocutors more readily assume that they are speaking the same language and differ only in their claims.

With the babel there also goes bedlam; inquiry suffers as seriously as communication. For with neglect of established meanings goes neglect of language in general as at least the codeterminant of truth. Hence,

> Not only do meanings fluctuate, and with them the criteria that might serve for verification; the conception of verification vacillates as well. Some look to faith, others to science, others to theology or metaphysics, others to personal perspectives. Language is seldom adverted to as in any way decisive. Yet the response to each such suggestion is the same: neither faith, nor science, nor theology, nor metaphysics, nor personal perspectives can determine when personhood begins, when humanity begins, when life begins. The uncertainty is verbal. Until that fact is recognized little progress toward consensus can be hoped for.[36]

Much the same analysis applies, I believe, to the dispute about performatives and to many another like it.[37] Disregard for established meanings leads to babel; disregard for language leads to bedlam. However, one point in this earlier account might be questioned: in such disputes, do new meanings proliferate, or just new "theories"? Observing people's claims and counterclaims and their reasons, we might opt for the former answer: different people mean different things by their words (for example, *person* and *human being*); their personal patterns of speech reveal personal meanings. However, the disputants do not view their assertions in this light; they do not see them as implicitly redefining the key terms of the debate but as advancing substantive claims. Hence they treat counterclaims as erroneous. Just as Graham is not ready to grant that what Austin says is true if judged by Austin's meanings, so too,

> The anti-abortionist is not inclined to say: "In the sense I give the word 'person' the fetus is a person, whereas in your sense, to be sure, it is not. We are both correct." Nor is the pro-abortionist any readier to reciprocate: "You are quite right that in your sense of the expression the fetus is a person, whereas my own denial requires a different sense." After all, they would not make their respective claims if they saw them in this light. Hence in such a confrontation neither common usage nor personal usage acts as a criterion. No verbal standard, distinct from the claims themselves, is adverted to or operative as arbiter of truth. Speech, cut loose from its moorings in language, drifts aimlessly, tossed this way and that by the waves of controversy.[38]

The remedy I would suggest for such confusion and uncertainty is to proceed as in nontheoretical discussion, accepting correspondence as a norm and customary senses as in general preferable. If, for example, Austin employs the word *true* as most speakers of English do, don't call his position "mistaken" or accuse him of "error." If you prefer a different use of the term, don't present it as a countertheory that refutes him. If you believe your alternate use has theoretical advantages, don't presume, without good reason, that the advantages require adopting the same use in ordinary contexts, or even in all theoretical ones.[39] And confirm the new use's supposed advantages before making your stipulation; compare the new sense with the old, hence examine the old with care. This Graham failed to do, with the result that he overlooked aspects of usage that would have placed his proposal in a very different light.

The Truth of Performatives

As a matter of fact we do speak of false promises,[40] though not, for example, of false bets, apologies, or christenings; for a promise refers to a future act, distinct from the promise, which the promiser may or may not intend to perform.

> I promise to go to the meeting. To the appropriate person at the appropriate time I use the sentence "I promise to come." But I do so without any intention of keeping the promise. I make a false promise. . . . A false promise is not identical with a sham promise.[41]

Thus, though Graham's verdict may agree at least in part with that of usage ("true promise" sounds less familiar than "false promise"), his reason does not. Not even in the following type of case, imagined by Justus Hartnack, is there a promise whose falsity consists in its falsely describing itself:

> Now take the sentence "I promise that I shall come." . . . It could be used descriptively. If I make a promise to come by signing a document I can at the same time answer the question: "What are you doing?" by saying "I promise to come" [or better: "I am promising to come"]. In this context the sentence "I promise to come" is used descriptively.[42]

It might therefore be a false description and to this extent fit Graham's account, but it would not be a promise that falsely described itself. For it would not be a promise but a report of a promise—the one allegedly performed by the signing.

Certain other performatives we also call true or false, but for neither of the preceding reasons—neither in view of the speaker's intention nor for the reason Graham cites. For example, in a courtroom,

> I swear that I did not commit the murder. The oath is made in accordance with prescribed rules. By performing the prescribed act, including the use of the

sentence "I swear that I did not murder him" I make an oath. But as I know quite well that I did murder him my oath is false. I swear but swear falsely. I have committed perjury.[43]

Similarly, a statement employing "I state" is called a true statement if what it states is true, false if what it states is false.[44] An assertion using "I assert" is true if what it asserts is true, false if what it asserts is false. And the like holds for attestations with "I attest," declarations with "I declare," and similar utterances.[45]

Most performatives, however, do not share with promises, declarations, or the like the features that elicit the assessment "true" or "false." They either contain no allusion to any act or event beyond themselves ("I apologize," "I welcome you," "I pardon you," "I baptize you," "I thank you," and so forth) or allude to it differently ("We praise you for your goodness," "We request your presence," "I order you to be there," "I thank you for coming," "I bet you ten dollars that Miami will win," and so on) and are not called true or false.[46]

Once we advert to this division of explicit performatives into those termed true or false and those that are not and to the reasons behind the division, we can see that usage makes good sense. It puts emphasis where it belongs, whereas Graham's suggestion does not. Calling the first class of performatives true on the mere ground that they succeed in promising, declaring, stating, or the like would resemble calling straightforward assertions of fact true or false according as they do in fact describe or report, whether accurately or inaccurately. Usage has a better idea. The verbal performance, heard with a person's own ears, can be taken for granted, as can the describing or reporting. What matters is whether the one who promises intends to do as he says and whether the one who declares "I claim p" or "I assure you that q" is right about p or q.

This analysis suggests that there may be more validity than Graham acknowledged in Austin's well-known claim: "Our common stock of words embodies all the distinctions men have found worth drawing, and the connexions they have found worth marking, in the lifetimes of many generations: these surely are likely to be more numerous, more sound, since they have stood up to the long test of the survival of the fittest, and more subtle, at least in all ordinary and reasonably practical matters, than any that you or I are likely to think up in our arm-chairs of an afternoon—the most favoured alternative method."[47] The distinctions drawn by usage with respect to truth and falsehood do in fact look wiser and sounder, both practically and theoretically, than those proposed by Graham.

Hence I think it is clear that before we abandon established meanings for unfamiliar ones, we should make sure that the latter really are advantageous. This we cannot do reliably on the basis of mere surmises as to how a new sense may work out overall or on the basis of equally hasty impressions as to how a word currently functions and why.[48]

More positively, I think the following approach is preferable to the popular one that Graham exemplifies:

1. Accept and follow usage until some clear advantage suggests a different use for a term (for example, *true*).
2. Weigh this advantage against possible disadvantages.
3. To do so, take a realistic look at usage.
4. If the revision still seems desirable, introduce the new sense explicitly as a new sense, explain the reasons for it, and indicate the contexts and types of discussion in which it seems preferable.
5. Distinguish clearly between the new meaning of the word and any theory stated by its means.
6. Recognize that even in the contexts indicated people who employ a different terminology may nonetheless be making true statements.[49] Statements' truth, in the common sense of *true*, is their agreement with the established uses of the terms they employ. And this common meaning of *true* is a good one. The present chapter again suggests, as did chapters 6 and 8, that it is better than any sense "you or I are likely to think up in our arm-chairs of an afternoon."

Borderline Debates

Applied to the question of performatives' truth, this approach renders a split verdict. Examples I have cited show that by the test of usage, some performatives are true or false, some not. This explains why I picked performatives to illustrate debates about the borderline of truth. Questions and commands are similarly contested,[50] but they do not straddle the borderline in this way. Only performatives do. Only they contribute interesting specimens to the class of true-false utterances.

Ralph McInerny contests this claim, and cites counter-instances: "Imagine a scene. Enter A and B, costumed as suburbanites. A: How can I get my lawn to look like yours? B: Keep off the grass. A: That's true. In order to see how utterly common such utterances are, it helps to have three actors. A: How can I get my trip to New York paid for? B: Read a paper. C: That's true."[51] These imagined specimens of verbal interchange look plausible enough, and in both of them it might appear that "true" characterizes a command ("Keep off the grass," "Read a paper"). However, it seems more accurate to say that in each instance "true" characterizes, not a command, but an answer to a question. For that is how each so-called command functions. In neither exchange does speaker B issue a command to speaker A either to keep off the grass or to read a paper. Rather, he employs an imperative form of expression to convey information.

The same distinction, between function and form, holds for questions and interrogative constructions. In parallel with McInerny's verbal sampling, we might envisage an exchange like the following:

A: What did C say to the boss?
B: "Who do you think you are, God almighty?"
C: That's true, but I didn't think he'd hear me.

Such a sample, rare and rather forced, does not show that questions are sometimes true or false. For, as B in McInerny's dialogue issues no command, so here B asks no question. The interrogative expression serves to inform.

Though informative or declarative utterances in interrogative form may thus count as true-false,[52] they do not do so ipso facto, by virtue of their function. A rhetorical question, for example, also has the force of a statement; the speaker is not requesting information, any more than McInerny's speaker B is issuing a command. Yet the appropriate response to such a veiled assertion is not "true" or "false."[53] Thus imagine another scenario, in which two speakers are arguing about Vietnam.

A: The money could be used for foreign aid rather than for bombing villages.
B: To be sure, it could be; but was it used that way before the war began?
A: No, but at least it *could* be used for foreign aid, if Congress preferred or the people permitted.

"True would be an inappropriate answer to B's rhetorical question, yet entirely appropriate as a reply to the straightforward assertion "It wasn't used that way before the war began." Here the verbal form makes a difference.

These contrasting examples reveal two configurations: despite its form, because of its function, we call the reply "Keep off the grass" true; because of its form, despite its function, we do not call the rhetorical question true. Now, the present chapter has revealed a third combination: despite its form, because of its function, we do not call an utterance like "I apologize" either true or false. Such a performative looks like a statement, we might say in explanation, but it does not function like one. It does not serve to inform, rightly or wrongly, and therefore it is not true or false.

However, when does an utterance "serve to inform"? Does "I promise to be there"? Do statements describing nonexistent referents? Do predictions? Do avowals? Do unverifiable assertions in mathematics? Do nonsensical utterances like "My neighbor grows binomials in his garden"? So should we—do we—call them true or false? A vast literature has grown up around these issues, and I shall not seek to survey it or adjudicate all the debates. What I have proposed is a manner of treating such questions. The next chapter will illustrate this manner further, in relation to another major class of utterances, as numerous and varied as performatives.

CHAPTER 10

MORAL TRUTH

For good reasons or bad, normal usage is often forsaken. For bad reasons, seldom for good, its verdict is frequently ignored. In the discussion of truth, as elsewhere, this disregard is variously shown, with theorists now stretching the boundary of *true*, now tightening it, now altering it in other ways. Thus many argue, in the manner we have noted, that questions, commands, christenings, congratulations, and various other kinds of speech act, though generally not called true or false, are in fact such. Others, as we shall see, restrict the range of truth, rather than enlarge it, and deny that moral and evaluative utterances, for example, which people commonly call true or false, are either. The speakers of the language are mistaken.

This verdict has manifold interest for the present inquiry. A treatise on truth should determine, first of all, whether the verdict is correct, and whether moral and evaluative utterances do or do not lie within the bounds of truth. If they do, we may then seek to discern in what the truth of such utterances consists. Does the correspondence account still apply in their regard? Or should their truth be differently explained and differently pursued? A third question, of still more general interest, is whether the considerations urged against normal usage or in place of normal usage, to exclude evaluative utterances, are valid. Should established word uses determine what we say? Does correspondence merit acceptance as a norm? Or should speculative discussion be freed from the restraints of even stipulated senses?

The debate about moral truth can shed new light on this normative issue. Often, it is true, the disputants' moves and motives resemble those already noted. Some parties cite familiar usage; many ignore it and proceed to argue the matter "theoretically." And the outcome is confusion of the kind we have come to expect. In certain respects, however, this borderline dispute differs from the preceding. New twists appear. In particular, a new challenge to usage arises, one that appears more plausible with regard to moral utterances than it would with regard to performatives, questions, or commands.

The chapter will therefore proceed as follows. At the start, to confirm and further illustrate the lessons of the last chapter, I shall trace the parallel between this debate and the preceding. Then I shall focus on the new reason for rejecting normal usage. Once this challenge, too, has been met and the verdict of established usage has been vindicated, I will then explain and analyze, rather than debate or defend. Granted that moral utterances are, and may legitimately be called, true or false, in what does their truth or falsehood consist? Does a correspondence account like that of chapter 3 apply to moral and evaluative utterances, as well as to historical claims, weather reports, or descriptions of the countryside? Can it function for them, too, as a test of what to say?

Familiar Features of the Debate

Cognitivists often affirm, noncognitivists often deny, that moral declarations are either true or false.[1] And both parties often argue in the manner we have seen, the one side urging similarities, the other dissimilarities, between moral or evaluative utterances on the one hand and factual utterances on the other.[2] Noncognitivists stress the strong emotive aspect of moral utterances, their imperative or persuasive function, their lack of agreed descriptive criteria. Cognitivists counter, for example, that evaluative judgments appear in indicative sentences, like judgments known to be cognitive; that they have negatives, whereas expressions of emotion do not; that they figure in indirect discourse as the objects of cognitive verbs like *know* and *believe;* that they "appear to function in arguments in precisely the same way that assertions do, while nonassertoric sentences cannot";[3] that we assess them in definite ways;[4] and so forth.[5]

In this debate, as in the preceding, standard usage is occasionally cited but is more commonly ignored. "It is completely obvious," one writer declares, "that there is moral truth." Not, however, because the verdict of usage is so evident. Rather, "life forces the perception upon us. There is something strangely frivolous and shallow in the frame of mind that can deny it."[6] Here, with verbal standards lost to view, moral criteria take their place. Or theoretical criteria. "Moral truth," the same author writes, "is based on the potential and inevitable ultimate agreement of reaction. . . . In their tastes and fancies men are utterly different, but in their vital needs, including the need of liberty for their tastes and fancies so far as not seriously hurtful to others, they are in a certain true sense one."[7] Accordingly, their moral judgments are objective, and therefore true or false.

Noncognitivists may cite supposedly contrary facts. But how and why any of the facts are pertinent is far from clear. For it is not evident how the nonlinguistic data relate to the expressions accorded or denied. Why apply the labels "true" and "false"? Why refuse them? If familiar usage may be ignored, may we not speak as we please? May we not label petunias true or false or equate the truth of statements with their loudness, length, or date of composition?

Surveying this debate as Houston surveyed the one on performatives, Arne Naess reaches similar conclusions. A priori arguments get us nowhere; a posteriori arguments are similarly indecisive. How, then, is a verdict to be reached? Unlike Houston, Naess at least considers normal usage; but he questions its relevance, for reasons that we shall see, and therefore concludes much as Houston did: "I cannot see any way leading to a rational decision. A suspension of judgment, an epoché, seems appropriate."[8] Once again, abandonment of shared meanings brings inquiry to a standstill.

Essentialist Reasoning

A further parallel between the two debates deserves close scrutiny. At one point in chapter 9 I noted briefly the essentialism implicit in Graham's thinking. His mode of reasoning seemed to assume invariant meanings beneath the varied applications of a term. Similar essentialism, with similar disregard for usage, appears in the debate on moral truth. Paradoxically, it appears with special clarity in the writings of the reputed ordinary-language philosopher G. E. Moore.

Early in his career, Moore declared apodictically: "What I wish first to point out is that 'right' does and can mean nothing but 'cause of a good result,' and is thus identical with 'useful.' "[9] If, as he then held, *good* was the name of a simple, "nonnatural" property, it would follow that moral judgments of right and wrong are as true and false as any other estimates of past or likely consequences. However, Moore offered no proof for his view of what the word *right* does and must mean, certainly none drawn from the actual employment of the word. And with this early dogmatism he himself later disagreed, denying both the necessity and the existence of the supposedly invariant meaning of the word. Even within the same early work he did not always define *right* identically. Sometimes he asserted that the consequences of an *action* are what make it right or wrong,[10] sometimes that the consequences of an *option* (including the action) are the sole criterion.[11] But apparently he did not notice this discrepancy or its significance. Had he done so, he might have questioned, even then, the alleged uniformity of *right*.

Moore's later misgivings about the constant, descriptive content of moral terms appear for instance in his *Commonplace Book*. However, so does his inveterate essentialism. He opens one discussion with the terse observation: " ' "Go away" is true' makes no sense." That is, it makes no sense to call a command true. Though not identical with any claim endorsed in the previous chapter, this assertion of meaninglessness looks plausible and interesting. However, Moore continues:

> Now it may be said that " 'You ought to go away' is true" also doesn't make sense; on the ground that a person who says the words "You ought to go away" is, if he's using them in the ordinary way, not *asserting* anything. The mere fact that an indicative form of expression is used does not shew that it makes sense to add before it "It's true that" or "It's false that." If a person who says "You oughtn't to do that" or "You oughtn't to have done that," is not *making any assertion*, then it will make no sense to say that what he said was true or was false.[12]

Here Moore's thinking proceeds as essentialistically as before, without regard for the vagaries of usage; only now he links moral utterances' truth or falsehood with their status as assertions. If they are assertions, then they are true or false; if they are not assertions, they are not true or false.[13] All (genuine, true, bona fide) assertions, it would seem, are essentially the same, with truth-falsehood pertaining to their single essence; and truth, conversely, is as rigidly restricted to (genuine, true, bona fide) assertions.

This reasoning, too, is simplistic; for truth is heterogeneous, and so are assertions. Reports, descriptions, explanations, evaluations, verdicts, avowals, performatives, predictions, and various other sayings may all be termed assertions and regularly are. Hence it is readily conceivable that some assertions may be true-false, others not. And consequently, whether moral utterances are true-false must be determined directly; it cannot be inferred from the mere fact that they are assertions, statements, propositions, or the like.[14]

Elsewhere, in similarly essentialist fashion, Moore made much of the incompatibility between conflicting ethical claims. On behalf of his former position that moral assertions are true-false and in opposition to Charles Stevenson's view that often, perhaps always, they are not, he proposed "at least one reason . . . , namely that it *seems as if* whenever one man, using 'right' in a 'typically ethical' sense, asserts that a particular action was right, then, if another, using 'right' in the same sense, asserts that it was not, they are making assertions which are logically incompatible. If this, which seems to be the case, really were the case, it would follow that Mr. Stevenson's view is false."[15]

This argument, too, is invalid. Either "logical incompatibility" simply means "true-false incompatibility," in which case the truth or falsehood of moral assertions must be determined along with their logical incompatibility, rather than deduced from it; or "logical incompatibility" has some other, unspecified meaning, which may or may not be linked with truth and falsehood. In neither supposition can the logical incompatibility of moral utterances serve without more ado as a basis for asserting their true-false status.

"Calculus reasoning" seems an apt name for thinking of the kind Moore exemplifies. For the moves are all formally valid, as they tend to be in a calculus, if one makes the supposition that the terms are all invariant, as they generally are in a calculus, and that their single, fixed content is the one assumed. If, for example, the expression "logical incompatibility" had an invariant sense, and that sense entailed truth-falsehood, it would follow that moral utterances, if logically incompatible, would also be true-false. Their being logically incompatible might similarly be deduced from their incompatibility if logical incompatibility were, by definition, the only kind possible for utterances. However, an expression like "incompatibility" or "logical incompatibility" could acquire the requisite invariance of sense only through stipulation, and personal stipulations validate no inferences. Hence this mode of argumentation, though common,[16] is invalid.

Calculus reasoning also begets much confusion, as does any reasoning that ignores established meanings and the rule of correspondence. Given his unconcern about discovering or stipulating meanings for key terms he employed, it is not surprising to see Moore incur the same perplexity as others I have quoted. He felt some inclination, he wrote, to say that people who make conflicting ethical assertions disagree merely in attitude, and a contrary inclination to say that they are making ("logically") incompatible assertions. Yet, "How on earth is it to be settled whether they *are* making incompatible assertions or not? There are hosts of cases where we do know for certain that people *are* making incompatible assertions; and hosts of cases where we know for certain that they are not, as, for instance, if one man merely asserts 'I approve of Brutus' action' and the other merely asserts 'I don't approve of it.' Why should there be this doubt in the case of ethical assertions? And how is it to be removed?"[17]

The solution, I would suggest, is to attend to the meanings of the expressions one employs (for example, *right, assertion, logical incompatibility*); to clarify them, if necessary, through observation or stipulation; and to abide thereafter by the meanings thus determined as one turns from the words to their referents and to substantive inquiry. Here is firm ground on which to stand; round about it lies morass.

The Hypothesis of Popular Error

A person who would determine whether moral utterances are true-false in the ordinary sense of *true* and *false* can take either of two routes. One is to examine directly whether speakers apply the words *true* and *false* to such utterances. Another is to examine their application to other types of utterance, ascertain from them the defining criteria of truth and falsehood, then determine whether moral utterances satisfy these criteria. If they do, they are true-false; if they do not, they are not true-false, regardless of what people may say about them.[18]

An obvious difficulty with this second approach is that it may falsify the words' meaning through its initial restriction, as would, for instance, an examination of *number* that excluded imaginary numbers or an examination of *game* that excluded solitaire. From a limited sampling we might derive a limited meaning, and from the limited meaning a limited extension of the concept. We might conclude that imaginary numbers are not numbers, that solitaire is not a game, that moral utterances are not true or false, despite what speakers of English may mistakenly suppose. Each such restriction, however, would be as arbitrary as the one that begot it. From a narrow sampling we may not infer a narrow class.

The only alternative, it would seem, is to consider all utterances commonly called true and false and learn from them the common concept. But to this approach, too, an objection is often made. People may err in their use of *true* and *false* as they may err in their use of other terms. They may call setters "terriers"; they may say that a blizzard is coming, and then it doesn't even snow; they may say that someone is sobbing, when she is merely blowing her nose. So, too, the suggestion goes, people may have mistaken notions about moral utterances and may therefore err when they call them true or false. Hence to consider indiscriminately all applications of *true* and *false* and thereby fix the words' meaning would be fallacious and misleading—as fallacious and misleading as examining setters to learn the meaning of *terrier* or the blizzard that didn't come to learn the meaning of *blizzard* or the woman blowing her nose to learn the meaning of *sob*.

One response to this objection is to note pertinent differences between these allegedly comparable cases and the one that interests us. This or that person might call a setter a "terrier." This or that person might mistake an instance of nose-blowing for sobbing. It is even conceivable that the populace as a whole might err concerning some individual member of a class (this planet's shape, that person's birthplace, and the like). But it is hardly conceivable that speakers of English generally might express mistaken judgments concerning all setters, all blizzards, all sobbing, or the like. If most people called most setters "terriers," doubtless that is what they would be: the common predication would reveal the common concept. If most people called most nose-blowing "sobbing," doubtless "sobbing" would be the name for that activity. So, too, if competent speakers of English regularly refer to moral utterances as true or false, the chances are good that their statements are not mistaken but reveal the standard meaning of the words *true* and *false*. The hypothesis of general error, in the double sense of error by all or most speakers concerning all or most instances, looks implausible.

Theorists often allege such mass error, but their allegations are seldom well founded. Russell, as we saw in chapter 8, was ready to suppose that all speakers of English (including himself) erred in their use of *see, hear, touch,* and the like and erred not just occasionally, but routinely. They never saw the things they said they saw, never heard the things they claimed they heard, never touched the objects they spoke of touching. However, Russell's charges were gratuitous. They came of his assuming that he knew these terms' senses, without troubling to determine them empirically. Had he attended to evident facts of usage, he could hardly have endowed the verbs of sensation with such fantastic meanings.

However, the allegation we are now considering differs sufficiently from Russell's claims and is sufficiently common that we had better examine it separately and judge it on its own merits. What may be said in favor of mass error concerning the truth of moral utterances? The general sentiment of many emotivists and other nondescriptivists is that such utterances diverge so significantly from other true-false sayings that it is misleading or mistaken to call them true or false.[19] Granted, people often do so designate them. But as Austin characteristically observed, "It is a matter for decision how far we should continue to call such masqueraders 'statements' at all, and how widely we should be prepared to extend the uses of 'true' and 'false' in 'different senses.' My own feeling is that it is better, when once a masquerader has been unmasked, *not* to call it a statement and *not* to say it is true or false."[20] Here Austin, like Russell, challenges common claims, and challenges them in the name of deeper insight. Just as Russell cited discoveries of science that cast new light on the facts of sensation, so Austin remarked: "Recently, it has come to be realized that many utterances which have been taken to be statements (merely because they are not, on grounds of grammatical form, to be classed as commands, questions, &c.) are not in fact descriptive, nor susceptible of being true or false."[21] Such are performatives. Such are value assertions, including moral utterances.

We have seen Austin's error with regard to performatives. What verdict shall we give concerning evaluative utterances? Does the common practice of calling them true or false[22] rest on an illusion? If so, on what illusion? The illusion that any utterances with the same verbal form as true-false utterances are also true-false? Hardly. For we have seen that even within the single class of performatives, usage makes distinctions, calling some true or false, some not. Indeed, concerning his varied collection of "masqueraders" Austin himself acknowledged that, despite their declarative form, "in ordinary life we should not call most of them statements at all, though philosophers and grammarians may have come to do so."[23]

A more plausible suggestion resembles Russell's concerning sensation.

As naive realists suppose that sense objects are rendered immediately present to the mind, similarly, it might be claimed, naive cognitivists suppose that actions are right or wrong in themselves, independently of our desires or preferences.[24] And this naive conception, it might be suggested, is the one expressed when people label moral utterances true or false. It would therefore seem better to call them neither. Popular agreement is not a sure guide.

Suppose, however, that someone were to suggest, in close parallel, that popular predications of heat and cold express the notion that heat and cold are present in objects themselves, that this notion is erroneous, and that the predications are therefore all false and should be discontinued. This, too, sounds plausible. For objects do seem endowed with heat or cold independently of our perceptions. And it has not occurred to most people to question this impression. Yet powerful arguments have been urged against it. If the arguments are valid, the impression is mistaken, and any statements that express it are likewise mistaken. It is wrong, or at least seriously misleading, we might therefore conclude, to assert that the weather is cold, the coffee is tepid, or the roof is red-hot; it is wrong to say that we enjoy the pleasant warmth of a fire. We should express ourselves differently.

Were innocent sayings like these arraigned as "masqueraders," we would probably feel misgivings, and rightly so. We should distinguish, first of all, between objective impressions and objectivist theories. We should distinguish, secondly, between epistemological statements that express the theories and everyday statements whose content is perhaps affected by the theories. We should distinguish, thirdly, between altering an everyday statement and altering the way we analyze or interpret it. And we should therefore beware of drawing the conclusion that statements whose content is affected by false theories are ipso facto false statements and should be withdrawn. People who believe that the earth is the center of the planetary system and say "The earth is round" do not make a false statement. People who believe that the earth is flat and say "The earth is inhabited by millions of people" do not make a false statement. So too, Berkeleyans, Kantians, phenomenalists, or naive realists, if mistaken in their conception of objects and their properties, do not utter false statements every time they assert that the sky is blue, the soup is hot, the water is cold, or Beth left her mittens in the hallway.

These points are familiar from chapter 8. Let us apply them to the question at hand. First, we should distinguish between the impression of value objectivity (the impression, say, that a painting is intrinsically ugly or a deed intrinsically admirable) and the metaethical theories to which the impression might perhaps give rise. Second, we should distinguish between statements which express the theories and are false if the theories are false and statements whose content may be affected by the theories but which are not thereby rendered false, mistaken, or even misleading. A person who calls a moral utterance true or false may wrongly conceive the functioning of moral utterances and may wrongly elucidate what it is for such utterances to be true or false; but his assertion of the utterance's truth or falsehood is not thereby invalidated. Even if most speakers were metaethicists and if most were mistaken in their metaethics, it would not follow that their assertions of truth or falsehood need revision. Their analysis of the assertions might be faulty but not the assertions themselves.

Even the most primitive, widespread theories may be contested, as they are for instance by a Berkeley or an Ayer, without calling into question the rightness of the terms employed by both parties in the debate or the truth of the assertions in which the terms occur. Realists and phenomenalists may give conflicting accounts of bodies; cognitivists and noncognitivists may give conflicting accounts of moral truth. Yet *body* or *truth* may nonetheless be the right word for both parties to employ. It may satisfy the principle of relative similarity.

An utterance that stated explicitly a mistaken ethical theory would not satisfy PRS and might be rejected. An ascription of moral truth in which the word *true* was rigidly defined by a mistaken theory (as *rain* is rigidly defined by drops of water falling from clouds) might not satisfy PRS and might be rejected. But everyday assertions of moral truth are neither explicit statements of moral theory nor rigidly defined by any theory. And I can think of no other way in which their extension of *true* to moral utterances might be convicted of error.

A More Fundamental Challenge

So far in this discussion the relevance of normal usage has not been called into question. Rather, the challenge mounted against the truth of moral utterances has been based on an intension supposedly revealed by normal usage. According to this objection, calling moral utterances true or false does not square with the meaning of *true* and *false* revealed in paradigm applications. People just think it does, because of their naive misconceptions concerning moral utterances. Their alleged error therefore resembles the error of those who called the earth flat or said that it was the center of the universe. No matter how widespread an assertion may be, it may still clash with established usage and therefore fail the test of correspondence. I have only questioned whether in this particular instance there is in fact any conflict with the words' established uses. There seems no good reason to assert that the standard meanings of *true* and *false* exclude moral or evaluative utterances.

A more basic challenge is therefore raised when Arne Naess dismisses the verdict of usage as irrelevant and indecisive. To some extent his reasons are familiar. "It is not the business of philosophy," he writes, "to ossify termi-nological regularities." And to cite established usage begs the question. "It presupposes that those beliefs are true[,] which makes it convenient to adhere to a terminology that is under consideration. Now, this is a presup-position which may turn out to be false. If so, the definition of truth or of proposition may be changed with good reasons, reasons which are good because of certain changes of opinion, due e.g. to new discoveries."[25] Here, as so often (see chapter 8), established word uses or forms of speech are equated with established beliefs, which may be superseded by new insights or discoveries. Their mere familiarity, therefore, is not seen as an argument in their favor; it does not figure at all as a motive, let alone a decisive one, for retaining the uses or forms of speech.

Naess's reasons take a new, more interesting turn when he further remarks: "Socalled definitions of truth must in order to be adequate have certain relationships to actual use. But occurrence analysis or other scien-tifically satisfactory technique[s] of studying actual use cannot yield (by induction or otherwise) just one definite socalled definition. The definitions are conceptual constructs with complicated and indirect relations to the observational data."[26] It follows, Naess believes, that no facile recourse to usage can resolve a question such as that which concerns us, with regard to the status of moral utterances. The issue is theoretical, he would say, and must be decided theoretically. But as noted earlier, what that means and how a decision may be reached, he is at a loss to suggest.

The apparent reason for his failure is that he approaches usage "theoret-ically" and therefore finds no solution for his theoretical difficulties. Mak-ing demands of usage which it cannot satisfy, he does not alter the demands but turns away from usage. If accurate observation cannot yield "just one definite socalled definition," then observation must be abandoned, and construction must take its place. Yet constructed definition vies with con-structed definition, and how are we to decide between them? After a few familiar remarks about "considerations of fruitfulness etc.," Naess acknowl-edges his perplexity. The fly, still imprisoned, continues to buzz in the fly bottle.

Naess's quandary epitomizes that of many theorists, who find no solution in familiar usage and no solution without it. If they turn to usage, contro-versy continues unabated. An Austin, say, gives one account of *true* and a Strawson another. The criterion of established use furnishes no remedy.

It does not, chapter 5 suggested, for two reasons. One is the urge to generalize—the insistence that usage yield a single, uniform theory. Thus Austin generalized in one direction, Strawson in another, and neither did justice to the vagaries of usage; neither recognized the asymmetry of *true*. The second, related reason is people's frequent failure to specify precisely the sense of the theories they propose. As Moore observed, we repeatedly proffer answers to questions we have not paused to understand. For instance, we debate, as Austin and Strawson did, the "reference" of some expression, or what we "talk about" when we utter it, but do not trouble to clarify the intended sense of *reference* or *talk about*. Were we to do so, we might have to abandon our theoretical aspirations and be content with accurate descriptions; but at least we might agree in our descriptions. And the basis might thereby be laid for eventual theories—as in biology, in which Ray's and Linnaeus's taxonomy preceded and prepared today's successful theorizing.

On occasion, it is true, established usage, even when carefully consulted, yields no verdict. "Consider William James's example," Feigl and Maxwell suggest, "of the dog [sic] running round a tree on the trunk of which is a squirrel that encircles the trunk so that he always faces the dog. Does the dog go around the squirrel? Or consider the old conundrum: When a tree falls out of earshot of any sentient being, is there or is there not any sound?"[27] From familiar usage's failure to answer either question, Feigl and Maxwell conclude: "Even in these extremely simple, perhaps puerile, 'philosophical problems,' a modest degree of reformation seems to be required." This inference suggests excessive eagerness to "reform." What need have we in either instance to sharpen usage? "Say what you choose," we may respond with Wittgenstein, "so long as it does not prevent you from seeing the facts." Thus, even when usage answers "Undecided," we can generally abide by its verdict. Indeed, as debates like the one about abortion demonstrate, it may be important that we do so.

The Moral Use of *True*

I see little reason, I have said, to suppose that the English-speaking population has erred en masse in calling moral utterances true and false. As for the claim that such ascriptions are "misleading," it might be at least as misleading, in view of existing usage, to *deny* that moral utterances are true or false. After all, there are analogies as well as disanalogies between these and other true-false utterances; and the denial would be as likely to obscure the analogies as the assertion to obscure the disanalogies. It seems better, then, to accept usage as it stands and try to understand it.

Just as Austin and Strawson both accepted existing usage but analyzed it differently, so many ethicists and metaethicists have accepted the verdict of usage that moral utterances are true-false but have offered different accounts of the utterances' truth and falsehood. Some of their analyses are Strawsonian, some Austinian. Charles Stevenson, for example, treats *true* as a mere endorsement or reiteration of another's moral judgment. Thus,

> When Mr. A says "Jones ought not to have done it," and Mr. B. replies, "that is true," what is the force of B's reply? Rather obviously he too has said, in abbrevi-

ated form, the equivalent of "Jones ought not to have done it." His "that is true" permits him as it were to repeat A's remark, thus expressing an attitude (apart from hypocrisy) that is in agreement with A's. The extent of their agreement in *belief* will usually not be evident until they go on to give reasons for their judgments.[28]

Similarly, for Alan Montefiore "the meaning of 'true' lies in this special sort of affirmatory or confirmatory function . . . while the criteria on which such confirmations may be based will obviously vary, as in the case of 'good,' from context to context."[29] For Carl Wellman, on the contrary, the epistemic terms *true* and *false* have critical meaning; in ethics, as elsewhere, "they function to make, press, withdraw, or concede the claim to rationality."[30] In like vein Richard Swinburne suggests: "It would appear to be a sufficient condition of judgments in a field of discourse being true or false (though perhaps not a necessary condition) that there are established ways of arguing for and against those judgments, where arguments are recognized as tending to establish conclusions."[31] In ethics there is considerable agreement of this kind.[32] Though consensus on moral issues may not always be reached within a finite time, "there are always ways of going on. We can adduce new cases, argue further about consistency, etc."[33]

Such insistence on the cognitivity of moral discourse seems warranted.[34] And a certain parallel may rightly be drawn between moral and nonmoral truth. For in ethics, too, as Wittgenstein suggested, there are such things as "criteria," in the sense of defining, constitutive traits for *right, just, should, obligation,* and the like, established by consistent practice or explicit statement within a given society, tradition, school, or individual's writings.[35] These criteria are satisfied or not satisfied in particular instances. Moral verdicts and assertions conform or fail to conform to them. They guide our own claims and our assessment of others' claims, determining which we call true and which we call false.

A major difference, however, disturbs this carefully stated parallel between moral and factual truth. It is not merely that moral criteria vary more from person to person and context to context than nonevaluative criteria do. Rather, the decisive difference between truth judgments passed on moral utterances and truth judgments passed on nonevaluative utterances is that only the latter take account of criterial variations. Thus, if one person says on a hot summer's day that the temperature is thirty-five degrees, another will take account of whether degrees centigrade or degrees Fahrenheit are meant before replying "True" or "False." When one person assesses another's moral assertion and calls it true or false, however, he generally disregards the other's criteria and whether they are satisfied and simply applies his own. It suffices for agreement that the statement assessed express the same verdict, for whatever reasons. Even if the speaker knows and contests both the other's criteria and his judgment that they are satisfied, he may still call his statement true.

Suppose, for example, that someone applies utilitarian criteria to warfare, judges that it never maximizes happiness, so asserts that it is always wrong. Another person may apply other (for example, agapistic) criteria, reach the same conclusion, and therefore declare the other's judgment "true"—without agreeing either with the other's criteria of morality or with the verdict that warfare fails to satisfy them. In his view, warfare might on occasion be moral if judged by utilitarian criteria; for it might maximize happiness. The test of happiness, however, is inadequate. We should ask instead, he would say, whether warfare can manifest love; and judged by that standard, it always fails. Hence warfare is indeed immoral, as the utilitarian asserts, and his verdict, though not his reasoning, is correct.

Kantians, voluntarists, natural-law theorists, and others would apply other tests, and the descriptive content implicit in their verdicts might vary accordingly; but these cognitive divergences would not matter: those who agreed that warfare should be banned would call a statement condemning it "true," regardless of who uttered it. They would ignore the speaker's criteria and whether they were satisfied. Their own criteria, however, would be decisive. In view of this basic duality—speakers' criteria irrelevant, critics' criteria conclusive in the application of *true*—it is not surprising that some theorists emphasize the noncognitivity of moral truth, whereas others stress its cognitivity. From one viewpoint, only verdicts seem to count, not criteria or their satisfaction; from the other viewpoint, criteria look crucial.

Correspondence?

Other reasons might be cited for stressing the cognitivity of moral discourse, and others for stressing its noncognitivity. Some of the former will surface if we now go on to ask: Given this clarification of *true*, does the analysis of chapter 3 still apply? If *true* functions in the way just described, can we spell out the truth of "It's wrong" or "It's right," as we did the truth of "It's raining," in terms of correspondence with established word uses?

Were we to equate "established uses" with standard, language-wide criteria or explicit, stipulated criteria, the reply would have to be negative; for the criteria by which moral statements are assessed are generally neither. On the other hand, were we to shift to the other extreme and equate "established uses" with the noncognitive aspects of moral terms' use, which are indeed standard, then, too, the answer would have to be negative; for *true* is not thus restricted in making moral appraisals. We do not call an ethical assertion true simply on the basis of its expressing approval, committing the speaker, commending, permitting, forbidding, or the like. By elimination, therefore, we can sense what it might mean for the use of ethical expressions to correspond with their established uses. When one person says "War is always wrong," and another says "That's true," the sense of the assessment is not "Your verdict agrees with the common criteria of right and wrong," or "Your verdict agrees with my criteria," but rather, "Your verdict agrees with correct criteria, as judged by the standards of rationality that underlie moral discourse. You have, in this sense, employed the terms in keeping with their established uses."

The standards of rationality in ethical discourse, as in scientific, are chiefly two: "In ethics as in physics, chemistry, astronomy, or the like, theories can be compared for their consistency and for their agreement with the clearest and surest of our immediate, concrete judgments."[36] I have spelled out the ethical term of this comparison elsewhere.[37] The scientific parallel emerges in the present essay, from chapter 11's confrontation between those who, like Neurath, stress coherence and those who, like Schlick, emphasize agreement with our surest concrete judgments.

Correspondence as Norm

In the light of this analysis, to urge that moral expressions be employed in accordance with their established uses would amount to urging that the judgments in which they occur be based on criteria, and that the criteria be rationally justified or justifiable. However, moral truth may consist in more than this, and the norm of correspondence therefore has a broader scope. Many ethical expressions have a strictly descriptive aspect; they categorize as well as prescribe. And the call for correspondence may focus on that aspect too, together with or apart from the grounds for the prescription.

Consider the kind of argument often encountered, for instance with regard to abortion. In favor of terminating the life of an embryo or fetus, one party cites various perils or hardships of the mother. Another rejoins that no consequences, no matter how serious, can ever justify murder. The truth of the implicit premise, that abortion is always murder, may be contested on two grounds, not one. For *murder* both condemns and classifies; it says that the act is wrong, and it says that it kills a human being. Thus the claim that abortion is murder may be challenged, first of all, as a gratuitous condemnation; better reasons must be provided than the speaker's mere opposition. Or it may be challenged on the ground that the fetus is not, or is not clearly, a human being. The deed might be immoral, as claimed, and the statement that abortion is murder might nonetheless be false, for this distinct, descriptive reason.

Chapter 9 observed that usage does not warrant the claim that a fetus or embryo is or is not a human being and went on to suggest how important it is, both for mutual understanding and for rational debate, to leave the concept *human being* or *person* alone and focus on substantive issues (for instance, the relative importance of actual versus potential development).

Disregard for correspondence has badly befogged the discussion of abortion.

A further dimension of moral truth and a further type of application for the rule of correspondence appears, for example, in the metaethical remarks of G. E. Moore. We have noted his views on the right and on the good. Concerning the latter, Geoffrey Warnock comments: "This question what 'good' means, Moore insists, is not a verbal one; it would be beside the point, even if it were possible, to excogitate some synonymous expression conforming with the use made of the word 'good' by those who speak English. The real question is: what is the property for which 'good' stands? What is the property which any subject has, in virtue of which it would be true to say that that subject is good?"[38] For Moore, the truth about good had to be determined independently of established word uses, and individual acts or objects could then be truly characterized as good or bad in light of the general doctrine. What *good* means, or what it stands for, is not to be learned by examining usage.[39]

How, then, can it be learned? What alternative is there? Shall we have recourse, like Plato, to a world of ideal forms, separate from and prior to all intercourse with words? Moore does not explain his procedure, but his thinking seems in fact to have resembled Plato's. As Geoffrey Warnock remarks:

> It appears to have been assumed by intuitionist philosophers that it is, in general, the business of an adjective to designate a quality, a property, or a character; or at any rate, if they would not have subscribed to this general view without qualification, they did not question that it was true of the adjectives "good" and "right." Thus, from the fact that goodness was felt not to be identifiable with any ordinarily discernible property of things that are good, Moore concluded merely that "good" must designate some *other* property; Prichard, finding that "obligatory" did not mean the same as "expedient," or "desirable," or "productive of good," inferred that "obligatory" must stand for some *other* character. On this view what distinguishes moral judgments from other things is simply that such judgments ascribe to things *different properties,* characters which are *sui generis* to moral judgment: the difference is simply a difference of subject-matter; moral judgments attribute moral qualities, and that is all there is to it.[40]

If a perusal of usage reveals no such properties, then they will have to be postulated. And so they are. Moore's doctrine of good as a simple, non-natural property is on a par with his doctrine of blue as a simple, nonvisible color common to all shades of blue.[41] From these examples it is clear, I trust, that truth-by-postulation is not a satisfactory substitute for truth-by-correspondence, and that before a thinker abandons the rule of correspondence, he or she had better have some better norm to go by.

By disregarding the actual use of *good,* Moore invited the general rejection his theory experienced. If most subsequent thinkers have judged his account deficient, the reason is not far to seek. Moore's account does not square with any sense of *good* established either by everyday usage or by stipulation within Moore's writings. It fails the test of correspondence.

Retrospect

With this illustration, I have reached the end of a two-chapter section that was meant to achieve two things. Various samples have served both to demonstrate the validity and relevance of the norm of correspondence first proposed in chapter 8 and to clarify the borderline of truth. Any halfway adequate account of language and truth must consider common claims that exclude large classes of utterances normally characterized as true-false and others which include large classes not normally so characterized. Since these exclusions and inclusions not only violate the norm of correspondence but often do so knowingly, for stated reasons, they serve as well as other theories to illustrate the issues at stake in accepting or rejecting the norm. Accordingly, it was possible to pursue the chapters' two aims concurrently, thereby avoiding much repetition and lengthy digressions on unrelated matters.

The tactic of using the concept *true* to illustrate the virtues of correspondence had a further advantage, grasped better here in retrospect than it would have been if stated at the start. If the points I wished to document—disregard for both usage and correspondence, the faulty reasons that support the disregard, and the chaos that results—can be exemplified so fully from discussion of this single concept out of thousands, the reader may sense how abundant is the evidence that might be adduced and how widespread the syndrome that concerns me. I recognize, however, that despite my initial explanations and declarations of intent, a double focus may have seemed to be no focus and readers may have become confused. So a retrospective survey, separating out the two themes—norm and border—may now prove helpful.

Chapter 8 sketched a case for accepting linguistic correspondence as a norm, first by pointing out its advantages for communication, verification, and human welfare generally, then by answering objections based on misunderstandings. To favor established uses, standard or stipulated, is not to oppose linguistic innovation; nor is it to ratify established beliefs. Thinkers may advance new hypotheses and debate conflicting theories while employing familiar expressions in their familiar senses. Chapter 9 went on to consider various negative and positive reasons for ignoring usage, and with it, correspondence: the alleged confusion, vacuity, or inconsistency of current ways of speaking and the supposedly greater coherence or explanatory power of alternate forms of expression. This resistance to the rule of correspondence was seen, once more, to rest on confusions and to generate deep puzzlement. The present chapter, finally, has made several important additions to the case for correspondence: it has examined more closely the essentialistic, or calculus, type of reasoning that ignores established meanings, standard or stipulated; it has weighed and found wanting the supposition that the whole population may consistently err in its application of everyday terms; and it has answered the complaint that established meanings offer no solution for theoretical perplexity. To provide an effective remedy, usage must be consulted and accepted, not dictated to. The norm of correspondence has not failed; it has been too rarely tried.

When consulted and accepted in this chapter and the previous one, usage gave a split verdict on performatives and a uniform verdict on moral utterances. Many performatives are neither true nor false; but others are—though not for the reasons often supposed. A genuine promise is not automatically a true promise; nor is an unsuccessful promise the same thing as a false one. Moral utterances, too, are true and false in their own special ways. Prescriptive criteria fluctuate, and a person's own criteria determine what moral verdicts he or she terms true or false. These criteria are held accountable, however; they must satisfy the standards of rationality that underlie moral discourse. Descriptive criteria, too, must be conformed to, when moral terms categorize, as well as prescribe. For these two reasons and in this double sense, moral truth, like factual, may be termed correspondence, and the correspondence merits acceptance as a norm.

CHAPTER 11

EMPIRICAL TRUTH

The truth of various other types of statement—empirical, trans-empirical, mathematical, logical—has sometimes been denied, as has that of moral and evaluative utterances, with similar disregard for usage and its supposedly fallible verdict. More frequently the nature of their truth has been obscured, rather than denied, through neglect of linguistic correspondence and its shifting configurations for different species of utterance. As I focus first on empirical statements, in this chapter, then on trans-empirical statements, in the next, I shall no longer urge the norm of correspondence, as I have in the last three chapters, but shall simply apply it, in ways that will illustrate its merits. In particular, the principle of relative similarity, introduced in chapter 7, will emerge as crucial not only for the truth of metaphysical, theological, and other trans-empirical utterances, but also for the truth of the most familiar empirical statements, concerning comets, traffic, TV commercials, or fishing in the Hudson. Its relevance for the former utterances is evident; its relevance for the latter may come as a surprise. It did to me.

Holistic versus Atomistic Views of Empirical Truth

At different times and in various ways, empirical truth has been assimilated to mathematical truth, and both have been explained in terms of "coherence" rather than "correspondence".

> The Coherence Theory of truth is characteristic of the great rationalist system-building metaphysicians, Leibniz, Spinoza, Hegel, and Bradley; but it has also had a vogue with several members of the Logical Positivist school, notably Neurath and Hempel, who were much influenced by systems of pure mathe-

matics and theoretical physics. According to the Coherence Theory, to say that what is said (usually called a judgment, belief, or proposition) is true or false is to say that it coheres or fails to cohere with a system of other things which are said; that it is a member of a system whose elements are related to each other by ties of logical implication as the elements in a system of pure mathematics, are related.[1]

Hempel has recounted the route by which he and Neurath reached their conclusion.[2] Their starting point was the *Tractatus* view defining the truth of everyday assertions in terms of elementary propositions, and the truth of elementary propositions as their conformity with reality. Their first difficulty was that no one could give a satisfactory account of this conformity. An intermediate solution, introduced by Carnap, was "to cut off the relation to 'facts,' from Wittgenstein's theory and to characterize a certain class of statements as true atomic statements."[3] However, to treat this class—so-called protocol statements—as though they were axioms seemed unwarranted. "There are no absolutely first statements for establishing Science; for each statement of empirical character, even for protocol statements, further justification may be demanded."[4] Thus, according to Neurath:

> In unified science we try to construct a non-contradictory system of protocol sentences and non-protocol sentences (including laws). When a new sentence is presented to us we compare it with the system at our disposal, and determine whether or not it conflicts with that system. If the sentence does conflict with the system, we may discard it as useless (or false), as, for instance, would be done with "In Africa lions sing only in major scales." One may, on the other hand, *accept* the sentence and so change the system that it remains consistent even after the adjunction of the new sentence. The sentence would then be called "true." . . . No sentence enjoys the *noli me tangere* which Carnap ordains for protocol sentences.[5]

With no fixed term of reference left, in reality or in language, truth becomes entirely relative to the system of accepted propositions. "By introducing the geographico-historical expression 'accepted by us at a certain time and at a certain place,' we intentionally avoid the 'absolutely' used term 'true' (and its opposite 'false'), which we do not know how to fit into a framework based on observation-statements."[6]

In their total rejection of correspondence, Neurath and Hempel went beyond the earlier type of theory that proposed coherence as the *test* of truth, but not its definition.[7] As Schlick noted, in their view it makes no more sense in physics than in pure geometry to ask whether statements agree with the facts.[8] And they were therefore exposed to the standard objection which Schlick urged against them: "If one is to take coherence seriously as a general criterion of truth, then one must consider arbitrary fairy stories to be as true as a historical report, or as statements in a textbook of chemistry, provided the story is constructed in such a way that no contradiction ever arises."[9] To this objection Hempel could only reply that in our culture fairy stories are not accepted as true, whereas "true" statements are.[10]

Against a coherentist view like Hempel and Neurath's it has also been observed that "we cannot consider such a system of judgments to have even any probability unless we can attribute to at least one of its constituents a probability which is derived from some other ground than its membership of the system."[11] Schlick sought firm, independent ground not in corrigible "protocol statements," but in "statements concerning what is 'immediately perceived.'"[12] Statements like "Here yellow borders on blue" and "Here now pain" cannot be mistaken, he maintained, since what gives them meaning likewise gives them truth, and to grasp their meaning is ipso facto to grasp their truth.

Suppose I say "Here now pain." These words say nothing about a person. They pick out a present experience and it alone. And since that is what they assert, their truth is assured. If they failed to denote any experience, they would lack meaning and would not constitute a statement. If they picked out some other experience, that would be the one they meant, and the assertion would be correct. Hence, whatever the words' meaning, provided they have one and indeed form a statement, they cannot conceivably go wrong. Their truth is as certain as that of an analytic assertion. Such, roughly, was Schlick's view.[13]

The seminal error in such theories (as Wittgenstein, their chief source, came to realize) is the supposition that momentary meanings are indeed meanings and may establish truth or falsehood. If the word *pain,* for instance, has its customary sense, or if it has a sense conferred by stipulation using familiar words with their familiar meanings, then "I have a pain" may be false, and so perhaps may be "Here now pain," provided the sentence-form is clarified. Furthermore, the utterer of such a statement may be in error. For in either supposition—customary sense or stipulated sense—the present use of the word may clash with its established use. The experience described may not be of the kind called "pain." If, however, no use has been established for the word, either publicly or privately, by usage or by stipulation, there can be no question of correctness or incorrectness. One may as well replace "Here now pain" with "Phiz boom bah." No amount of mental gazing, no matter how intense, can confer meaning on these marks or sounds or turn them into a statement.[14]

Not surprisingly, Neurath and Hempel betrayed the same oversight as Schlick and slighted the role of established word meanings. For they too started from the *Tractatus;* and the *Tractatus* based truth not on words or their established meanings, but on elementary propositions whose sole components were atomic names for atomic objects. The most plausible candidates for atomic objecthood were the experienced yellows, blues, pains, and the like that Schlick viewed as basic. Schlick clung to such items as the sole foundation of knowledge; whereas Neurath and Hempel abandoned them and were left with nothing but the remaining parts of the scheme—that is, with believed propositions and their relationships. If these were mutually consistent, that was enough; truth as correspondence was a chimera. Neither Neurath nor Hempel thought to replace the bogus atomic meanings of Wittgenstein and Schlick with the nonbogus, nonatomic meanings whose place they had usurped. A likely reason for this remains to be examined.

Empirical Meaning and Truth

Schlick and his opponents, I would say, represent the thesis and antithesis of a dialectical confrontation, each halfway right and each halfway wrong by virtue of a common oversight. Schlick was wrong in supposing that the utterers of basic empirical statements cannot err, Neurath and Hempel in equating empirical truth with coherence. And both parties went astray, I suggest, because they overlooked the fundamental role of established word uses. It is these that are missing both from Schlick's account of observation statements and from Neurath and Hempel's stress on mere coherence. Schlick was right, however, in clinging to empirical verification as somehow fundamental. And Neurath and Hempel were right in maintaining that truth is far more holistic than Schlick recognized. For truth depends on meanings, and meanings are necessarily holistic.

Several steps toward this conclusion can be traced in Wittgenstein's thought. First came the realization that no word meanings are or can be as simple as those postulated in the *Tractatus*. A truly elementary proposition was to be logically independent; its truth was to be compatible with the truth or falsehood of any other equally elementary proposition. Hence a predicate like *soft* or *sweet* or *yellow* could not occur in such a proposition, for being soft or sweet or yellow conflicts with countless alternatives. The yellowness of a spot, for example, precludes the spot's being concurrently brown, mauve, blue, purple, orange, green, and many other shades. These exclusions belong both to the truth-conditions of a statement employing *yellow* and to the cognitive content it directly conveys (see chapter 8).

It is an intriguing fact that all names or descriptive terms are similarly exclusive, and that none is atomic. Indeed, Wittgenstein came to realize that none could be. Search as he might, he could discover no candidate that might serve as a logically simple object of reference. The colors, sounds, tastes, feelings, and smells that experience reveals are all at odds with other colors, sounds, tastes, feelings, and smells. Pick any one you please to describe or report; the resulting proposition will thereupon conflict with many other equally simple propositions.[15]

Furthermore, even the simplest assertion has far broader implications than those of any term it contains. Wittgenstein reached this second realization when he went looking for "primary" propositions which, though not logically independent of one another, might be used to spell out the meaning and establish the truth of more complex empirical assertions.[16] "Here now pain" will hardly do. Is it to be accompanied by a gesture indicating the spot? And will the spot be, for instance, the speaker's stomach or tooth? In that case the statement made will be equivalent to "I have a stomachache" or "I have a toothache." And either of these assertions not only includes a wide variety of possible sensations and excludes a still wider variety of others, but also requires, for example, a tooth, a mouth, a nervous system, and a human being. The meaning is far from "primary."

This, too, Wittgenstein came to see as a necessary feature of existing languages and of any we might construct by their means. Suppose I try to leave out the human subject and say simply "There is a pain." Any sort of pain will now qualify (mental or physical) in any location (tooth, toe, or missing limb) of any organism equipped with a nervous system (person, porpoise, or tree toad). The statement's content is now far broader, not narrower. All these disjunctive possibilities belong to the statement's truth-conditions and to its cognitive content for typical speakers. Suppose, instead, that I take a different tack and attempt to bracket the painful part; suppose I say, "I seem to have a toothache," rather than "I have a toothache." It would appear that a tooth no longer figures in the statement's truth-conditions. However, "seeming to have a toothache" is logically parasitic on "having a toothache," and its truth-conditions are therefore more, not less, complex. Twist as he might, Wittgenstein could find no way to reverse this order and spell out the meaning of "I have a toothache" by means of a simpler proposition stating just the pain, or of "The chair is brown" by means of simpler propositions stating just the sensible color, or the like.[17] It was, he later remarked, as though he were trying to repair a spiderweb with his fingers.[18] The verbal means at his disposal seemed so clumsy—so logically complex.

The two moves made so far—to the complexity of even the simplest predicates and to the still greater complexity of even the simplest assertions—leave Schlick and Tractarian atomism far behind. One further step, easily taken, might bring us to Neurath and Hempel's position and make the truth of empirical statements appear as holistic as they claimed. Abstractly stated, the step would consist in denying any distinction between defining and nondefining traits, incorporating both in the meaning of a term, then judging the truth of a statement by the comprehensive meaning that results.

Take the term *water*. *Water*, it might be said, is H_2O by definition. But the dictionary notes with equal legitimacy the boiling point, the freezing point, and various other traits as firmly fixed as the chemical composition. As for the composition, hydrogen and oxygen in turn have their own defining traits and their own atomic structure; and their constituent subatomic particles are further defined in terms of contemporary theory—quanta, relativity, and the rest. It might therefore appear that even so simple a statement as "There is water on the floor" implicitly affirms the better part of modern chemistry and physics.[19] Asserting the presence of water, it asserts the presence of molecules composed of atoms, of atoms composed of subatomic particles, of the particles' characteristics and the laws they obey—the whole bundle. Let a statement allude to a human being—say, "John mopped up the water"—and the implicit content might appear to embrace contemporary biology, psychology, physiology, anatomy, and the like, as well as contemporary chemistry and physics. Get all of this right, and the statement will be true; get any of it wrong, and the statement will be false. Truth might thus appear a distant ideal, not achieved by any empirical statement.[20]

However, usage draws a line; we do not in fact judge the truth of statements so severely. Aware though we are that no area of science is error-free, we readily concede the truth of statements like "There is water on the floor" or "John mopped it up." We are not troubled by the fact that some of our ideas about water, people, and floors may be mistaken. Evidently, then, the truth-conditions of individual statements stop well short of the whole corpus of contemporary science. But where they stop and why may prove puzzling.

PRS Again

One solution would be to delimit the meanings of individual expressions and thereby preserve the truth of statements in which they occur. For example, with regard to the statement "There's water on the floor," it might be suggested that molecular, atomic, and subatomic theories, no matter how widely accepted, do not belong to the meaning of the word *water*. Yet why not? We say that water consists of hydrogen and oxygen, as we say that rain consists of water and comes from clouds. And we characterize oxygen and hydrogen in accordance with contemporary chemistry and physics. These are facts of usage, and usage establishes meanings. No distinction has been drawn, explicitly or implicitly, between the defining and nondefining traits of water. Granted, in certain contexts a line may be traced. If, for instance, the presence of subatomic particles in water were challenged and debated, no doubt it would be clear that in that setting subatomic particles did not count as defining traits of water. The dispute would be factual, not semantic. However, if someone says simply, "Watch out—there's water on the floor," no such sharpening occurs.

We may therefore rightly wonder why this assertion may be perfectly true, despite hidden errors in current scientific thinking about water, hydrogen, protons, and the rest. And chapter 8 may appear to have sharpened the difficulty, for it made clear that popular agreement does not guarantee truth. If everyone says that water is H_2O and it is not, then everyone is wrong. If everyone says that hydrogen and oxygen are composed of subatomic particles and they are not, again, everyone is wrong. Linguistic correspondence, rightly understood, condemns them. And if "There's water on the floor" is implicitly defined by erroneous theory, it, too, is false. The popular verdict "True" is unduly lenient.

Here PRS confirms its worth by suggesting a way to clarify and justify both our use of the term *water* and our judgment that the statement is "true." Alternative terms such as *kerosene, milk, cream,* or *crude oil* would carry the same erroneous implications as *water* and would add other, more evident deviations of their own. And no better, tailor-made term is available, as *gulf* was for my niece when she described the Gulf of Mexico as a "big bathtub." No ideal terminology exists, expressing the whole truth and nothing but the truth about water. Hence "There is *water* on the floor" typically satisfies PRS—this refinement on the rule of correspondence—and is true.[21]

I am not suggesting that *true,* as customarily employed, is a regrettably lax expression, tolerating deficiencies that more discriminating speakers would abjure. Even an omniscient speaker could do no better were he or she obliged to speak English. And only for an omniscient being might a "better" language be feasible or desirable (supposing there were other omniscient beings with whom to communicate and any need to do so). The idea that we human beings might have a separate term for every conceivable defining configuration—a thousand in place of *water,* ten thousand replacing *person,* ready for any variation or advance, foreseeable or unforeseeable, in a speaker's biology, psychology, physics, metaphysics, or theology—is an evident absurdity. And to judge speech acts as though speakers were so equipped would be palpably unhelpful and unfair. Hence PRS indicates not only how we do speak and how we do employ the word *true,* but also how we should. It is a reasonable norm.

It might be suggested that we need not have a separate term for every conceivable defining configuration, since we already possess words from which each and every definition might be constructed. Thus, right now we might, for instance, replace the word *water* in "There's water on the floor" with a definite description lengthy enough to identify the stuff as water but accurate enough to eliminate at least one common error concerning water (supposing we had detected it). And wouldn't such an expression be a rival expression, and wouldn't it come closer than *water?* Granted, it too would doubtless be infected with further, undetected error. But couldn't that too be eliminated, employing the linguistic resources of our existing language?

Ideally, perhaps, but not really. And if we can never eliminate all error from the theoretical content of a statement, why attempt such lengthy rewording? The more closely we examine this supposedly superior mode of discourse, the more patent its absurdity becomes. If, for instance, someone disagreed with the majority concerning the complicity of Nixon in the Watergate affair, he could never thereafter refer to "Nixon" until the majority came to agree with him. He would have to replace the proper name with some such phrase as "the president of the United States who resigned from office, but who did not cover up the Watergate affair." Thereupon the majority—those with whom he wished to communicate—would doubtless contest the existence of any reference for his description. Thus, instead of successfully reporting the sale of Nixon's memoirs or the marriage of his granddaughter, our ideal speaker would get involved in an argument about Watergate. And so it would be for countless other words and names on countless other occasions. The all-important distinction between shared terminology and shared opinions would have broken down, and chaos would ensue. These reflections suggest once again, as did those in chapter 9, that there is more wisdom in the common use of *true* than straightway meets the eye. And PRS, as worded and explained in chapter 7 (with "rival *terms*" rather than "rival *expressions*"), is indeed a reasonable norm.

The principle is reasonable both in what it endorses and in what it does not. For in permitting the use of *true* for everyday assertions, it does not countenance any error or direct expression of error. It does not approve our saying, for instance, that there are subatomic particles or that water is composed of them, if there are in fact no such entities. Such a statement would not satisfy PRS, since it would employ the term *particle* where *field, fiction,* or the like would be more appropriate. Employing some alternative term available in the language, we might achieve closer correspondence between our use of words and their established uses. However, for the stuff on the floor we could do no better than "There is water on the floor"—even though a full explanation of that statement revealed the same erroneous conviction as was stated by the words "Water is composed of subatomic particles."

Further Applications

PRS fits many a lock and is handy on many an occasion. It permits a ready answer, for example, to Joachim's challenge in *The Nature of Truth:*

> If it be said that the contention is not that any judgement is *the whole truth,* but that any true judgement is *wholly true,* we must doubt whether this distinction will stand examination, or whether those who put it forward quite realize to what they are committed. For how do they conceive the relation of these wholly-true judgements to the whole of truth, these little bits of perfect knowledge to the larger perfect knowledge which they constitute? And how do they conceive the "truth"

either of the single judgements, or of the system of judgements into which they enter?[22]

Conceive a judgment as including a person's complete conception of water, say, and Joachim's objection to "wholly true" judgments may stand. Conceive a judgment's truth as determined by its statement's truth, and its statement's truth as determined, without qualification, by correspondence, and his objection may still stand. But add PRS, and the answer becomes: A particular judgment may be wholly true because it wholly satisfies a criterion of truth which reasonably allows for imperfections of correspondence. "There's water on the floor" may then be perfectly true, despite residual inaccuracies in our current conception of water.

As a further illustration of the principle's utility, consider the puzzle Winston Barnes recounts: "Very early in his career, in 1906, Moore noted that from different metaphysical standpoints a statement such as *Hens lay eggs* would mean very different things. On an idealist metaphysics it would refer to the activity of minds or spirits; on a materialist metaphysics, to the movements of invisible particles; on a sensationalist metaphysics, to an actual or possible relation between groups of the speaker's sensations."[23] After noting these various senses and without committing himself to any one of them, Moore added: "But whatever the proposition 'Hens' eggs are generally laid by hens' may *mean*, most philosophers would, I think, allow that in some sense or other, this proposition was true." So Barnes perceives a difficulty: "If we know it to be true that hens lay eggs, must we not know what the statement means? If it has several meanings, must we not know in which of its meanings it is true? And, in fact, is not *Hens lay eggs* the very type of an unambiguous statement, *i.e.* a statement which has only one meaning? And if it is only in some sense which is not its ordinary meaning that it is true, would it not be better to say that the statement is false?"[24]

PRS resolves such puzzlement. For it is satisfied by all three terms—*hens, lay,* and *eggs*—in all three viewpoints mentioned: idealist, materialist, and sensationalist. And the statement "Hens lay eggs" is therefore true in all three. The theoretical content might vary still more widely, and the verdict would still be "True." *Hens* and *lay* and *eggs* might still come closer than any rival terms.

W. H. Newton-Smith cites more recent conundrums, arising from a neo-positivist conception of meaning:

> The meaning of a theoretical term was said to be determined by the entire set of sentences within the theory containing the term. Consequently any change in the postulates containing a given theoretical term was claimed to bring a change in the meaning of that term. . . . On this account of the matter the assertion by the Newtonian 'Mass is invariant' and the assertion by the Einsteinian 'Mass is not invariant' are not logically incompatible, as the meaning of 'mass' is not constant across the theories.[25]

It would therefore appear that supposedly rival theories do not in fact conflict. And if we suppose not only that the meaning of a term is given by its role in a theory, but also that the referent of a term, if any, is determined by the meaning of that term, the consequences become still more counterintuitive. If, for instance,

> we look at the theories of Thomson and Bohr from the perspective of our current theories, we shall have to say that there are neither such things as Bohr electrons nor such things as Thomson electrons. For we shall not find anything having the properties which their theories associate with being an electron. Since they attempted to discourse about what does not exist, all their assertions involving the term "electron" are false. Thus, their theories are totally false. This is incompatible with our assumption that there has been growth in scientific knowledge to which their theories contributed.[26]

Here the solution is the same as for Nixon, hens, or water on the floor. Thanks to PRS, *electron* has the same reference, if any, in Thomson's, Bohr's, and contemporaries' theories; the same entities merit the designation and are in fact so designated.[27] Hence the claims do conflict when, for instance, Thomson asserts and Bohr denies that electrons are well defined with regard to spatial volume, or when Bohr asserts and contemporary theorists deny that electrons can have any energy level.[28] And science has indeed progressed if more descriptions of electrons are true now than formerly.

Noting the inadequacies of both holistic positivism and holistic anarchism in the philosophy of science, Putnam is led to inquire: "If we agree that rationality (in the wide sense, including Hume's 'reasonableness') is neither a matter of following a computer program nor something defined by the norms of the culture, or some subset of them, then what account *can* we give of it?" The problem, he notes, has analogues in other areas.

> Some years ago I studied the behavior of natural kind words, for example, *gold*, and I came to the conclusion that here too the extension of the term is not simply determined by a 'battery of semantical rules,' or other institutionalized norms. . . . We are prepared to count something as belonging to a kind, even if our *present* tests do not suffice to show that it is a member of the kind, if it ever turns out that it has the same essential nature as (or, more vaguely, is "sufficiently similar" to) the paradigmatic examples (or the great majority of them).[29]

I would suggest that, when spelled out by PRS, "sufficient similarity" is a sharper criterion than "sameness of nature," not a vaguer one, and that, when seen in the light of the preceding four chapters, it appears not merely as an analog, but as an instance of the "reasonableness" Putnam seeks to clarify.

The introduction of PRS complements, but does not contradict, Putnam's own account. "What the essential nature is," he comments, "or what counts as sufficient similarity, depends both on the natural kind and on the context (iced tea may be 'water' in one context but not in another); but for gold what counts is ultimate composition, since this has been thought since the ancient Greeks to determine the lawful behavior of the substance." To "kind" and "context" as determinants of what to say, I would add "relation to other terms available in the language, and in particular to rival, incompatible terms." And I therefore see no opposition between Putnam's general statement and his example. If a substance's composition resembles that of gold, and its composition determines its lawful behavior, and it therefore resembles gold both innerly and outerly, *gold* is the term to use for it. PRS is satisfied.

Looking Back

Detach science from truth's domain, and a principal fiefdom would be denied it; remove the whole of empirical discourse, and the erstwhile monarch of Western thought would become a mere pretender to the throne, forced to find refuge in the regions of logic and mathematics—if even there. Both moves have been recommended, for reasons sampled in this chapter.

Neither Schlick, on the one hand, nor Hempel and Neurath, on the other, denied in word the truth of scientific or empirical statements; they just denied or bypassed the reality. Where meaning and truth coincide, as in Schlick's elementary utterances, there is no empirical truth. Where thinking a thing is so, coherently and all together, suffices to make it so, as in Hempel and Neurath's alternative position, there is no empirical truth. The tactic of labeling coherence "truth" when no correspondence can be found resembles the stratagem, scrutinized in the next chapter, of redefining God in purely moral terms when no meaning or truth can be discerned in traditional statements of belief. Just as some may prefer open atheism to atheism decked out as theism, so some have preferred to abandon talk of truth when *truth* becomes a name for something else and have proposed, for example, to replace the search for truth with the search for solutions to problems. There was interest, therefore, in taking a look at how such thinking has arisen, thinking that challenges truth's long reign.

The atomist troubles of Schlick and the coherentist troubles of Neurath and Hempel arose from a common source and had a common explanation. Starting from the *Tractatus,* neither party recognized the role of established word uses. Once such uses are taken account of, it appears that true empirical statements are never as atomic as Schlick supposed or as holistic as Neurath and Hempel maintained. They fall in a middle range. They do, that is, if they ever occur. Since, however, words typically get their meanings from the way they are employed, and they are employed to express current views, and current empirical views always contain some falsehood, it may appear that empirical statements always contain some falsehood. They may approximate the truth, but are never in fact true. PRS corrects this impression. Neither rational, effective speech nor the concept *true* by which speech is judged requires total correspondence. The realities we label need not possess all the properties suggested by previous applications of the label, the false as well as the true. It suffices that the term come closer than any rival term. Thus *water* will do for the stuff on the floor.

CHAPTER 12

TRANS-EMPIRICAL TRUTH

As the preceding chapter has shown, were it not for the principle of relative similarity, practically all empirical statements might have to be judged false. So too might most trans-empirical statements, concerning animal sensations, unconscious thoughts, subatomic particles, Kantian things-in-themselves, attributes of God, and the like. Indeed, were it not for PRS, many such assertions might not even count as meaningful. The principle not only indicates their truth-conditions, but also reveals thereby the intelligibility often thought to be lacking by critics unacquainted with the principle.

A Theological Illustration

In the area of theology and religious discourse, where the issue of meaningfulness has been debated most thoroughly, "Flew's challenge" has received special attention. The challenge, as Flew himself explained, ran as follows:

> Some theological utterances seem to, and are intended to, provide explanations or express assertions. Now an assertion, to be an assertion at all, must claim that things stand thus and thus; *and not otherwise.* Similarly an explanation, to be an explanation at all, must explain why this particular thing occurs; *and not something else.* Those last clauses are crucial. And yet sophisticated religious people—or so it seemed to me—are apt to overlook this, and tend to refuse to allow, not merely that anything actually does occur, but that anything conceivably could occur, which would count against their theological assertions and explanations. But in so far as they do this their supposed explanations are actually bogus, and their seeming assertions are really vacuous.[1]

For example,

> Someone tells us that God loves us as a father loves his children. We are reassured. But then we see a child dying of inoperable

cancer of the throat. His earthly father is driven frantic in his efforts to help, but his Heavenly Father reveals no obvious sign of concern. Some qualification is made—God's love is "not a merely human love" or it is "an inscrutable love," perhaps—and we realize that such sufferings are quite compatible with the truth of the assertion that "God loves us as a father (but, of course, . . .)." We are reassured again. But then perhaps we ask: What is this assurance of God's (appropriately qualified) love worth, what is this apparent guarantee really a guarantee against? Just what would have to happen not merely (morally and wrongly) to tempt but also (logically and rightly) to entitle us to say "God does not love us" or even "God does not exist"?[2]

Religious apologists have for the most part been surprisingly unsuccessful in their answers to this query. I say "surprisingly" because, paradoxically, Flew's demand focuses on the least problematic aspect of the statements he questions.

A loving father may permit his child to suffer, indeed, may even inflict suffering on the child, but only in view of some compensating good, whether of the child or of others (for example, members of the family) whose good he also has at heart. He may give the child unpleasant medicine or consent to a painful operation for the sake of its health, may send it to school or deny it TV for the sake of its intellectual development, may punish or scold it to improve its character, and so forth. What an assertion of fatherly love excludes is any suffering permitted or inflicted on the child without a compensating reason. So it is for human fathers. So it is for God, according to believers. Thus the difficulty Flew's challenge highlights is not logical, as he supposed, but epistemological.

A small child might truly and meaningfully believe that its father loved it, yet it could hardly apply Flew's test and determine accurately what its father might do or permit and still be a loving parent. Too many facts, values, and likely consequences lie outside the child's ken. And doubtless the father cares about other people too and must balance their needs against those of the child, without thereby counting as an unloving father. Similarly, but still more clearly, an adult human being cannot second-guess God and determine the best overall course of events for himself, the human race, and the universe at large. Yet the adult's limited understanding doesn't entail any shift in the meaning of the word *love* any more than the child's does. If we had a comprehensive grasp of all facts, all values, and every kind of causal relation, both here and hereafter, we might answer Flew's challenge in a manner appropriate to the belief he questions—that is, belief in a love that embraces the whole universe and seeks the good of all. We might be able to indicate in detail and person by person just what would have to happen to entitle us to say "God does not love us." But obviously we do not possess such knowledge.[3]

More problematic, as some have noted, than the idea of God's acting for our *good* is the idea of his *acting* at all. Thus Kai Nielsen writes: "We cannot understand what it would be for such a being to act and thus to be loving, merciful or just, for these predicates apply to things that *a person does*. But we have no understanding of 'a person' without 'a body' and it is only persons that in the last analysis can act or do things. We have no understanding of 'disembodied action' or 'bodiless doing' and thus no understanding of 'a loving but bodiless being.'"[4]

Clearly, we cannot understand these things in the sense of imagining them; but *understand* is not synonymous with *imagine*. As one author remarks, "Whether I can imagine it or not, a thousand-sided polygon, an animal that's a cross between a walrus and a wasp, and a color different from any we have ever seen, are all *logically possible;* we need not stop to ask whether we can *imagine* them."[5]

Elsewhere, in a nontheological context, Nielsen himself makes much the same point, with similar emphasis. In an article that urges confirmability, at least in principle, as a criterion of factual statements, he writes: "Mackie gives us no evidence that there is a *logical ban* on observing mesons. Technically and even physically, it is impossible to observe them, but Mackie gives no evidence that the acceptance of the physical theory in which 'meson' plays a functional part commits us to the claim that it would be *contradictory* to say that even an infinitely observant observer, with very different sense organs and in a very different situation, could observe them."[6]

Nielsen does not spell out this closing suggestion. He does not specify in what respects the putative "observer," "situation," "sense organs," or "observations" would be similar to the things customarily called observers, situations, sense organs, or observations, and in what respects dissimilar. He does not need to. For his surmise to make sense, it suffices that he should mean that there might conceivably exist a being sufficiently similar to us to merit the name "observer," endowed with perceptual equipment sufficiently similar to ours to merit the name "sense organs," related to mesons in a fashion sufficiently similar to what we call "observing" to merit the same appellation. Each time, the test of sufficient similarity would be PRS, or some variant thereof. Without some such explanation, it is difficult to see how Nielsen's supposition would be intelligible. For as he himself notes, "We have no idea of what it would be like to observe a meson."[7]

In the same sense, we "have no idea"—or, as Nielsen puts it, "have no understanding"—of what it would be like for God to act on our behalf and therefore be "loving." However, the same principle that saves his supposition applies to this one too, and assures it meaning. If the effects of God's providence for his people resemble those of a loving father, and if he can be said to bring them about, in the sense that what he does comes closer to causing, doing, or bringing about than it does, for instance, to suffering, receiving, enduring, or the like, then he may truly be said to be loving. And if this is what is meant, then, regardless of whether it is true, the belief is meaningful. It has determinate truth-conditions.

The combination revealed by this analysis of God's *acting* for our *good*—close empirical similarity, on the one hand, together with indeterminate, perhaps more distant trans-empirical similarity, on the other, grounding the use of a term—is a common one. It appears, for instance, in our assertions concerning the sensations of animals and insects. When we say that a mouse hears a noise, a bee sees a flower, an earthworm feels a robin hop nearby, we ground our assertions partly on organs, stimuli, and movements we perceive which are analogous to our own, and partly on experiences we can only surmise. Here, too, *surmise* does not mean *imagine*. For the statements to be true, it suffices that the mouse's experience resemble more closely what is commonly called hearing than what is commonly called seeing, tasting, running, or hiding; that the bee's experience resemble more closely what is commonly called seeing than what is commonly called hearing, flying, mating, or sleeping; and so forth. And for the statements to be meaningful, it suffices that such be our understanding—reflective or unreflective—of the words. PRS assures both their meaning and their truth.

In certain respects, talk of animals' "pleasure" or of secretions ants find "attractive" may resemble more closely the theological example than does talk of animals' or insects' sensations. So too may various psychoanalytic, scientific, and metaphysical assertions. On the basis of visible behavior, we surmise unconscious "thoughts" and "mechanisms" whose intrinsic nature remains nebulous.[8] On the strength of perceptible phenomena, we posit subatomic "particles" as their "causes."[9] Analogously, we relate our sensations to noumena or things-in-themselves which in some sense "cause" the sensations.[10] In theological and religious discourse, various other parallels come to mind. Assertions of divine "wisdom," "knowledge," "foresight," and "power," for example, combine empirical and nonempirical elements in somewhat similar fashion.

The Need for PRS

Trans-empirical utterances are often problematic, not just epistemologically, but also semantically; and PRS greatly improves their chances of being acknowledged as at least making sense. Yet this principle, or any like it, is strangely absent from the literature.[11] Even those most inclined to champion trans-empirical discourse pay the principle little heed. Indeed, their assertions may implicitly deny it. Thus it has, for instance, been stated: "Since we cannot know what God is like, it makes no sense to ask whether or not one has a true notion of him. This is but another way of remarking that any notion we have of God is inadequate, and hence none could be said to be true."[12] If *notion* here means "mental representation," then, to be sure, we have no adequate notion of God. But neither, in that case, do we have an adequate notion of atomic power, friendship, Ibsen's plays, inflation, sorrow, or the cost of potatoes (see chapter 2). If, however, by *notion* is meant "content of an intelligible assertion," we may indeed have a true notion of God, as we may of those other things. The assertion may satisfy PRS.

Usually, PRS is simply absent from discussion, not implicitly denied. Thus it has for instance been said:

> The appeal to analogy is . . . an attempt to find a position between the two extremes; in speaking about God and man the term "love" is to be used neither in two absolutely different senses nor in one exactly identical sense, but in an analogical sense, which is to say that one love is *similar* to the other, where "similar" means neither "absolutely different" nor "absolutely identical." To be similar is therefore to combine sameness and otherness, continuity and discontinuity in a peculiar way.[13]

But in *what* peculiar way? As an analysis of the concept *similarity,* this is too narrow; as an analysis of successful predication, it is merely a blank check. And the check cannot be filled in without mentioning what here receives no mention—namely, the expression's relation not only to the reality named, but also to the alternative expressions available in the language.

Sometimes the sheer fact of similarity is considered sufficient justification. For instance, Norris Clarke, in replying to Kai Nielsen, insists on "the principle, handed down to St. Thomas by both the Neoplatonic and the Aristotelian traditions, that *every effect must in some way resemble its cause.* In a word, every causal bond sets up at the same time a bond of intrinsic similarity in being."[14] Hence the Creator resembles his creatures, and creaturely predicates can be applied to him. Evidently, though, not just any kind or degree of similarity warrants their application, or else we would have to say that the creator of trees is a tree, the creator of mice is a mouse, and so forth. But once we try to indicate more precisely the nature and degree of the requisite similarity, then, as we saw in chapter 7, no account that fails to mention alternative expressions can succeed. Even close similarity may fail the test of truth if it is not "relative similarity"—that is, the kind specified by PRS.

Similarly inadequate is a defense in terms of "open texture" or the like. Theological employment of the words *cause, make, love,* and so forth cannot be vindicated by observing: "The justification for using such terms of God is that they already have a very wide range of uses in non-religious contexts, and that we are merely continuing an on-going process of stretching. Such a process is in any case a natural feature of any living language, particularly with regard to the development of metaphors."[15] Unless further refined, such a defense might endorse the worst abuses.[16] Extending our concepts "naturally," resemblance by resemblance, we might feel entitled to say that a booklet is a book, then that a brochure is, then a flier, then a single page, a single sentence, a single word. After all, did not the concept *number* develop in much the same manner, first embracing cardinal numbers, then integers, rational numbers, real numbers, and finally complex and hypercomplex numbers, so that the numbers at the end of the series bear no resemblance to those at the start?[17] To such a vindication the answer must be a firm negative. No, the two developments are not comparable. For every step in the extension of *number* conformed to PRS, whereas no step in the proposed extension does. Nor is there any other justification for calling a single word or a single page a book. Thus, to strike a happy balance between license and rigidity, we have need of some such norm as PRS.

We need it for an adequate account of speech, that is, but not—or not primarily—for adequate speech. The importance of this distinction becomes apparent when Nielsen remarks: "The catch is, however, that believers and nonbelievers alike, once they give up an anthropomorphic conception of divinity, do not understand what it would be like for such statements to express true statements. But then the very discourse of the believer lacks the kind of intelligibility requisite for Christian or Jewish religious belief."[18] This inference from lack of understanding to lack of intelligibility is not sound. Those who say it is raining, who call books, but not booklets, "books," who refer to complex numbers as "numbers," doubtless do not understand, reflectively, "what it would be like for such statements to express true statements." They could not specify the requisite correspondence, either generally in the manner of chapter 3 or more specifically in the manner of chapter 7. But this does not mean that their statements all lack sense.

It is just as well that linguistic awareness is not a condition of sense; for, as chapters 1 and 2 made clear, such awareness has often been wanting. Even now, I have found, the present account may elicit the remark: "Isn't your point simply this, that when we resort to analogy, we should choose the nearest analog? If electrons resemble particles more than they do fields of force, we should call them 'particles.' If God resembles loving humans more than he does unloving, we should call him 'loving.' And so forth. Is there really any need to mention rival *expressions*?"

This suggested simplification obscures the fact that we would still be choosing between rival expressions, and preferring the *name* for the nearest analog to the *names* for more distant analogs. Furthermore, the suggestion appears to assume such a complete supply of names that each rival analog invariably possesses a name we can employ. But this assumption is unrealistic. To give a simple illustration: suppose I have just seen a flying saucer. While its shape is still clearly etched in my memory, I sketch it or model it in clay. There now exists an analog far closer than a saucer in the cupboard. But the saucer has a name, and my analog does not. So I call the thing I have observed a "flying saucer." Generally, then, it can be seen that an adequate norm of *predication* had better speak of *predicates*, hence of rival expressions and not just of rival analogs. PRS is not a needless complication.

Prospects for Acceptance

The chances are fair, I believe, that both opponents and proponents of trans-empirical discourse, for instance in theology, may accept the mediating services of PRS. This surmise may sound optimistic, especially with regard to opponents. Recall, however, Nielsen's own way of speaking when he was not criticizing theological assertions. And notice the implication of my saying that PRS has been overlooked; it follows that the accounts so far rejected by critics are not of the kind proposed here. Furthermore, when critics state their demands clearly and without begging the question (not confusing truth with verification, for example, or making statements meaningless or nonfactual by arbitrary redefinition of *meaningful* or *factual*), PRS readily satisfies the conditions they set.

To illustrate, in a passage Nielsen quotes with approval Bernard Williams writes: "To believe is to believe *something*, and if there is anything that one believes, one ought to be able to say in some way—if not in the very narrow terms of sense-experience—what the difference is between what one believes being true and what one believes not being true."[19] A merit of PRS is that it permits a reply to this request. A believer can answer that he believes in a reality that satisfies PRS, as opposed to one that does not. If, for instance, he believes in subatomic particles, he believes in realities which resemble more closely the sort of things called particles than the sort of things called fictions or fields of force. The reverse might be true: there might be no such realities as those he speaks of, or they might resemble more closely some rival paradigm; but such is not his belief. Similarly, a believer in noumenal causality, unconscious desire, insect consciousness, life on other planets, or divine love believes in a reality that meets the same basic requirements: he believes there is something that comes closer to what we customarily call causality, desire, consciousness, life, or love than it does to what goes by any other, incompatible name.

Such, at any rate, is the type of explanation open to believers. Whether they adopt it is another question. Some may find it too nebulous, others too definite. I suspect, however, that on reflection such an account may prove acceptable to both the dogmatically and the mystically inclined. The former may be reassured by the fact that relative similarity may be close, the latter by the fact that it may be distant. For example, the life believed to exist on far-off planets may be just like that on ours, or it may surpass the wildest fancies of science fiction. A bee's image of a flower may be just like ours or may be so dissimilar that we would have difficulty recognizing it even as an image, never mind the image of a flower. God's love and knowledge may resemble ours more closely than we suppose, or they may be exceedingly dissimilar. Yet in either supposition PRS may be satisfied, and it may therefore be true to say that there is life on other planets, that the bee has an image, that it sees the flower, that God is loving or knowing.

Because PRS accommodates both the dogmatic and the mystical traditions, the analysis it suggests seems realistic. It conforms with the understanding of believers. Thus it fits hand in glove, for example, with the type of theological analysis most favored through the centuries, combining affirmation with negation. Consider a typical sample: "We cannot form an adequate idea of the divine simplicity as it is in itself," writes Copleston, "since it transcends our experience: we know, however, that it is at the opposite pole, so to speak, from simplicity or comparative simplicity in creatures."[20] Truly at the opposite pole from creaturely simplicity would be creaturely complexity. But divine simplicity, the tradition would doubtless hold, is not as far removed as that. It resembles creaturely simplicity more than it does creaturely complexity. Otherwise, why call it "simplicity," rather than "complexity"?[21]

Implicit in the "affirmative way" of traditional theology is the conviction that the word employed—*simple, wise, good, powerful, provident,* or the like—is somehow legitimate. Implicit in the "negative way" is recognition that the word's legitimacy does not derive from close similarity. All that is missing from these traditional two ways is a clear grasp of what kind and degree of similarity would suffice. Such understanding is not achieved or expressed by asserting, as in the "way of eminence," that divine simplicity, wisdom, goodness, or the like is higher or more perfect: it must be higher or more perfect *simplicity, wisdom,* or *goodness.* The same word must apply. And it does if PRS is satisfied.

The general agreement of PRS with theological tradition comes out negatively as well as positively—in what it does not countenance as well as in what it does. It is no more favorable than the majority of believers are to various reductive analyses proposed in recent decades.[22] "Sophisticated apologists have," for example, "urged that credal affirmations may, without significant loss, be treated as equivalent to recommendations of the behaviour and attitudes that are agreed on all hands to be their proper corollaries. 'There is a God' thus becomes equivalent, or nearly equivalent, to something like: 'Treat all men as brothers, and revere the mystery of the universe.' "[23] Similarly, "Paul van Buren, for example, interprets Christ's resurrection in terms of 'a new perspective upon life' . . . opened up for the Apostles and for modern man, rather than as a physical rising from the dead which is a sign of Christ's divinity and a pledge of man's future resurrection."[24]

As Sherry, the author of these words, observes: "Such reinterpretations may or may not make Christian doctrines more palatable to people today, but they are certainly far removed from the intentions of the Fathers of the Church who originally formulated the doctrines."[25] Furthermore, they are hardly what the words suggest and no longer satisfy PRS. "He rose from the dead" might be verified by an event, however mysterious, that was rightly called a rising from the dead, but hardly by a new perspective upon life. Other, more appropriate words are available to express that reality—for instance, "new perspective upon life." Likewise, "God loves us" might be verified by a reality, however transcendent, that was rightly called loving, but not by the supreme value of love. "Love is supremely valuable" would be a more accurate formulation of this latter claim.

The same reductive readings that fail to satisfy PRS and that fail to win acceptance from most believers and theologians are likewise unacceptable to most critics of theological discourse. A "bizarre enterprise" and "a mockery of the faith of the Saints and the Fathers" are Flew's epithets for the efforts of those who "have tried to analyse the meaning of religious utterances entirely in normative, as opposed to descriptive or would be descriptive terms."[26] This agreement between the verdict of PRS and that of critics is a further reason for surmising that the principle may win their approval.

A Broader Perspective

The significance of such a principle seems great regardless of its preferable formulation, whether in terms of greater similarity or of equal similarity, whether as a sufficient condition or as a necessary condition, or both. The important thing is that the principle calls attention to a neglected, yet essential, aspect of analogical discourse. Proper predication cannot be assessed word by word; the claims of alternative expressions must also be considered. Yet they seldom are, at least explicitly. Though the issue of relative similarity is pertinent, even crucial, to most discussions of analogy, it is hardly ever noted, much less addressed and resolved.

One outcome, as we have seen, is the inadequacy of both critics' and defendants' observations. Another is their narrowness. PRS has the virtue of loosening rigid categories and broadening perspectives. By way of illustration, let me quote again from the Nielsen-Clarke exchange concerning talk about God. In defense and explanation of analogy, Clarke writes: "An analogous concept is not a composition of one part exactly identical and another part different, as Scotus, Ockham, and Nielsen seem to imply; rather it is an indissoluble unity where the similarity itself is through and through diversified in each case. As a result there is quite a bit of 'give,' flexibility, indeterminacy, or vagueness right within the concept itself, with the result that the meaning remains essentially incomplete."[27]

Clarke is right, I would say, to contest the narrow notion that similarity entails at least partial sameness. As I pointed out earlier when explaining PRS, *resemblance* or *similarity* is not a sharp or uniform concept. Thus, if all we know is that two things resemble each other—or that they resemble each other more than they do some other thing, as PRS prescribes—we cannot then infer any identity; the things may share multiple traits or a single trait or no traits at all. It follows, however, that Clarke's account, too, is unduly narrow. PRS accommodates either type of resemblance and either type of analysis—the kind Nielsen insists on, as well as the kind Clarke prefers.

A child hears certain shades called "blue," say, then extends the term to other shades; an adult, familiar with activities called "games," invents a somewhat similar activity and calls it, too, a "game" (for instance, a "video game"). Analyzing these cases, we might say that in the first there is no discernible identity between the old blues and the new, whereas when the adult extends the term *game*, there is considerable overlap between his invention and the activities previously called "games": it too has rules, is played by human beings, has winning and losing, and so forth. Or, applying stricter criteria of identity, we might say that neither from game to game nor even within the same game do rules, people, playing, winning, or the like reveal any single essence or perfect similarity. Regardless of which mode of analysis we prefer, though, PRS still applies. Both analyzable and unanalyzable resemblances may merit the accolade "True" for a statement, provided the resemblances are greater for the terms it employs than for rival terms.

As these various samples suggest, there seems to be some further narrowness in Clarke's talk of "analogous concepts," with its apparent implication that analogy is a trait of certain words and not of others.[28] All words may be extended in accordance with PRS, and most words are so extended in the course of their history. Thus it is even truer than appears from Clarke's account that in analogical talk, and in discourse generally, there may be "quite a bit of 'give,' flexibility, indeterminacy, or vagueness." *Every* word is flexible and vague, in the sense that every word may be extended in accordance with PRS. And the extension thus permitted may be of either variety, the analyzable or the unanalyzable. The vagueness and flexibility reside not so much "within the concept itself," as Clarke puts it, but within the concept as related to other concepts. The looseness resides in the language as a whole and in its mode of predication.

This mode calls for nothing more than relative similarity; it does not require that a validating similarity be surveyable, as even Clarke appears to suggest. "The similarity involved," he writes, "cannot be isolated from its qualitatively diversifying modes and expressed by itself clearly, as it can be in the case of a univocal concept. It can indeed be caught or recognized by an act of intellectual insight as we run up and down the scale of examples. It can be *seen,* and *shown forth* by our meaningful linguistic behavior, as Wittgenstein would say, but it cannot be *said* or expressed clearly by itself."[29] Such an account may apply to the range of blues or reds or to the variety of games; but it does little to clarify trans-empirical discourse—for instance, about God. We can look and see what blues or games are like, as Wittgenstein advised; but we cannot look and see what God is like and thereby justify our choice of words. However, neither meaningfulness nor truth requires that we do so. Once again, PRS is less restrictive. For trans-empirical *truth,* it suffices that the terms used in fact come closer than rival terms. For trans-empirical *meaning,* it suffices that such be our understanding of the terms.

CHAPTER 13

A COMPARISON WITH TARSKI AND DAVIDSON

Formulating one version of the so-called paradox of analysis, Joseph Hanna writes: "In order to know that the explicatum and explicandum are synonymous one must already know the meaning of the explicandum, in which case the explication is unnecessary. But if the explicatum and explicandum are not synonymous, then the explication is inadequate. Hence, an explication is either trivial or it can never be known to be adequate."[1] What Hanna and others like him overlook is the difference between knowing reflectively and knowing unreflectively.[2] Most word meanings we know unreflectively; we use words with ease, yet have little awareness of how we use them. Often, though, it is desirable to pass from unreflective to reflective knowledge of a word or concept. The preceding twelve chapters offer a notable example. The unreflective content of the concept *true* revealed by part 1 turned out in part 2 to be a basic norm that merits reflective acceptance and observance.

I have not tried to encapsulate either the concept or the norm in a rigorous definition of *true* or *true statement*. The chances of success for such an enterprise are slight, especially when the defining terms, as well as the one to be defined, are everyday, nontechnical expressions. In that case, to expect all-and-only equivalence between *definiens* and *definiendum* is like expecting exact coincidence between the form of one cloud and that of several others combined. We *may* achieve such a match, even outside the exact sciences, but we should not expect to do so.[3]

We have seen that the contours of *true*, like those of a cloud, are both varied and indefinite. The variety appeared in the word's functioning (now descriptive, now performative); in what the word describes (for example, beliefs and propositions, as well as utterances); in the various types of utterance it characterizes (performative, evaluative, empirical, trans-empirical, and other); and in the slight shifts of meaning it acquires in these applications. The word's indefiniteness appeared, for example, in the vagueness of the border between its descriptive and nondescriptive uses and between utterances that are clearly true or false and those that are neither. It became especially evident in the assessment of PRS, first as a sufficient, then as a necessary, condition of truth. Applied to such an imprecise, heterogeneous concept, a defining formula that aspired to exactness would stand little chance of success.

Viewed as a norm, the concept *true* reveals further dimensions of indefiniteness. As chapter 6 noted, utterances can be good or bad in various ways and for various reasons. It is not always good, overall, to speak truthfully; it is not always bad to speak falsely. Just what considerations may or should weigh in the scales of decision, how heavily, against the standard benefits of truth, it is difficult to say very definitely or comprehensively. In a work like the present it seemed reasonable merely to suggest what are the standard benefits of truth when truth is envisaged as linguistic correspondence and not to append an ethical treatise on truth-telling.

Some readers, accustomed to technical terminology and to definitions, "explications," and succinctly formulated theories, may find unsatisfactory an account that leaves so much vagueness. My treatment may appear regrettably fuzzy and unsystematic by comparison, say, with Alfred Tarski's famed explication of truth[4] or Donald Davidson's well-known extensions of Tarksi's findings. An appropriate way, therefore, to review the preceding chapters, confirm their validity, and highlight their significance may be to compare their results with those of these two authors.

Tarski

Tarski's semantic theory, writes Susan Haack, "has been, of late, probably the most influential and most widely accepted theory of truth. His theory falls into two parts: he provides, first, *adequacy conditions,* i.e. conditions which any acceptable definition of truth ought to fulfil; and then he provides a definition of truth (for a specified formal language) which he shows to be, by his own standards, adequate."[5] In amplification of this summary, I might say something about Tarski's Convention T ("'S' is true iff p") and its role as a test of acceptable definitions, about his stipulations for an acceptable formal language, and about his recursive definition of truth in terms of satisfaction. However, I have not attempted a strict definition of truth, much less a formal one like Tarski's, which might be compared with his definition or tested by his standards. Our projects, aims, and criteria—indeed, our whole worlds of discourse—differ. Rather, then, than attempt to compare what cannot be compared, I shall suggest why it is that Tarski and I take such disparate approaches to the common topic, truth. Two initial divergences look especially decisive.

At a first parting of our ways Tarski also departs from Aristotle, whose thinking he intends to follow. "We should like our definition," he writes, "to do justice to the intuitions which adhere to the *classical Aristotelian conception of truth*—intuitions which find their expression in the well-known words of Aristotle's *Metaphysics: To say of what is that it is not, or of what is not that it is, is false, while to say of what is that it is, or of what is not that it is not, is true.*"[6] Here Aristotle speaks of statements—of "saying that." Yet Tarski proceeds to speak only of sentences. The explanation of this discrepancy, which he neither notes nor justifies, lies in the decisive move made several paragraphs earlier.

"We begin," Tarski there observes, "with some remarks regarding the extension of the concept of truth which we have in mind here. The predicate *'true'* is sometimes used to refer to psychological phenomena such as judgments or beliefs, sometimes to certain physical objects, namely, linguistic expressions and specifically sentences, and sometimes to certain ideal entities called 'propositions.'"[7] Remarking merely that the meaning of the term *proposition* "is notoriously a subject of lengthy disputations by various philosophers and logicians" and "seems never to have been made quite clear and unambiguous," Tarski concludes: "For several reasons it appears most convenient to *apply the term 'true' to sentences,* and we shall follow this course."[8]

Notably absent from Tarski's brief list is any mention of true statements, in the sense of true speech acts. Yet, as was explained in chapter 4, it is statements that are true in the primary sense of *true,* whereas beliefs, propositions, and sentences are true only in a derivative, functionally dependent sense. Further, it is statements that relate the expressions of a language (the mere marks or sounds) to the objects or states of affairs they mention or describe. Thus, from the start, Tarski eliminates most of the contents of this present study. Excluded are the uses of words and therefore their correspondence with established uses (chapter 3). Excluded are refinements like the principle of relative similarity, stating the closeness of the correspondence (chapters 7, 11, and 12), and inquiries relating linguistic to nonlinguistic truth (chapter 4), contrasting descriptive and nondescriptive uses of *true* (chapter 5), situating *true* with other cognitive comparatives (chapter 6), and so forth. No such analyses are possible once expressions are viewed as mere physical objects.

Equally responsible for the gulf that divides us is Tarski's option for a formal definition of truth, for formal languages, rather than an informal definition or description, for natural languages. The need for a formal treatment, he argues, and for theoretical semantics in general, is shown by antinomies like that of the Liar.[9] In ordinary English, for instance, one may write just these words on a page: "The only sentence on this page is false." If this self-referring sentence is true, then what it says is the case; so it is false. If, on the other hand, it is false, then what it says is not the case; so it is true. Hence, if it is either true or false, it is both, and we are caught in a contradiction.

One way out would be to deny that the sentence is either true or false, thus abandoning the so-called laws of bivalence and excluded middle.[10] This should not prove troubling. Many other sentences are neither true nor false—for example, those that apply terms to borderline cases. In such instances some resemblances point one way, some another, and usage yields no verdict. Similarly, we might suggest, a sentence like the one just imagined—"The only sentence on this page is false"—straddles the border between *true* and *false* and accordingly is neither true nor false. Or it might be compared with nonsensical utterances which depart so far from usage that we have no idea what it would be like for them to be true or false. "I have three sisters" makes sense, and so does "I have three and a half dollars," but "I have three and a half sisters" does not. Similarly, "This sentence is *short*" makes sense, and so does "*That* sentence is false," but "*This* sentence is *false*," we might say, does not; for we have no idea what state of affairs might verify it.[11] Even PRS cannot help us.

The norm of correspondence permits a still firmer response. For this much is clear: Whoever insists on the truth or falsehood of paradox-generating sentences lacks the backing of usage and therefore of the norm. No one contends that such sentences are simply true. No one asserts that they are simply false. Some, for theoretical reasons, maintain that they are both true and false. Some, for different reasons, maintain that they are neither. Many, perplexed, seek to escape from the dilemma, without deciding one way or the other. Hence no verdict is forthcoming from usage, any more than it is in the debate about the humanity of fetuses or many a similar imbroglio. The charge that natural languages are inconsistent therefore lacks a basis.

Tarski, possessing neither an analysis of the everyday concept *true* nor a norm of predication by which to resolve the problem that concerned him, took a step that precluded his ever attaining either the analysis or the norm that he needed. In view of the antinomies that arise in natural languages, he resolved to "abandon the attempt to solve our problem for the language of everyday life and restrict myself henceforth entirely to *formalized languages*."[12]

Even if he had acknowledged the norm of correspondence and its verdict, Tarski might still have been unhappy with my solution of the paradoxes, resulting as it does in assertions which are neither true nor false. "We have classical laws of logic," we can imagine him replying, "and according to those laws, all the sentences or statements of a language must be either true or false. If they are not, so much the worse for the language; we shall have to look for a substitute."[13] I would judge, on the contrary, "So much the worse for the laws, if they really make such demands." There is nothing amiss, for example, in a language whose concepts draw imprecise borders, permitting occasional non-true-false assertions. For purposes of communication, no other kind of language is conceivable.[14] As for the antinomies, I agree with Alan White: "The confusions which the logician overcomes [as Tarski did] by a distinction between an object-language and its higher order meta-language are not confusions in our everyday language, but are due . . . to various abuses of that language and, hence, to be overcome by ceasing to abuse it."[15]

In summary, then, I suggest that neither of Tarski's key moves had a sound basis, and that from his double fixation, on sentences rather than statements and on ideal notations rather than actual languages, a double diminishment resulted. Tarski himself might have agreed with White's assessment that "whatever the virtues of the semantic theory of truth for the artificial languages of logicians, it is no help—beyond its insistence that 'p' is true if and only if p—for an examination of the notion of truth in everyday thinking or of the meaning of 'true' in everyday language."[16] Even White's parenthetical concession we shall see reason to reconsider. However, I shall now turn to an author whose views here merit fuller consideration. Davidson does attend to statements and does attend to natural languages; hence his treatment of truth is more comparable to mine and appears a more serious rival.

Davidson

Davidson envisages greater benefits from Tarski's theory than did Tarski himself. He believes, for one thing, that

> a recursive theory of absolute truth, of the kind required by Convention T, provides an answer, *per accidens* it may at first seem, to quite another problem. This problem may be expressed as that of showing or explaining how the meaning of a sentence depends on the meanings of its parts. A theory of absolute truth gives an answer in the following sense. Since there is an infinity of T-sentences [satisfying Convention T or a variant] to be accounted for, the theory must work by selecting a finite number of truth-relevant expressions and a finite number of truth-affecting constructions from which all sentences are composed. The theory then gives outright the semantic properties of certain of the basic expressions, and tells how the constructions affect the semantic properties of the expressions on which they operate.[17]

"In sum," writes Putnam, "Davidson's idea is to *invert* Tarski's argument. Instead of taking 'true' as the word whose meaning is to be explained and the object language as understood, Davidson takes the object language as what is to be explained and 'true' (or whatever the word for truth is in the language in which the explanation is to be given) as what is already understood. In this way, any truth definition for a language (in Tarski's sense) can be viewed as a *meaning theory* for that language."[18]

More directly germane to the topic of truth, "Davidson goes further and argues the converse; that any meaning theory for a language, i.e., any finite description which projects meanings for the infinitely many sentences of the language, is implicitly a truth definition for the language, and that the explicit Tarski form is the ideal form for formalized meaning theories."[19] The notion of truth, as purified and formalized by Tarski, can be applied to natural languages and yield a full extensional representation of their truth-conditions. It is as though Davidson had turned the Wittgensteinian tables on an account like mine and said: "I cannot suggest the essential nub of truth, by means of a single formula, any more than I might disclose the essence of an artichoke, hidden beneath its many leaves; however, grasping the common stem (Convention T), I may succeed in depicting the individual leaves, one by one, and thereby reveal the whole artichoke."[20]

Prior to this option for piecemeal clarification in preference to a generalized account, Davidson's views and mine run closely parallel. He, too, notes the murkiness of the questions often asked about truth.[21] He, too, traces past failures to the notion "that truth must be explained in terms of a relation between a sentence as a whole and some entity, perhaps a fact, or state of affairs."[22] He, too, recommends that attention focus on statements, rather than mere sentences;[23] on components of statements, rather than on statements as wholes; and specifically on the components' conventional uses. "I think there is a fairly simple explanation," he writes, "for our frustration: we have so far left language out of account. Statements are true or false because of the words used in making them, and it is words that have interesting, detailed, conventional connections with the world. Any serious theory of truth must therefore deal with these connections, and it is here if anywhere that the notion of correspondence can find some purchase."[24]

"If I am right," he therefore concludes, "by appealing to Tarski's semantical conception of truth we can defend a theory that almost exactly fits Strawson's description of Austin's 'purified version of the correspondence theory of truth' "[25]—that is, "roughly, . . . to say that a statement is true is to say that a certain speech-episode is related in a certain conventional way to something in the world exclusive of itself." The same description fits my treatment equally well. However, beyond this point our paths diverge; in order to discern the "conventional way" in which true statements connect with the world, I examine the use of *true* in the language which is its home, whereas Davidson examines the standard use of other everyday expressions, but not that of *true* itself. The chief rationale for this omission, it appears, is his acceptance of Tarski's verdict, with which I have shown reason to disagree, that the colloquial concept *true* leads to insoluble antinomies.[26]

Davidson himself notes various limitations which his indirect, formal approach entails, as well as misgivings to which it may legitimately give rise.

> First, it is certainly reasonable to wonder to what extent it will ever be possible to treat a natural language as a formal system, and even more to question whether the resources of the semantical method can begin to encompass such common phenomena as adverbial modification, attributive adjectives, talk of propositional attitudes, of causality, of obligation, and all the rest. At present we do not even have a satisfactory semantics for singular terms, and on this matter many others hang.[27]

Davidson sees reasons, nonetheless, for being optimistic; I see more for being pessimistic. His enterprise appears too reminiscent of the *Tractatus*, with its unredeemed promissory notes, now recognized as unredeemable, and its tendency to suppose "that if anyone utters a sentence and *means* or *understands* it he is operating a calculus according to definite rules."[28]

Consider, for example, the class of attributives, to which Davidson often adverts and on which chapter 6, most of whose sample expressions are attributives, casts new light. "The problem," he explains, "is to frame a truth definition such that ' "Bardot is a good actress" is true if and only if Bardot is a good actress'—and all other sentences like it—are consequences. Obviously 'good actress' does not mean 'good and an actress.' . . . The problem is not peculiar to the case: it is the problem of attributive adjectives generally."[29] Although attributives, when contrasted with nonattributives, may occasion a common problem, it appears improbable that they can all receive a common treatment. Their truth-conditions vary so. Even chapter 6's sampling, restricted to cognitive-comparative attributives, reveals diversity within diversity. *Good* itself has different attributive senses, one comparative ("better than the majority"), the other not ("satisfying the criteria for a good thing of that kind"). Looking farther afield, we note that neither *typical* nor *accurate*, for example, reveals the same cognitive pattern as either use of *good;* nor can *typical* and *accurate* be analyzed identically (the criteria for one are interdependent, those for the other are not). And both these terms, being complex cognitive comparatives, differ in their truth-conditions from simple cognitive comparatives like *big* and *fast*. These latter reveal further diversity, sometimes meaning "bigger than most" or "faster than most," sometimes not, depending on the composition of the subject class. Again, some words have both attributive, cognitive-comparative uses and nonattributive, noncomparative uses. Other samples slip between even these compartmentalizations. (Where, for example, shall we situate the adjective *white* in the expression "white men," or the adjective *beautiful* in the expression "beautiful dancer"?) Such is one small tract of the wilderness

Davidson plans to schematize. And I have ignored the still more varied attributives which are not cognitive comparatives ("utter fool," "third edition," "nuclear physicist," and so forth).

Davidson admits that "there is something arbitrary in how much of logic to pin on logical form."[30] Not all the truth-conditions of a statement can be given uniform treatment or counted as "logical structure." It suffices that we "uncover enough structure to make it possible to state, for an arbitrary sentence, how its meaning depends on that structure, and we must not attribute more structure than such a theory of meaning can accommodate."[31] I suspect there will be a great deal that his theory cannot accommodate. And if, for example, all attributives, despite their great diversity, are somehow stretched on a single Procrustean bed, the theory is likely to obscure more than it reveals.

Witness Davidson's handling of a second difficulty "of the many kinds . . . that must be overcome if we are to have a comprehensive theory of truth for a natural language":

> We have suggested how it might be possible to interpret attributions of truth to statements or to sentences relativized to occasions of use, but only in contexts of the sort provided by the left branch of (7) [Sentence s is true (as English) for speaker u at time t if and only if p]. We have given no indication of how the analysis could be extended to apply to sentences like
>
> (8) It is true that it is raining.
> (9) The statement that it is raining is true.
>
> Here is how we might try to meet the case of (8). We have, we are supposing, a theory of truth-in-English with truth treated as a relation between a sentence, a speaker, and a time. . . . The problem is to find natural counterparts of these elements in (8). A speaker of (8) speaks the words "it is raining," thus performing an act that embodies a particular sentence, has its speaker, and its time. A reference to this act can therefore serve as a reference to the three items needed to apply the theory of truth. The reference we can think of as having been boiled down into the demonstrative 'that' of (8) and (9). A long-winded version of (8) might, then, go like this. First (reversing the order for clarity) I say "It's raining." Then I say *"That* speech act embodied a sentence which, spoken by me now, is true." On this analysis, an utterance of (8) or (9) consists of two logically (semantically) independent speech acts, one of which contains a demonstrative reference to the other.[32]

The same generalizing tendency that vitiated Austin's and Strawson's one-sided accounts (chapter 5) can here be seen at work. And here, as there, it is evident that such a tendency, even if it does not lead "into complete darkness,"[33] may beget more darkness than light. A simpler, more perspicuous, less misleading account than this can be given of the difference between the descriptive and nondescriptive uses of *true*—or of other asymmetrical expressions such as those employed in performatives and avowals. (Again, see chapter 5.)

Mention of these classes of utterances, some true-false, some not, evokes a third difficulty. After citing some of "a staggering list of difficulties and conundrums" that remain to be dealt with by his theory, Davidson adds: "Finally, there are all the sentences that seem not to have truth values at all: the imperatives, optatives, interrogatives, and a host more. A comprehensive theory of meaning for a natural language must cope successfully with each of these problems."[34] So must a comprehensive theory of truth, of Davidson's piecemeal, leaf-by-leaf variety. It must investigate the special logic—the special truth-conditions—of each category or subcategory of statements. And it must determine which categories have truth-conditions. But this it cannot do, as it stands. For it possesses no criterion, such as that provided by chapters 3–8, by which to discriminate between true-false utterances and non-true-false utterances, in the manner of chapters 9–13.

This is no peripheral or picayune detail. As we have seen, some theorists have challenged the truth not only of moral and evaluative utterances, but even of empirical and mathematical statements; whereas others, at the opposite extreme, have claimed truth-status for imperatives, interrogatives, and the full spectrum of performatives. A theory of truth which ignores the everyday concept *true*, both descriptively and normatively, is ill equipped to adjudicate such disputes and trace the borderline of truth; nor is it any better equipped, once the borderline has been drawn, to sort out the truth-conditional patterns that differentiate one class of utterances from another (mathematical from empirical, empirical from moral, moral from performative, and so forth).

Elsewhere Davidson cites still another "of the considerations that have led linguists and philosophers to doubt whether it is possible to give a formal theory of truth for a natural language":

> Bar-Hillel gives an example like this: "They came by slow trains and plane." We can take "slow" as modifying the conjunction that follows, or only "train." Of course an adequate theory would uncover the ambiguity; a theory of truth would in particular need to show how an utterance of the sentence could be true under one interpretation and false under another. So far there is no difficulty for a theory of truth. But Bar-Hillel makes the further observation that the context of utterance might easily resolve the ambiguity for any normal speaker of English, and yet the resolution could depend on general knowledge in a way that could not (practically, at least) be captured by a formal theory. By granting this, as I think we must, we accept a limitation on what a theory of truth can be expected to do. Within the limitation it may still be possible to give a theory that captures an important concept of meaning.[35]

Comparable to this case are shifts in the logic of simple cognitive comparatives such as the notes of chapter 6 imagine or surmise: "tall acrobats" in the majority, for a population of fifty-one seven-footers and fifty five-footers; "small cars" likewise in the majority, when compacts become popular. Far from being mere occasional oddities, such shifts call attention to the exuberant spontaneity of speech, surveyed in chapter 7. Though it brings some order to the chaos, PRS nonetheless contrasts with theories which, like Davidson's, construe the meanings of statements as functions of the meanings of the statements' constituent expressions, without considering any other terms than those employed. The reference to relative similarity suggests a comparison: Davidson's account is Newtonian; mine is Einsteinian. For mine takes due notice of apparent aberrations which in fact reveal a principle that applies to nonextended predications, as well as extended ones. Both types of true utterance, the humdrum as well as the expansive, exemplify a general principle—PRS—for which Davidson makes no allowance. His is a calculus "according to definite rules."

PRS is not a definite rule, sharply dividing true utterances from false or true-false utterances from other varieties; for in neither respect is *true* a sharp concept. As chapter 9 observed and chapter 7 illustrated most fully, "The concepts *true* and *false*, like most others, have a broad, indefinite borderline; and linguistic acts that fall on or within that border rather than on one side or the other cannot truly be described as being or not being true or false. The assertion or denial would lack linguistic backing." Even on those occasions when the concept *true* clearly applies, the constituent concepts of the statements assessed may not.[36] For both these reasons, plus others,[37] many an assertion whose "logical form" is the same as that of assertions which are true or false is neither.

A further complication for Davidson's theory, therefore, is its reliance on a principle which, as Haack observes, makes no allowance for sentences or statements which are neither true nor false.[38] Feed an English sentence like "Fetuses are persons" into Convention T, and it will reject it. Even if relativized to specific times and speakers, " 'Fetuses are persons' is true if and only if fetuses are persons" will fail the test of equivalence. A like difficulty can arise for countless other sentences in any natural language ("It is raining," "My uncle is bald," "Orchids are expensive this year," and the like), since all the concepts of such a language are more or less fuzzy at the border, and specific predications may therefore fall on or within the border, rather than on one side or the other.[39]

Of the shortcomings I have catalogued so far, some are serious, some not; some restricted, some more general. For Davidson, specifically, it is not serious that he lacks a valid criterion by which to separate out true-false utterances from other kinds (imperatives, interrogatives, and so on); he can make use if he wishes of the norm here provided or of the verdicts resulting from its application (for example, in chapters 9–12). For formal semanticists generally, the occurrence of statements that are neither true nor false is not fatal; many-valued logics are available. No formal system, however, either does or reasonably could furnish what seem most necessary—namely, an adequate analysis of truth, and a valid norm of predication, for natural languages.[40] If a Russell, for example, maintains that no one has ever seen a tree, touched a table, or heard a nightingale sing, formal semantics cannot say him nay. Cite him truth-conditions for *see, touch,* and *hear,* and he will want to know where you got them. Tell him you found them in English usage, among the standard applications of these terms, and he will be unimpressed, to say the least.

The implications of this further limitation for Davidson's enterprise can be sensed from the fact that in his theory, T-sentences are to be empirically verifiable. Consider, for example, the sentence Ian Hacking proposes for verification: "The German sentence 'Es regnet' is true if and only if it is raining"; and observe the sample evidence he suggests: " 'Es regnet' is with regularity uttered only when it is in fact raining, by people who are in a position to know that fact, in contexts where some remark about the weather is apropos."[41] Hacking notes that "all sorts of assumptions underlie any use we might make of this simple analysis" and goes on to cite half a dozen. To his list (liberally sprinkled with unchallenged appearances of the words *true* and *truth*) I would add the assumption that we can somehow tell whether "it is in fact raining." Even for so simple an assertion there is a problem. Examples like those in chapter 8 and theories like some in chapter 11 demonstrate the need to ask: How can we know that lights flash? that objects are red? that tables are solid? that people grow up? that animals act? that words have meaning? How can we answer, not fatuous skeptics, but sophisticated thinkers who maintain the contrary? As Esa Itkonen observes, "There is no point in trying to define the *correct* T-sentences in terms of what people actually believe, because they may actually entertain the most curious beliefs."[42]

Reading Davidson's proposals,[43] one is reminded of Bishop Butler's confident declaration: "Let any plain honest man, before he engages in any course of action, ask himself, Is this I am going about right, or is it wrong? Is it good, or is it evil? I do not in the least doubt, but that this question would be answered agreeably to truth and virtue, by almost any fair man in almost any circumstance."[44] In ethics such assurance is clearly misplaced; with regard to even the simplest empirical matters (color attributions, the identity of persons, the object or location of sensations, and so forth) it would not be much more realistic. To be sure, let us be reasonable; let us speak the language as it is spoken; let us say that snow is white, iron is solid, and people see the sun rise. However, as chapters 8–10 attest, the appeal to common sense or to established word use carries little weight in many quarters.

Western culture has long suffered from a form of schizophrenia. Its central concept is *true,* and its central pursuit is truth; yet the concept and the pursuit do not agree. Analysis of the word's standard meaning reveals an implicit norm which is widely resisted in theory and still more widely ignored, especially in speculative inquiry.[45] Reflection on the norm verifies its validity and suggests why the concept, though embattled, has survived; linguistic correspondence merits the massive, albeit unreflective recognition it still receives as arbiter of truth. Yet, repeatedly, resoundingly, its authority is repudiated both in word and in act. An important reason for this schism, I suggest, has been the lack of an adequate analysis of the concept *true,* and the consequent lack of an adequate defense of the norm the concept enshrines. Neither Tarski nor Davidson fills either of these lacunae; my principal aim in this study has been to fill both.

NOTES

Preface

1. This is Alvin Goldman's view, as summarized by Hilary Putnam in his *Philosophical Papers*, vol. 3, *Realism and Reason* (Cambridge: Cambridge University Press, 1983), p. 200.

Introduction to Part 1

1. Max Black, *Models and Metaphors: Studies in Language and Philosophy* (Ithaca, N.Y.: Cornell University Press, 1962), p. 69.
2. Samuel Gorovitz, Merrill Hintikka, Donald Provence, and Ron G. Williams, *Philosophical Analysis: An Introduction to Its Language and Techniques*, 3d ed. (New York: Random House, 1979), p. 139.
3. Ibid., pp. 139–40. In like vein, see Wolfgang Stegmüller, *Das Wahrheitsproblem und die Idee der Semantik: Ein Einführung in die Theorien von A. Tarski und R. Carnap* (Vienna: Springer, 1957), pp. 15–16, 219–21. For remarks on this procedure which complement mine, see Winfried Franzen, *Die Bedeutung von 'wahr' und 'Wahrheit': Analysen zum Wahrheitsbegriff und zu einigen neueren Wahrheitstheorien* (Freiburg and Munich: Karl Alber, 1982), pp. 16–17.
4. William James, *Pragmatism* (Cambridge, Mass.: Harvard University Press, 1975), pp. 96–97.
5. Quoted in John W. Yolton, "Philosophical and Scientific Explanation," *Journal of Philosophy* 55 (1958): 137.

Chapter 1: The Isomorphic Tradition

1. Ludwig Wittgenstein, *Philosophical Investigations*, trans. G. E. M. Anscombe, 2d ed. (Oxford: Blackwell, 1967), §96.
2. Though often used in the sense of mere matching, the term *isomorphism* is sometimes given a fuller sense like that of *correspondence*. See, e.g., Albert Wohlstetter, "The Structure of the Proposition and the Fact," *Philosophy of Science* 3 (1936): 168–69.
3. Clement of Alexandria *Stromata*, 8, ch. 8, n. 23.
4. John Wisdom's formulation is broad enough to cover all versions. A judgment or a proposition is true, he explains, if it accords with the facts; more specifically, "'My judgment that Cameronian beat Orpen *accords* with a fact' means 'There is some fact such that (i) the elements in that fact are identical with the objective constituents in my judgment, (ii) the order of the elements in the judgment *reflects* the order of the elements in the fact'" (*Problems of Mind and Matter* [Cambridge: Cambridge University Press, 1963], p. 202).
5. Plato *Sophist* 263–64.

6. Frederick Copleston, *A History of Philosophy*, vol. 1 (London: Burns and Oates, 1966), p. 187. Copleston cautions: "To postulate Forms of Sitting and Flying may be a logical application of Plato's principles, but it obviously raises great difficulties. Aristotle implies that the upholders of the Ideal Theory did not go beyond postulating Ideas of natural substances (*Met.* 1079a)." And Plato's misgivings in the *Parmenides* are well known (see ibid., p. 181).

   For a different interpretation of the *Sophist*, which does not stress forms, see, e.g., W. K. C. Guthrie, *A History of Greek Philosophy*, vol. 5 (Cambridge: Cambridge University Press, 1978), pp. 155–56. My interest extends beyond the *Sophist* to Plato's thinking as a whole and to its influence: to subject-predicate dichotomy, unitary reference for each part, and truth achieved through symbolic combination, according as the referents are similarly joined.

7. Aristotle *Metaphysics* 9. 10. 1051b3 (trans. W. D. Ross, in *The Basic Works of Aristotle*, ed. R. McKeon [New York: Random House, 1941], p. 833). See also ibid., 9. 10. 1027b, and *On the Soul* 430a, b; Marten Ringbom, "Thoughts and Facts—An Aristotelian Problem," *Ajatus* 34 (1972): 9–18.

8. Aquinas *Summa theologiae* I, q. 16, a. 2 (trans. Thomas Gornall in vol. 4 of the Blackfriars edition [New York: McGraw-Hill, 1964], p. 81). See also ibid., q. 16, a. 3; q. 17, a. 3; q. 58, a. 5; idem, *De veritate*, q. 1, a. 3; idem, *In Perihermenias* I, lect. 8, n. 3; idem, *In IX Metaphysicorum*, lect. 11, n. 1898; Patrick Lee, "Aquinas on Knowledge of Truth and Existence," *The New Scholasticism* 60 (1986): 46–71; Gerald B. Phelan, "Verum Sequitur Esse Rerum," in *Philosophy of Knowledge: Selected Readings*, ed. R. Houde and J. Mullally (Philadelphia: Lippincott, 1960), pp. 205, 210–15; Steven P. Marrone, *William of Auvergne and Robert Grosseteste: New Ideas of Truth in the Early Thirteenth Century* (Princeton: Princeton University Press, 1983), pp. 83–84.

9. Aquinas *Summa* I, q. 16, a. 8, *ad* 3 and 4. See also ibid., q. 13, a. 1.

10. Locke, *An Essay concerning Human Understanding*, book 4, ch. 5, n. 6 (A. C. Fraser edition, Oxford: Clarendon Press, 1894).

11. Aquinas *Summa* I, q. 84, a. 1.

12. Aquinas *In XII Metaphysicorum*, lect. 8, n. 2541. "Aquinas often uses the word 'similitude' in this context because while there is identity in form or content, the mode of being of the form in the thing is different from its mode of being in the intellect's act, and 'similitude' means identity in form together with difference in other aspects" (Lee, "Aquinas," p. 58, citing *Summa* I, q. 4, a. 3, and q. 93, a. 9).

13. Locke, *Essay*, book 3, ch. 3, n. 6; see also book 2, ch. 11, n. 9.

14. Ibid., book 3, ch. 3, n. 12.

15. Aquinas *Truth*, vol. 1, trans. R. Mulligan (Chicago: Henry Regnery, 1952), p. 425 (q. 9, a. 4).

16. Ibid.

17. Locke, *Essay*, book 3, ch. 2, n. 7; see also book 2, ch. 18, n. 7; book 3, ch. 9, n. 4.

18. Ibid., book 3, ch. 9, n. 4; see also book 3, ch. 9, n. 6.

19. Ibid., book 2, ch. 18, n. 2. On Locke's "thought-transference theory of communication," see Godfrey Vesey, "Locke and Wittgenstein on Language and Reality," in *Contemporary British Philosophy*, 4th ser., ed. H. D. Lewis (London: Allen and Unwin, 1976), pp. 254–60.

20. Locke, *Essay*, book 2, ch. 22, n. 9.

21. George Berkeley, *A Treatise concerning the Principles of Human Knowledge*, part 1, nn. 10–13.

22. Bertrand Russell, *The Analysis of Mind* (London: Allen and Unwin, 1921), pp. 273–74. See also idem, *The Problems of Philosophy* (New York: Oxford University Press, 1959), pp. 125–28.

23. Bertrand Russell, *Logic and Knowledge: Essays 1901–1950*, ed. R. C. Marsh (London: Allen and Unwin, 1956), p. 319.

24. Ibid., p. 308.

25. Wittgenstein, *Philosophical Investigations*, §449. "It is now fairly commonplace for philosophers to pursue Berkeley's line of questioning and conclude that some terms fail to have corresponding mental images. This point of view was anything but a truism for 19th century German psychology. Titchener, for example, claimed that all thought was imagistic and sought by introspection to describe the pictures associated with words like 'but,' 'patriotism,' and 'triangularity'" (Elliott Sober, "Mental Representations," *Synthese* 33 [1976]: 102).

26. Augustine *Confessions*, book 10, ch. 8.

27. Ibid., book 10, ch. 15 (my translation). This passage makes clear that the word *image* is not synonymous with *visual image*.

28. Russell, *Logic and Knowledge*, p. 302. See also Henry H. Price, *Thinking and Experience*, 2d ed. (London: Hutchinson, 1969), pp. 253–54.

29. Russell, *Analysis of Mind*, p. 278.

30. Ludwig Wittgenstein, *Tractatus Logico-Philosophicus*, trans. D. F. Pears and B. F. McGuinness (London: Routledge and Kegan Paul, 1961). The parenthetical references in the text are *Tractatus* numbers.

31. See also Ludwig Wittgenstein, *Notebooks 1914–1916*, ed. G. H. von Wright and G. E. M. Anscombe, trans. G. E. M. Anscombe (Oxford: Blackwell, 1961), p. 53.

32. Ibid., p. 68.

33. Garth L. Hallett, *A Companion to Wittgenstein's "Philosophical Investigations"* (Ithaca: Cornell University Press, 1977), p. 39. I have deleted many parenthetical references; those that remain are to manuscripts in Wittgenstein's *Nachlass*.

34. William James, *The Principles of Psychology* (London: Macmillan, 1901), vol. 1, pp. 219, 252, 281.

35. Aquinas *De veritate*, q. 1, a. 2.

36. Ibid., q. 1, a. 1.

37. See J. L. Mackie, *Problems from Locke* (Oxford: Clarendon Press, 1976), pp. 85–88.

38. Aquinas *De veritate*, q. 4, a. 1. Compare Plato *Cratylus* 389d; Augustine *De Trinitate*, book 15, ch. 10, n. 19; James, *Principles of Psychology*, vol. 1, p. 29.

39. Aristotle *De interpretatione* 16a. Compare Clement of Alexandria, n. 3 above, and Roy Harris's account of the medieval *modistae* (*The Language-Makers* [Ithaca: Cornell University Press, 1980], p. 66).

40. Locke, *Essay*, book 3, ch. 7, n. 1.

41. Wittgenstein, *Tractatus*, 4.0312; idem, *Notebooks 1914–1916*, p. 119.

42. G. E. Moore, *Some Main Problems of Philosophy* (New York: Allen and Unwin, 1967), p. 301.

Chapter 2: Critique of Isomorphism

1. See Gerasimos X. Santas, *Socrates: Philosophy in Plato's Early Dialogues* (London: Routledge and Kegan Paul, 1979), pp. 93–96, on Socrates; or G. P. Baker and P. M. S. Hacker, *Wittgenstein: Understanding and Meaning* (Chicago: University of Chicago, 1980), p. 56, on Russell.

2. W. David Ross, *Plato's Theory of Ideas* (Oxford: Clarendon Press, 1951), p. 225.

3. Plato *Theaetetus* 146E; idem, *Euthyphro* 6D.

4. See Plato *Republic* 596A6–8: "We have been in the habit, if you remember, of positing a Form, wherever we use the same name in many instances, one Form for each many."

5. For an indication of isomorphism's continuing appeal, see Thomas Storer, "Linguistic Isomorphisms," *Philosophy of Science* 19 (1952): 78; Robert N. Binkley, "Change of Belief or Change of Meaning?," in *Conceptual Change*, ed. G. Pearce and P. Maynard (Dordrecht: Reidel, 1973), p. 63; N. J. Brown, "Judgment and the Structure of Language," *Proceedings of the Aristotelian Society* 52 (1951–52): 23.

6. James, *Pragmatism*, p. 96. Compare Franz Brentano, *The True and the Evident*, ed. O. Kraus;

English ed. R. Chisholm, trans. R. Chisholm, I. Politzer, and K. Fischer (New York: Humanities Press, 1966), p. 21. For difficulties not raised here, see pp. 16–19.

7. See Wittgenstein, *Philosophical Investigations*, §396; William P. Alston, "Meaning," in *The Encyclopedia of Philosophy*, ed. P. Edwards, vol. 5 (New York and London: Macmillan, 1967), p. 235.

8. Actually, an image is not blue in the same sense that an object is; in the case of the image, there is no contrast between being blue and looking or seeming blue.

9. Sober, "Mental Representations," p. 102.

10. Quoted in Roger Brown, *Words and Things* (Glencoe, Ill.: Free Press, 1958), p. 91.

11. See Ludwig Wittgenstein, *The Blue and Brown Books* (Oxford: Blackwell, 1960), pp. 36–37.

12. See ibid., pp. 31–32.

13. Similarly, "nothing in the picture itself carries the message that it reproduces reality in this way. Pictures are not by their nature assertions" (Keith Graham, *J. L. Austin: A Critique of Ordinary Language Philosophy* [Atlantic Heights, N.J.: Humanities Press, 1977], p. 189).

14. James, *Pragmatism*, p. 102.

15. On occasion, James identifies truth, not with verification, but with verifiability. The potency, however, must be understood in terms of the act, not vice versa. Truth as verification is the primary notion.

16. See, e.g., *Translations from the Philosophical Writings of Gottlob Frege*, ed. P. Geach and M. Black, 2d ed. (Oxford: Blackwell, 1970), p. 194a: "Signs would hardly be useful if they did not serve the purpose of signifying the same thing repeatedly and in different contexts, while making evident that the same thing was meant." By "same thing" Frege evidently did not mean merely "thing(s) signified by the same sign."

17. Wittgenstein, *Philosophical Investigations*, §67.

18. See Garth L. Hallett, *Logic for the Labyrinth: A Guide to Critical Thinking* (Lanham, Md.: University Press of America, 1984), pp. 29–31. I have found it necessary to point out that in speaking of these various possibilities I am not speaking of rival theories or alternative generalizations; I am not proposing various essences of general terms with a view to some single definition.

19. Ludwig Wittgenstein, *Philosophical Remarks*, trans. R. Hargreaves and R. White (Oxford: Blackwell, 1975), p. 63.

20. Ludwig Wittgenstein, *Lectures and Conversations on Aesthetics, Psychology and Religious Belief*, ed. C. Barrett (Oxford: Blackwell, 1966), p. 67.

21. Wittgenstein, *Philosophical Investigations*, §107.

Chapter 3: Linguistic Truth

1. Wittgenstein, *Blue and Brown Books*, p. 42. The word *calculus* carries connotations of ideal precision and rigor against which Wittgenstein would later warn (e.g., in *Philosophical Investigations*, §81).

2. According to the view I shall propose, isomorphists were right: the truth of judgments or statements does consist in correspondence, in the straightforward sense of resemblance. James was right too: the correspondence does not consist in mental copying. But both were mistaken in largely ignoring language, and therefore taking no note of linguistic correspondence.

3. I address the issue of truth-bearers in chapter 4, and indicate multiple respects in which the application of *true* to statements is primary. In a typical instance of what chapter 10 characterizes as "calculus reasoning," it has been objected that we do not speak of acts as true, and that it is therefore deviant to speak of speech acts as true. Similar argumentation, if valid, would tell equally against true utterances, since they too are acts; against true sentences, since they are groupings of words, and we do not call groupings true; against

true beliefs, since beliefs are dispositions, and we do not call dispositions true; and so forth. Though fallacious, such reasoning is all too common.

4. Some linguists might deny that words, names, and the like have meaning, save indirectly; this disagreement, however, seems mainly verbal. See, e.g., Wallace L. Chafe, *Meaning and the Structure of Language* (Chicago: University of Chicago Press, 1970), p. 74.

5. Friedrich Waismann, *How I See Philosophy*, ed. R. Harré (New York: St. Martin's Press, 1968), p. 173.

6. Chapter 6 calls them *cognitive comparatives*, for reasons explained there.

7. In "Token Sentences, Translation and Truth-Value," *Mind* 79 (1970): 45, R. J. Haack and Susan Haack appear to overlook these aspects of truth, plus others, when they write: "It is still open to speak of *some* sentence-types as being true or false; we propose, for instance, the following condition under which we might do so:

(H) A sentence-type will take the truth-value 'true' if all its token instances are true, and will take the truth-value 'false' if all its token instances are false.

On this condition a sentence-type will lack a truth-value if, either, at least one token instance of it is neither true nor false, or one token instance of it is true and another false." No sentence-types, I would say, including those given as examples, ever satisfy either of the conditions stated in (H). For instance, "3 + 2 = 2 + 3," cited as always true, does not; nor does "4 > 3 + 2," cited as always false. In answer to many a question, the first might be false, the second true. In many a context neither might make sense.

8. From another perspective, to understand the interplay of truth-making conditions in an utterance would be to grasp how we come to understand new utterances using familiar expressions according to familiar rules. See Bernard Harrison, *An Introduction to the Philosophy of Language* (New York: St. Martin's Press, 1979), p. 212.

9. It is in this Wittgensteinian sense that I shall generally use the term *criterion* and not in the other common sense of a sure extrinsic clue.

10. On what we do say, see Herman Tennessen, "Vindication of the Humpty Dumpty Attitude towards Language," *Inquiry*, 3 (1960): 187ff.

11. In confirmation, see Frederic T. Sommers, *The Logic of Natural Language* (Oxford: Oxford University Press, 1982), p. 209: "Thus 'my car broke down' in excuse of lateness is false and not merely 'misleading' if I have no car." In the context of Sommers's discussion, *false* is not misleading; as a reply to the excuse, it probably would be. Hence the restriction on *false* does not hold for all utterances that lack reference, but for certain contexts in which they are referred to.

12. Susan Haack, *Philosophy of Logics* (Cambridge: Cambridge University Press, 1978), p. 86.

13. My account goes beyond Wittgenstein, but in a direction suggested by his later writings. In the light, say, of Manuscript 116, p. 110, in Wittgenstein's *Nachlass*, I would put more weight on §§241 and 429 in the *Investigations* than on the Ramseyan equivalence at the start of §136. See my *Companion*, e.g., pp. 118, 236–37, 463–65, 467. For a contrary reading, see, e.g., Saul Kripke, *Wittgenstein on Rules and Private Language* (Cambridge, Mass.: Harvard University Press, 1982), p. 86.

14. Ludwig Wittgenstein, *Zettel*, ed. G. E. M. Anscombe and G. H. von Wright, trans. G. E. M. Anscombe (Oxford: Blackwell, 1967), p. 31.

15. Wittgenstein, *Philosophical Investigations*, §429.

16. Wittgenstein, Manuscript 109, p. 191.

Chapter 4: The Primacy of Linguistic Truth

1. Wittgenstein, *Blue and Brown Books*, p. 3.

2. Bertrand Russell, *Philosophical Essays* (New York: Simon and Schuster, 1966), pp. 148–49.

See, e.g., John H. Muirhead, "The Problem of Truth and Some Principles in Aid of Its Solution," in *The Problem of Truth*, ed. G. Adams, J. Loewenberg, and S. Pepper (Berkeley: University of California Press, 1928), pp. 5–6; W. R. Dennes, "Practice as the Test of Truth," in *The Problem of Truth*, p. 89 ("Truth is a character which all serious judgments claim, and which nothing but a judgment can claim"); J. Loewenberg, "The Fourfold Root of Truth," in *The Problem of Truth*, p. 210 ("From the bald assertion that there is no truth without judgment few philosophers would perhaps dissent").

3. Brentano, *The True and the Evident*, p. 6.

4. See also Hugo Meynell, "Truth, Witchcraft and Professor Winch," *Heythrop Journal* 13 (1972): 166.

5. See Hallett, *Companion*, pp. 43, 463–65; Philip Wheelwright, *Metaphor and Reality* (Bloomington, Ind.: Indiana University Press, 1962), pp. 26–29.

6. To say that the content of a person's belief is fixed linguistically does not signify, of course, that the object is itself linguistic, any more than to say that the referent of a statement is determined by the words it employs implies that the referent is linguistic.

7. See H. P. Grice, "Meaning," *Philosophical Review* 66 (1957): 387; Peter A. Facione, "Meaning and Intending," *American Philosophical Quarterly* 10 (1973), pp. 280–81.

8. See John Finnis, *Fundamentals of Ethics* (Washington, D.C.: Georgetown University Press, 1983), p. 63; D. W. Hamlyn, "The Correspondence Theory of Truth," *Philosophical Quarterly* 12 (1962): 200.

9. D. R. Cousin, "Truth," *Proceedings of the Aristotelian Society*, suppl. vol. 24 (1950): 164.

10. "The lesson of Grice's early work must be that a complete theory of meaning will provide compatible theories of signification and utterer's-meaning without identifying the two. Questions will arise as to which kind of meaning is more primitive and whether one kind is definable in terms of the other or not" (Facione, "Meaning," p. 281). See also Garth L. Hallett, *Darkness and Light: The Analysis of Doctrinal Statements* (New York: Paulist Press, 1975), pp. 9–11.

11. Wilfrid Sellars, *Science, Perception, and Reality* (London: Routledge and Kegan Paul, 1963), p. 200.

12. John Stuart Mill, *A System of Logic Ratiocinative and Inductive*, 10th ed. (London: Longmans, Green, 1879), vol. 1, p. 18. Compare Alan R. White, *Truth* (Garden City, N.J.: Doubleday, 1970), p. 8: "It is what is said, and not what is done when one says something, that is true or false."

13. Frank P. Ramsey, *The Foundations of Mathematics and Other Logical Essays*, ed. R. Braithwaite (London: Routledge and Kegan Paul, 1931), p. 142.

14. A. J. Ayer, *Language, Truth and Logic*, 2d ed. (New York: Dover, 1952), p. 88. See also A. C. Ewing, *The Fundamental Questions of Philosophy* (London: Routledge and Kegan Paul, 1951), p. 54; Geoffrey Warnock, "A Problem about Truth," in *Truth*, ed. G. Pitcher (Englewood Cliffs, N.J.: Prentice-Hall, 1964), p. 55; Irving Copi, *Symbolic Logic*, 2d ed. (New York: Macmillan, 1965), p. 4.

15. Ayer, *Language, Truth and Logic*, p. 88. See also White, *Truth*, pp. 15–18.

16. Priority such as I have noted between verbal truth and mental or propositional truth, some have extended to other cases, not treated here. See Meynell, "Truth, Witchcraft and Professor Winch," p. 166; Bernard Mayo, "Truth as Appraisal," *Mind* 68 (1959): 81.

17. Moore, *Some Main Problems of Philosophy*, p. 64.

18. Brentano, *The True and the Evident*, p. 5.

19. Think, for instance, of successive, independent derivations from the same root sense (e.g., *square* for a location, then *square* for a person).

20. Wittgenstein, *Philosophical Investigations*, p. 216.

21. The difference between these two sorts of dependence comes out in Jeffrey Tlumak's definitions: "Xs are identificationally prior to Ys *iff* for any person S, S could not identify

things of kind Y without reference to things of kind X, but not conversely. . . . Xs are conceptually prior to Ys *iff* for any person S, S could not understand what it is to be a Y (have the concept Y . . .) without understanding what it is to be an X, but not conversely" ("Cross-Categorial Priority Arguments," *Metaphilosophy* 14 [1983]: 32).

22. Such operational dependence should also be distinguished from definitional dependence of the kind Gilbert Ryle asserts, rightly or wrongly, when he writes: "Knowing is not one definable species of 'consciousness of . . .' among others, it is something anyhow partly in terms of which believing, fancying, guessing, wanting and the rest have to be defined. Belief, *e.g.*, is a state of mind involving *ignorance* of such and such a *knowledge* of so and so: it involves more than that, but at least it involves this double reference to knowledge" ("Phenomenology," in *Analytic Philosophy and Phenomenology*, ed. H. Durfee [The Hague: Nijhoff, 1976], p. 26). From the fact that I cannot define *X* without using the word *Y*, it does not follow that I cannot use *X* without applying the criteria for *Y*. For further refinements and related distinctions, see William P. Alston, *Philosophy of Language* (Englewood Cliffs, N.J.: Prentice-Hall, 1964), pp. 101–02.

23. See, e.g., Aquinas, *De veritate*, q. 9, a. 4.

Chapter 5: Performatives, Avowals, and the Asymmetry of *True*

1. I agree with Austin that true opinions, propositions, and the like are best explained in terms of true utterances, and true utterances in terms of the agreement between their use of words and the words' established uses. I shall here argue, however, that he slighted the nondescriptive uses of *true*, which lend such plausibility to Strawson's counterclaims. And the specific manner in which he spelled out the agreement with established word uses leaves many true-false utterances out of account. See Peter F. Strawson, "Truth: A Reconsideration of Austin's Views," *Philosophical Quarterly* 15 [1965]: 294. Further differences will become apparent in chapters 9 and 10.

2. John Austin, "Truth," in *Truth*, ed. Pitcher, p. 19.
3. Ibid.
4. Ibid., p. 20.
5. Ibid.
6. Ibid., p. 22.
7. Geoffrey Warnock later suggested, and Austin apparently approved, a revision like the following: "A statement is said to be true when the historic state of affairs to which the words used in making it are, as *then* used, correlated by demonstrative conventions is of a type with which those words are, *standardly*, correlated by descriptive conventions." See Strawson, "Truth: A Reconsideration," p. 290.
8. Austin, "Truth," p. 31.
9. Peter Strawson, "Truth," in *Truth*, ed. Pitcher, pp. 52–53.
10. Ibid., p. 33.
11. Ibid., p. 34.
12. Ibid., p. 33.
13. Ibid., p. 34.
14. As I note in the next chapter, in ordinary parlance, "talk about" abstracts from cognitive content and focuses on verbal formulation. (E.g., "big dog" may be equivalent to "dog bigger than the average dog"; yet, when I say a dog is big, I am not "talking about" other dogs.) It is far from evident, though, that Strawson intends any such restriction when he debates the "actual functioning of the word 'true.'"
15. Austin himself observes: "Names for speech-acts are more numerous, more specialised, more ambiguous and more significant than is ordinarily allowed for: none of them can be safely used in philosophy in a general way (*e.g.*, 'statement' or 'description') without more

investigation than they have, I think, yet received" ("How to Talk," *Proceedings of the Aristotelian Society* 53 [1952–53]: 243).

16. On "blind uses," such as *"Whatever* the pope says is true," see, e.g., Peter Geach, *Mental Acts: Their Content and Their Objects* (New York: Humanities Press, 1957), p. 97; Gertrude Ezorsky, "Performative Theory of Truth," in *The Encyclopedia of Philosophy,* ed. P. Edwards, vol. 6, pp. 89–90; idem, "Truth in Context," *Journal of Philosophy* 60 (1963): 117, 123; White, *Truth,* p. 94; J. Kincade, "On the Performatory Theory of Truth," *Mind* 67 (1958): 395; John Knox, Jr., "Truth, Correspondence, and Ordinary Language," *Personalist* 52 (1971): 519–20; L. Jonathan Cohen, "Mr. Strawson's Analysis of Truth," *Analysis* 10 (1949–50): 136–40; Richard T. De George, "Reason, Truth, and Context," *Idealistic Studies* 4 (1974): 39.

17. Or in others. For other samples, which, though not "blind," likewise cast doubt on the alleged eliminability of *true,* see Bede Rundle, *Grammar in Philosophy* (Oxford: Oxford University Press, 1979), p. 359. In a later paper Strawson acknowledged that "at least part of what anyone does who says that a statement is true is to make a statement about a statement" ("A Problem About Truth—A Reply to Mr. Warnock," in *Truth,* ed. Pitcher, p. 69).

18. See Warnock, "A Problem About Truth," p. 63.

19. Chapter 9 distinguishes between certain performatives which are true-false, for a different reason, and the majority, which are not.

20. John Austin, *Philosophical Papers* (Oxford: Clarendon Press, 1961), p. 222.

21. For a still more diversified account, see Strawson's review of Wittgenstein's *Philosophical Investigations,* in *Wittgenstein: The Philosophical Investigations,* ed. G. Pitcher (Garden City, N.Y.: Doubleday, 1966), p. 56. On the asymmetry of psychological verbs, see also Norman Malcolm, *Problems of Mind: Descartes to Wittgenstein* (New York: Harper and Row, 1971), pp. 82–91.

22. Wittgenstein, *Philosophical Investigations,* §441.

23. Ibid., §452.

24. See William Hasker, "Theories, Analogies, and Criteria," *American Philosophical Quarterly* 8 (1971): 247; Peter F. Strawson, *Individuals: An Essay in Descriptive Metaphysics* (London: Methuen, 1959), pp. 104–05.

25. Wittgenstein, *Philosophical Investigations,* p. 192.

26. Wittgenstein, Manuscript 169.

Chapter 6: Cognitive Comparatives and *True*

1. Antoine Arnauld, *The Art of Thinking. Port-Royal Logic,* trans. J. Dickoff and P. James (Indianapolis: Bobbs-Merrill, 1964), p. 90.

2. Ibid., p. 33. See also Price, *Thinking and Experience,* p. 261, on talk about universals, abstract ideas, concepts, and even images: "People introduced them because they wanted to make clear to themselves how it is that *thinking,* though conducted in absence, could nevertheless be a form of *cognition,* in touch with the real world" (emphasis added).

3. See, e.g., Hallett, *Darkness and Light,* pp. 21–22, 25–28.

4. For a typical class—of dogs, cats, hats, trees, nails, or noses—"larger than average" is roughly equivalent to "larger than most"; and the difference between these two, when and if there is one, is not known or attended to by speakers. Hence I shall use the two expressions interchangeably when discussing cognitive comparatives.

5. They are sometimes referred to as "relative" expressions, but that is a broad, vague characterization, covering many other terms as well.

6. See Carl G. Hempel, *Fundamentals of Concept Formation in Empirical Science* (Chicago: University of Chicago Press, 1952), p. 54.

7. Friedrich Waismann, "Are There Alternative Logics?," *Proceedings of the Aristotelian Society* 46 (1945–46): 86–87.

8. Compare "the rush of shoppers" and "the rush of traffic," "He rushed from the room" and "The jet rushed down the runway," "She walked quickly" and "She ran quickly." Many a cognitive comparative is also an *attributive*—that is, "an adjective or adverb which, when paired with a substantive or stuff-predicate or verb, yields sentences which cannot correctly be given a conjunctive account" (Samuel C. Wheeler III, "Attributives and Their Modifiers," *Nous* 6 [1972]: 311). "That's a big tent," for example, is not equivalent to "That's big" and "That's a tent," whereas "That's a plastic tent" is equivalent to "That is plastic" and "That is a tent." However, the two classes of expressions—attributives and cognitive comparatives—are not coextensive. Many attributives (e.g., *partial, former, alleged, fake, left-handed*) are not cognitive comparatives in the sense just explained, and many cognitive comparatives (e.g., verbs and nouns) are not attributives. *True* is of their number when used, for instance, of statements. On predicative versus attributive uses of *true*, see White, *Truth*, pp. 3–4.

9. See Zeno Vendler, "The Grammar of Goodness," *Philosophical Review* 72 (1963): 450. Noting a rare use of *red*, in "red lobster," which he assimilates to the use of terms like *big*, Wheeler concludes that *red*, too, and "most of the words that occur in what grammarians call 'attributive position' are really two-place predicates and cannot correctly be given a conjunctive account" ("Attributives and Their Modifiers," p. 331). Once an attributive, always an attributive. Consider what such reasoning might make of an item like that noted by Max Black: "If I'm using the 'white' pieces on the chess board, 'white' there may cover green, gray, a great many colors" ("Logic and Ordinary Language," in *Language, Belief, and Metaphysics*, ed. H. Kiefer and M. Munitz [Albany: State University of New York Press, 1970], p. 47).

10. Midway between *red* and *big* fall numerous terms such as *rude* and *devout*, which are, in a sense, comparative, yet differ in important ways from *big* and its kin. A "devout Muslim" is likely to be a devout person (devout in comparison with people in general) who happens to be a Muslim, not a Muslim more devout than most Muslims.

11. See Nicholas Rescher, *The Logic of Commands* (New York: Dover, 1966), p. 9: "From the fact that Smith *said* 'No Tuesdays are sunny days' on some occasion it certainly does not follow that Smith *said* 'No sunny days are Tuesdays' on that occasion, although to be sure the second quoted statement is logically equivalent with the first."

12. Haig Khatchadourian, "Truth," *Man and World* 2 (1969): 73.

13. See Patrick Sherry, *Religion, Truth and Language-Games* (New York: Barnes and Noble, 1977), pp. 173–75.

14. See John Knox, *Myth and Truth: An Essay on the Language of Faith* (Charlottesville: University Press of Virginia, 1964), pp. 18–19. For more in the same vein, see Friedrich Waismann, "Language Strata," in *Logic and Language*, 2d ser., ed. A. Flew (Oxford: Blackwell, 1966), p. 23; Donald A. Wells, "Some Implications of Empirical Truth by Convention," *Journal of Philosophy* 48 (1951): 185–86. A discussion of mathematical truth in an earlier, longer version of the present book concluded: "The composition of forces, and therefore the correspondence, works out differently for a typical mathematical proposition like 'Seven times eleven is seventy-seven' than it does for a typical empirical proposition like 'It rained all night.' "

15. Stephen D. Ross, "Truth in Science: Unrestricted Validity," *Transactions of the Charles S. Peirce Society* 6 (1970): 47.

16. J. O. Wisdom, "Conventionalism, Truth, and Cosmological Furniture," *Canadian Journal of Philosophy* 4 (1974–75): 443.

17. Contrast the familiar, yet misleading, way of speaking: "So great are the cultural shifts, says Dillenberger, that 'contradictory statements made in different cultural periods may in fact

be closer to one another than the repetition of the same statements from different cultural periods'" (Avery Dulles, *The Survival of Dogma* [Garden City, N.Y.: Doubleday, 1971], p. 19, quoting John Dillenberger, *Contours of Faith* [Nashville, Tenn.: Abingdon Press, 1969], p. 35). These "contradictory statements" are sentences which in different circumstances than those described might be used to make contradictory assertions.

18. The distinction is not as sharp as it might appear at first glance. See J. A. W. Kamp, "Two Theories about Adjectives," in *Formal Semantics of Natural Language,* ed. Edward L. Keenan (Cambridge: Cambridge University Press, 1975), p. 141.

19. The word *average* itself has been suggested. For suppose one person asks, "Is she intelligent?," and another replies, "Just average." The answer places her midway between *stupid* and *bright.* It does so, however, thanks to the adjective *intelligent;* by itself it does not place her anywhere on any continuum, as *large* or *intelligent* does. In this it resembles *rather:* "*Rather* forms adjectives out of adjectives, e.g. *rather tall* out of *tall, rather clever* out of *clever,* etc." (Kamp, "Two Theories about Adjectives," p. 145), which then mark off a narrow, almost central zone.

20. Wheeler objects: "My problem with this analysis arises from the following sort of case: The population of acrobats consists [let us suppose] of 101 individuals, 51 of which are exactly seven feet tall, and 50 of which are exactly five feet tall. It seems to me that the 51 are tall acrobats, but they are not taller than most acrobats" ("Attributives and Their Modifiers," p. 319; see also John Wallace, "Positive, Comparative, Superlative," *Journal of Philosophy* 69 [1972]: 777). With Wittgenstein, I would answer that if we imagine certain general features of the world or some segment of it to be different from what we are used to, as here, our terms may indeed then have quite different meanings—or none at all. I am describing the meanings that *tall, big,* and the like typically have in the world as it actually is. (Compare the critique of Graham in chapter 9.)

   An objection of Kamp ("Two Theories about Adjectives," p. 126) draws attention to a possible real-life analog of Wheeler's hypothesis. What in England are called "small cars," notes Kamp, are a majority of cars in England. In reply, one might point out that they are not called "small *English* cars." However, given recent trends, the cars called "small" in England may belong to the majority of cars worldwide.

21. Doubtless the availability of negatives largely accounts for this fact, since a minority term together with a negative does designate a majority. (A majority of dogs are *not small, not large,* and so forth.)

22. Such is the lesson of Wheeler's objection, in n. 20 above.

23. Compare Ernst Cassirer, *The Logic of the Humanities* (New Haven: Yale University Press, 1961), p. 137.

24. A case might perhaps be made that for basic terms to acquire the meanings they have, the majority of their uses must be truthful. See Wittgenstein, *Philosophical Investigations,* §§240–42; idem, *On Certainty,* trans. Denis Paul and G. E. M. Anscombe, ed. G. E. M. Anscombe and G. H. von Wright (Oxford: Blackwell, 1969), p. 59.

25. Thus, whereas for Patrick Nowell-Smith, "comparisons are always implied" in the use of the word *good* ("The Meaning of 'Good,'" in *Readings in Ethical Theory,* 2d ed., ed. W. Sellars and J. Hospers [New York: Appleton-Century-Crofts, 1970], p. 309, Dorothy Mitchell makes no mention of a comparative sense when she writes: "To make the more general claim that something is good is to claim either that it has the appropriate virtues for a thing of its kind, or that it has some virtues appropriate to its kind, or that it has some virtues, or, as in the claim that courage is good, that it *is* a virtue" ("The Truth or Falsity of Value Judgments," *Mind* 81 [1972]: 67).

26. "'Good' in this usage means 'better than average' or perhaps 'considerably better than average,' and 'bad' 'worse than the average' or 'considerably worse than the average'" (W. David Ross, *The Right and the Good* [Oxford: Clarendon Press, 1930], p. 67). See also David L. Perry, "What Things Can Be Evaluated?" *Journal of Philosophy* 61 (1964): 188–92;

Nowell-Smith, "The Meaning of 'Good,' " p. 309. Whether used comparatively or noncomparatively, *good* is still an attributive. See Peter Geach, "Good and Evil," *Analysis* 17 (1956–57): 33–34.

27. See Richard M. Hare, *The Language of Morals* (Oxford: Clarendon Press, 1952), p. 138; J. O. Urmson, "Some Questions Concerning Validity," in *Essays in Conceptual Analysis*, ed. A. Flew (New York: Macmillan, 1966), pp. 127–28.

28. See, e.g., Joseph Ratner, "The Correspondence Theory of Truth," *Journal of Philosophy* 32 (1935): 149: " 'The application of the adjectives true and false,' says W. E. Johnson, 'coincides with the imperatives "to be accepted" and "to be rejected" respectively.' "

29. See C. J. Ducasse, *Truth, Knowledge and Causation* (London: Routledge and Kegan Paul, 1968), pp. 135–37.

30. John Dewey, *Experience and Nature* (Chicago: Open Court, 1925), p. 209.

Introduction to Part 2

1. De George, "Reason, Truth, and Context," p. 42.

Chapter 7: The Relativity of Linguistic Truth

1. In *Darkness and Light*, I used the same name for an analogous principle of meaningfulness. For a discussion that complements the present one, see there, pp. 30–40.

2. Compare, e.g., these various samples: (1) "A four-year-old boy saw a blanket on a horse and called it an 'apron' " (Edgar H. Sturtevant, *Linguistic Change: An Introduction to the Historical Study of Language* [Chicago: University of Chicago Press, 1917], p. 90). (2) " 'Hippopotamus' is from Greek *hippo* (horse) and *potamos* (river), hence 'the river horse' " (John Ciardi, *How Does a Poem Mean?* [Boston: Houghton Mifflin, 1959], p. 766). (3) "Compare the way children say 'car' when they see a picture of a car, even though they have been taught the word 'car' in relation to actual cars. No doubt they do this even before they have any conception of what a picture is: certainly they do it before they learn the *word* 'picture' " (J. J. C. Smart, *Philosophy and Scientific Realism* [London: Routledge and Kegan Paul, 1963], p. 37). (4) "In the *Charmides* we find a boy of this name presented by his elder cousin and guardian, Critias, to Socrates as a perfect specimen of that comeliness and grace and modesty, united with strength and self-mastery, which gave to the youth of that age and land their peculiarly androgynous charm. He is the embodiment of the much-lauded and much-desired virtue of *sôphrosyne*, which, for lack of a better equivalent, we translate 'temperance' " (Paul Elmer More, *Platonism* [London: Oxford University Press, 1917], p. 33). (5) " 'The American Idiom,' William Carlos Williams used to say; and 'the Variable Foot.' . . . His problem was inherited terminology. 'Idiom' was not the word he wanted, nor was 'Foot.' These were simply nouns he could hear learned men uttering in the general vicinity of what he meant" (Hugh Kenner, "William Carlos Williams's Rhythm of Ideas," *New York Times Book Review*, 18 Sept. 1983, p. 15).

3. See, e.g., Jaakko Hintikka's discussion ("Theories of Truth and Learnable Languages," in *Philosophy and Grammar*, ed. S. Kanger and S. Öhman [Dordrecht: Reidel, 1981], pp. 37–58) of "what Davidson calls the *Frege Principle*, that is to say, the principle which says that the meaning of a complex expression is a function of the meanings of its constituent parts" (p. 37). Hintikka argues "that compositionality fails in natural languages in a wide variety of ways" (p. 38). Baker and Hacker agree (*Wittgenstein: Understanding and Meaning*, pp. 258–83). Yet Uriel Weinreich's attitude is common: "The goal of a semantic theory of a language, as we conceive it, is to explicate the way in which the *meaning of a sentence of specified structure is derivable from the fully specified meanings of its parts*" (*Explorations in Semantic Theory* [The Hague: Mouton, 1972], p. 44).

4. Compare the contention that "a predicate 'φ' can be correctly applied to an object if and

only if that object satisfies a *suitable majority* of those descriptions believed to be true of φs" (Peter Smith, *Realism and the Progress of Science* [Cambridge: Cambridge University Press, 1981], p. 15; emphasis added). Smith backs into this thesis, arguing for the "if," but not the "only if," against essentialistic or Fregean demands. To settle for mere minority resemblance would clearly not do; but he neither envisages nor assesses any alternative, such as PRS, relating the predicate to rival expressions. This oversight is typical.

5. Richard Swinburne, *The Coherence of Theism* (Oxford: Clarendon Press, 1977), p. 61. Compare Austin, "How To Talk," p. 240.

6. Compare I. M. Crombie, "The Possibility of Theological Statements," in *Religious Language and the Problem of Religious Knowledge,* ed. R. Santoni (Bloomington, Ind.: Indiana University Press, 1968), pp. 60–61; H. D. Lewis, *Philosophy of Religion* (London: English Universities Press, 1965), p. 152; Stuart C. Brown, *Do Religious Claims Make Sense?* (New York: Macmillan, 1969), p. 178.

7. Gustaf Stern, *Meaning and Change of Meaning* (Bloomington, Ind.: Indiana University Press, 1968), p. 194.

8. For Scotus, see *Opus oxoniense,* book 1, dist. 8, q. 3, nn. 9–12. For Nielsen, see "Talk of God and the Doctrine of Analogy," *The Thomist* 40 (1976): 40, 60. See, e.g., Robin Attfield, "Religious Symbols and the Voyage of Analogy," *International Journal for Philosophy of Religion* 11 (1980): 229–30, 232; William L. Power, "Musings on the Mystery of God," *International Journal for Philosophy of Religion* 7 (1976): 306–08; C. J. Ducasse, "Are Religious Dogmas Cognitive and Meaningful?," in *Religious Language,* ed. Santoni, pp. 284–85.

9. Elizabeth A. Johnson, stating Pannenberg's view, in "The Right Way to Speak about God? Pannenberg on Analogy," *Theological Studies* 43 (1982): 683–84.

10. See Raphael Demos, "Are Religious Dogmas Cognitive and Meaningful?," in *Religious Language,* ed. Santoni, p. 278; W. Norris Clarke, "Analogy and the Meaningfulness of Language about God: A Reply to Kai Nielsen," *The Thomist* 40 (1976): 70–71.

11. C. A. Campbell, *On Selfhood and Godhood* (New York: Macmillan, 1957), p. xxxii.

12. Daya Krishan, "Religious Experience, Language, and Truth," in *Religious Experience and Truth,* ed. S. Hook (New York: New York University Press, 1961), p. 236.

13. See Stern, *Meaning and Change of Meaning,* pp. 341–42.

14. Thomas S. Kuhn, "Metaphor in Science," in *Metaphor and Thought,* ed. A. Ortony (Cambridge: Cambridge University Press, 1979), pp. 412–13.

15. "We speak of the 'lip' and the 'ears' of a cup, the 'teeth' of a saw or a comb, the 'legs' of tables and other immobile articles of furniture, the 'elbows' of pipes and macaroni, the 'hands' of a clock, the 'tongue' of a balance or a bell, the 'eye' of a needle, and the 'head' of a hammer. When we travel we encounter the 'foot' of a mountain, the 'mouth' of a river, a 'head'-land, the 'shoulders'—even the 'soft shoulders'—of a road, the 'brow' of a hill, and the 'neck' of the woods" (Margaret Schlauch, *The Gift of Language* [New York: Dover, 1955], p. 111).

16. Wittgenstein, *Philosophical Investigations,* §385.

17. See Alston, *Philosophy of Language,* p. 89.

18. Stephen P. Schwartz, ed., *Naming, Necessity, and Natural Kinds* (Ithaca: Cornell University Press, 1977), p. 30, on Kripke and Putnam.

19. See Putnam, *Realism and Reason:* "What makes something gold is having the same nature as the paradigms; in current physical theory this is unpacked as having the same composition, since it is the atomic composition that determines the law-like behavior of a substance" (p. 73). "Indeed, what makes composition important, when it is, is its connection with laws of behavior" (p. 74).

20. Ibid., pp. 70–71, and Hilary Putnam, *Philosophical Papers,* vol. 2, *Mind, Language and Reality* (Cambridge: Cambridge University Press, 1975), pp. 310–11.

21. Mary Hesse, *Revolutions and Reconstructions in the Philosophy of Science* (Bloomington, Ind.: Indiana University Press, 1980), p. 72.

22. See Thomas McPherson, *The Philosophy of Religion* (New York: Van Nostrand, 1965), p. 189.
23. Schlauch, *The Gift of Language*, p. 111.
24. Samuel I. Hayakawa, *Language in Thought and Action* (New York: Harcourt, Brace, 1949), p. 120. See also Stern, *Meaning and Change of Meaning*, pp. 310–12. Much metaphor—for instance, the use of the word *lion* to denote a brave man (ibid., p. 301)—admits a similar response. As Stern notes, "Hyperbole is often combined with metaphor, so that a word is both hyperbolical and metaphorical (*I have oceans of time*)" (ibid., p. 310).
25. Implicit in this response is an extension, or clarification, of my initial remarks concerning rival terms. I cited synonyms among the types of terms that do not count as rivals, but did not distinguish between established synonyms (e.g., *big* and *large*) and occasional synonyms (e.g., *dead* and *tired*). Samples like Hayakawa's alert us to the latter variety and justify their inclusion. In order for a statement like "I'm simply dead" to be true, it suffices that its hyperbolic use of words approximates more closely their established uses (including the hyperbolic) than would, for instance, "I'm not tired" (literal rival) or "I'm really revved up" (figurative rival).
26. Galen K. Pletcher, "Mysticism, Contradiction, and Ineffability," *American Philosophical Quarterly* 10 (1973): 207. The reference is to W. T. Stace, author of *Mysticism and Philosophy* (New York: Lippincott, 1960).
27. R. C. Zaehner, *Mysticism: Sacred and Profane* (New York: Oxford University Press, 1961), p. xiii.
28. Wittgenstein, *Philosophical Investigations*, p. 202.
29. This line of interpretation does not figure among the four which Stace considers and rejects as possible solutions to mystical paradoxes, nor would it merit his closing criticism: "All attempts to show that the mystical paradoxes can be got rid of by some logical or linguistic device are just so many attempts to reduce mysticism to common sense, to take away its unique character, and reduce it to the level of our everyday experience" (*Mysticism and Philosophy*, pp. 251–65).
30. Wittgenstein, *Philosophical Investigations*, p. 204.
31. Wittgenstein, *The Blue and Brown Books*, pp. 129–30. See also Richard Boyd, "Metaphor and Theory Change: What is 'Metaphor' a Metaphor for?," in *Metaphor and Thought*, ed. Ortony, p. 356; John Searle, "Metaphor," in *The Philosophy of Language*, ed. A. P. Martinich (New York: Oxford University Press, 1985), pp. 426–29.
32. For similar examples, see Stern, *Meaning and Change of Meaning*, pp. 325–26.
33. Hallett, *Darkness and Light*, p. 34. In his treatment of metaphors based on "similarity of perceptual or emotive effect," Stern acknowledges that "it is somewhat doubtful what the precise nature of the common element really is" (*Meaning and Change of Meaning*, p. 322).
34. James F. Ross, "Analogy and the Resolution of Some Cognitivity Problems," *Journal of Philosophy* 67 (1970): 731. "So too with 'has' in: (a) 'John has a comb with him.' (b) 'John has a home of his own.' (c) 'John has a wife already.' (d) 'John has a cold' " (ibid., p. 733). See Baker and Hacker, *Wittgenstein: Understanding and Meaning*, p. 268, for a richly varied collection of samples and for similar remarks, and Hallett, *Darkness and Light*, pp. 40–46, for closer analysis of such contagion.
35. Hesse, *Revolutions and Reconstructions*, p. 116.

Chapter 8: The Concept *True* as Norm

1. See Hallett, *Logic for the Labyrinth*, chs. 8–10.
2. Wittgenstein, *The Blue and Brown Books*, p. 17.
3. See David K. Lewis, *Convention: A Philosophical Study* (Cambridge, Mass.: Harvard University Press, 1969), p. 179.
4. Wittgenstein, *Philosophical Investigations*, §129.

5. "What I wish to question," writes Richard Gregory, "is whether linguistic usage is ever a valid criterion for accepting or rejecting a concept" ("Discussion," in *Philosophy of Psychology*, ed. S. C. Brown [New York: Barnes and Noble, 1974], p. 232). Compare John Rawls, *A Theory of Justice* (Cambridge, Mass.: Harvard University Press, 1971), p. 130.
6. See Mary G. Forrester, *Moral Language* (Madison, Wis.: University of Wisconsin Press, 1982), p. 52.
7. Bertrand Russell, *The Analysis of Matter* (London: Allen and Unwin, 1954), p. 155.
8. Bertrand Russell, *The Scientific Outlook* (Glencoe, Ill.: Free Press, 1931), p. 78.
9. See Garth Hallett, "The Theoretical Content of Language," *Gregorianum* 54 (1973): 314–15; J. L. Cobitz, "The Appeal to Ordinary Language," *Analysis* 11 (1950–51): 9–10.
10. "Why should philosophers expect each other, as they nowadays often do, to take seriously the reproach 'That's not how we use the word'? Is it not that the unexplained 'we,' whose identity so puzzles the critics, necessarily includes (because the two can understand each other) the speaker *and the person addressed?* The reproach is an appeal to the philosopher to recognize the implications of his own verbal habits, and thus to correct his own analysis or censor his own extravagance in the light of *his own* actual usage" (F. E. Sparshott, *An Enquiry into Goodness* [Chicago: University of Chicago Press, 1958], p. 57).
11. Stuart Chase, *The Power of Words*, p. 103, quoted by E. R. Emmet, *Learning to Philosophize* (Harmondsworth: Penguin Books, 1968), p. 54.
12. Hayakawa, *Language in Thought and Action*, pp. 187–88.
13. E.g., George Berkeley, *Three Dialogues between Hylas and Philonous*, in *The Works of George Berkeley*, ed. A. Fraser, vol. 1 (Oxford: Clarendon Press, 1901), p. 386: "Intense heat is nothing else but a particular kind of painful sensation; and pain cannot exist but in a perceiving being." See Alasdair MacIntyre, *A Short History of Ethics* (New York: Macmillan, 1966), p. 15; William K. C. Guthrie, *The Greek Philosophers from Thales to Aristotle* (New York: Philosophical Library, 1950), p. 67.
14. Berkeley, *Three Dialogues*, p. 416: "In truth and strictness, nothing can be *heard* but *sound*."
15. Wendell Johnson, *People in Quandaries: The Semantics of Personal Adjustment* (New York: Harper and Row, 1946), p. 118.
16. Dewitt H. Parker, *Human Values* (New York: Harper, 1931), p. 21; A. L. Hilliard, *The Forms of Value* (New York: Columbia University Press, 1950), p. 47.
17. Isaac Newton, *Opticks* (London: G. Bell and Sons, 1931), pp. 124–25.
18. Heraclitus, Fragments 12 and 91.
19. B. F. Skinner, *Science and Human Behavior* (New York: Free Press, 1953), p. 72.
20. Hayakawa, *Language in Thought and Action*, p. 165. See also Arthur Eddington, *The Nature of the Physical World* (Cambridge: Cambridge University Press, 1928), p. 342; Benson Mates, "On the Verification of Statements about Ordinary Language," in *Ordinary Language: Essays in Philosophical Method*, ed. V. C. Chappell (Englewood Cliffs, N.J.: Prentice-Hall, 1964), p. 70; Urmson, "Some Questions Concerning Validity," pp. 121–22; L. Susan Stebbing, " 'Furniture of the Earth,' " in *Philosophy of Science*, ed. A. Danto and S. Morgenbesser (New York: Meridian Books, 1960), p. 74.
21. Hanna F. Pitkin, *Wittgenstein and Justice: On the Significance of Ludwig Wittgenstein for Social and Political Thought* (Berkeley: University of California Press, 1972), p. 319; Carl Sagan, *Cosmos* (New York: Random House, 1980), p. 189.
22. Plato *Phaedo* 115E.
23. Max Scheler, *Formalism in Ethics and Non-Formal Ethics of Values: A New Attempt toward the Foundation of an Ethical Personalism*, trans. M. Frings and R. Funk (Evanston, Ill.: Northwestern University Press, 1973), p. 85.
24. George Herbert Palmer, *Altruism: Its Nature and Varieties* (Westport, Conn.: Greenwood Press, 1970), p. 95.
25. Norman Malcolm, *Thought and Knowledge. Essays* (Ithaca: Cornell University Press, 1977), p. 48, on Descartes, and p. 113, on Reid.

26. Silvano and James Arieti, *Love Can Be Found: A Guide to the Most Desired and Most Elusive Emotion* (New York: Harcourt Brace Jovanovich, 1977), p. 11.

27. Samuel E. Stumpf, *Socrates to Sartre: A History of Philosophy*, 2d ed. (New York: McGraw-Hill, 1975), p. 18, on Parmenides; Stephen Toulmin, *An Examination of the Place of Reason in Ethics* (Cambridge: Cambridge University Press, 1950), p. 60, on Anaxagoras.

28. W. Edgar Moore, *Creative and Critical Thinking* (Boston: Houghton Mifflin, 1967), p. 6; Norwood R. Hanson, *Patterns of Discovery* (Cambridge: Cambridge University Press, 1958), p. 6, on Brain, Mann, Arber; Romano Harré, *Theories and Things: A Brief Study in Prescriptive Metaphysics* (London and New York: Sheed and Ward, 1961), p. 108, on G. E. Moore.

29. Lindsay Dewar, *Moral Theology in the Modern World* (London: Mowbray, 1964), p. 76; J. Mason, review of Justus Hartnack, *Language and Philosophy*, in *Mind* 85 (1976): 467.

30. Malcolm, *Thought and Knowledge*, p. 46, on Descartes.

31. For numerous quotations, see David A. J. Richards, *A Theory of Reasons for Action* (Oxford: Oxford University Press, 1971), p. 297, n. 28.

32. John Hospers, *An Introduction to Philosophical Analysis* (New York: Prentice-Hall, 1953), p. 75.

33. Peter G. van Breemen, *As Bread That Is Broken* (Deveille, N.J.: Dimension Books, 1974), p. 165.

34. Karl Mannheim, *Ideology and Utopia: An Introduction to the Sociology of Knowledge*, trans. L. Wirth and E. Shils (New York: Harcourt, Brace, 1936), p. 3.

35. Kurt Baier cites various philosophical examples in "The Ordinary Use of Words," *Proceedings of the Aristotelian Society* 52 (1951–52): 57–59.

36. See Hallett, *Logic for the Labyrinth*, ch. 10.

37. Alan R. White, "Moore's Appeal to Common Sense," *Philosophy* 33 (1958): 221.

38. For ample kindred cases, consult the Russellian listing above.

39. For illustrations, see A. J. Ayer, *The Concept of a Person and Other Essays* (New York: St. Martin's Press, 1963), pp. 17–18; Bertrand Russell, "The Cult of 'Common Usage,'" *British Journal for the Philosophy of Science* 3 (1952–53): 303–07; Stephan Körner, "Some Types of Philosophical Thinking," in *British Philosophy in the Mid-Century: A Cambridge Symposium*, ed. C. A. Mace (London: Allen and Unwin, 1957), p. 122 (e.g., "These standards are embodied in the common sense of the ordinary man, or, as it is nowadays often put, in his habits of speech"); Richard M. Rorty, "Recent Metaphilosophy," *Review of Metaphysics* 15 (1961–62): 310; Morris Weitz, "Philosophy and the Abuse of Language," *Journal of Philosophy* 44 (1947): 545–46 (e.g., "The language of common sense and its belief in cognitive certainty"); Henry H. Price, *Truth and Corrigibility* (Oxford: Clarendon Press, 1936), p. 4; Jason Xenakis, "Ordinary Language and Ordinary Belief," *Philosophical Studies* 5 (1954): 41–42; Waismann, *How I See Philosophy*, p. 180 ("Grammar draws a *cordon sanitaire* against any rebellious ideas that dare to crop up"); Edwin A. Burtt, *In Search of Philosophic Understanding* (New York: New American Library, 1965), p. 42; Hesse, *Revolutions and Reconstructions*, pp. 79–80; Herbert Hochberg, *Logic, Ontology, and Language: Essays on Truth and Reality* (Munich: Philosophia, 1984), pp. 39–40.

40. John H. Randall, Jr., "Talking and Looking," *Proceedings of the American Philosophical Association* 30 (1956–57): 16.

41. Harold N. Lee, "Methodology of Value Theory," in *Value: A Cooperative Inquiry*, ed. R. Lepley (New York: Columbia University Press, 1949), p. 155. In like vein, see Burtt, *In Search of Philosophic Understanding*, pp. 49, 55.

42. Wittgenstein, *Philosophical Investigations*, §127.

43. Against the supposedly necessary connection between scientific progress and conceptual revision, see Peter Achinstein, "Rudolf Carnap, I," *Review of Metaphysics* 19 (1965–66): 521–23. A still more striking counter-instance than those I have cited is Darwin's concept of *species*, which was more traditional in *The Origin of Species* than it was at an earlier stage of his thinking. His theory advanced; his concept regressed. See Ernst Mayr, *The Growth of*

Biological Thought: Diversity, Evolution, and Inheritance (Cambridge, Mass.: Harvard University Press, Belknap Press, 1982), pp. 265–69 ("Darwin's Species Concept").

44. Stephen E. Toulmin, *Human Understanding*, vol. 1 (Princeton: Princeton University Press, 1972), pp. 11–12.
45. On "the tendency to confuse or conflate concept and conception," see Putnam, *Realism and Reason*, p. 194.
46. For further illustration, see Hallett, "The Theoretical Content of Language," pp. 307–22. There is considerable truth in Wittgenstein's remark: "The essential thing about metaphysics: it obliterates the distinction between factual and conceptual investigations" (*Zettel*, §458). And the failing is not confined to metaphysicians.
47. See the section below entitled "Senses in which a Language is and is not Theory-laden."
48. See Hallett, *Logic for the Labyrinth*, pp. 82–85.
49. Ibid., pp. 82–89. Compare Grover Maxwell, "The Ontological Status of Theoretical Entities," in *Minnesota Studies in the Philosophy of Science*, vol. 3, ed. H. Feigl and G. Maxwell (Minneapolis: University of Minnesota Press, 1962), pp. 23–24.
50. "A favorite theme is that every language, even ordinary everyday language, commits one to hypotheses which could be false. Every term is theory laden; and every language is a theory" (James A. Martin, reviewing Paul Feyerabend's *Realism, Rationalism, and Scientific Method*, in *Philosophical Review* 93 [1984]: 280).
51. See Hallett, "The Theoretical Content of Language," pp. 328–29.
52. See Willard van Orman Quine, *From a Logical Point of View: Logico-Philosophical Essays* (Cambridge, Mass.: Harvard University Press, 1961), pp. 44–45.
53. Compare Saul A. Kripke, "Naming and Necessity," in *Semantics of Natural Language*, ed. D. Davidson and G. Harman, (Dordrecht: Reidel, 1972), pp. 318–19.
54. Brand Blanshard, "The Philosophy of Analysis," in *Clarity Is Not Enough*, ed. H. D. Lewis (London: Allen and Unwin, 1963), p. 102. Compare Joel J. Kupperman, *Ethical Knowledge* (New York: Humanities Press, 1970), p. 69.
55. Ashley Montagu, ed., *The Meaning of Love* (New York: Julian Press, 1953), p. v.
56. Robert Faricy, *Spirituality for Religious Life* (New York: Paulist Press, 1976), p. 27.
57. Brown, *Do Religious Claims Make Sense?*, p. 116. See also Roderick M. Chisholm, "Philosophers and Ordinary Language," *Philosophical Review* 60 (1951): 318.
58. See Renford Bambrough, introduction to *Reason and Religion*, ed. S. C. Brown (Ithaca: Cornell University Press, 1977), pp. 17–18.
59. Kuhn, "Metaphor in Science," p. 417.
60. Hayakawa, *Language in Thought and Action*, p. 63.
61. Willard van Orman Quine, *Word and Object* (Cambridge, Mass.: M.I.T. Press, 1960), p. 16. See also J. J. C. Smart, "The Reality of Theoretical Entities," *Australasian Journal of Philosophy* 34 (1956): 4.
62. Rollo Handy, *Methodology of the Behavioral Sciences. Problems and Controversies* (Springfield, Ill.: Charles C. Thomas, 1964), p. 117.
63. For concrete illustration of this sixth point, see Thomas S. Kuhn, *The Essential Tension: Selected Studies in Scientific Tradition and Change* (Chicago: University of Chicago Press, 1977), pp. xi–xii ("I did not become an Aristotelian physicist as a result, but I had to some extent learned to think like one").
64. Hallett, "The Theoretical Content of Language," p. 336. See also Alan R. Anderson, "Mathematics and the 'Language Game,'"in *Philosophy of Mathematics: Selected Readings*, ed. P. Benacerraf and H. Putnam (Englewood Cliffs, N.J.: Prentice-Hall, 1964), pp. 482–84 (e.g., "The point that we never escape completely from natural languages into ideal languages, where the air is purer, is an important one, and bears repetition"). My quoted claim might be contested by those who maintain (in a pertinent sense?) that "the way a thing is said is part of what's being said." See George McClure, "The Special Jargons of Philosophy: Insights, or Barriers to Understanding?" *Metaphilosophy* 12 (1981): 62, 66.

65. Max Black, *Margins of Precision: Essays in Logic and Language* (Ithaca: Cornell University Press, 1970), pp. 265–66.

66. In *The Concept of a Person*, p. 18, A. J. Ayer goes further and observes that in a society which believed in witchcraft it might be perfectly correct to describe a person as "bewitched" if he showed the commonly accepted marks of demonic possession, but that this would not entail that there were actually demons at work. See Sherry, *Religion, Truth and Language-Games*, p. 31.

67. See Frederick Suppe, *The Structure of Scientific Theories*, 2d ed. (Champaign, Ill.: University of Illinois Press, 1977), pp. 193–94, on Scheffler; Ayer, *The Concept of a Person*, pp. 18–19; Peter Winch, "Language, Belief and Relativism," in *Contemporary British Philosophy*, 4th ser., ed. H. D. Lewis (London: Macmillan, 1976), pp. 324–25.

68. See Hallett, *Companion*, p. 316.

69. Wittgenstein, *Notebooks 1914–1916*, p. 44.

70. Wittgenstein, *On Certainty*, §114.

71. See Putnam, *Mind, Language and Reality*, pp. 353–54; Ayer, *The Concept of a Person*, pp. 17–20.

72. For comparable remarks on moral concepts, which I endorse, see R. M. Hare, *Moral Thinking: Its Levels, Method, and Point* (Oxford: Oxford University Press, 1981), pp. 17–18.

73. There is no conflict, say, between the doctrine of determinism as usually understood and an argument like Antony Flew's: "Since the meaning of 'of his own freewill' can be taught by reference to such paradigm cases as that in which a man, under no social pressure, marries the girl he wants to marry (how else *could* it be taught): it cannot be right, on any grounds whatsoever to say that no one *ever* acts of his own free will" ("Philosophy and Language," in Flew, *Essays in Conceptual Analysis*, p. 19).

74. See Hallett, *Companion*, pp. 26–34.

75. Wilbur M. Urban, *Language and Reality: The Philosophy of Language and the Principles of Symbolism* (New York: Macmillan, 1939), p. 743.

76. Ibid., p. 746.

77. Baier, "The Ordinary Use of Words," p. 64.

78. This series of points is made on pp. 64–65.

79. Notice the term *such*. My claim is not as general as Michael Scriven's assertion that well-justified redefinition, of any kind, for any reason, is "enormously difficult in areas outside the physical sciences and—from the record—almost always unsuccessful" ("The Argument from Ordinary Language," in *Principles of Philosophical Reasoning*, ed. J. Fetzer [Totowa, N.J.: Rowman and Allanheld, 1984], p. 275. See also ibid., pp. 270–71.

80. E.g.: "When the 'atom' was first imported into physics, it was defined as the ultimate and indivisible particle of matter. Now, notoriously, it has been subdivided so often that there seems to be room in it for an unending multitude of parts; and its exploration is the most progressive part of physics. The word remains, but its definition has been radically changed" (F. C. S. Schiller, "How Is 'Exactness' Possible?," in *The Language of Wisdom and Folly: Background Readings in Semantics*, ed. Irving J. Lee [New York: Harper, 1949], p. 146).

81. For similar recommendations, see Herbert Feigl and Grover Maxwell, "Why Ordinary Language Needs Reforming," *Journal of Philosophy* 58 (1961): 496; Herman Tennessen, "Permissible and Impermissible Locutions," *Synthese* 12 (1960): 506; idem, "Vindication of the Humpty Dumpty Attitude towards Language," p. 187.

82. Experience suggests that a recurring difficulty may block acceptance of this and similar assertions. When people read that "though theory-laden, word meanings are not themselves theories," that "words can be used with identical senses to assert or deny the same theory," that "established word meanings can be used to express any debatable theory," and the like, they may conclude that my whole account is vitiated by belief in core meanings devoid of theoretical content. So a comparison may prove helpful. Suppose that, while

boating on Lake Erie, I draw up one bucketful of water and pour in another: people would typically say I was still afloat on the same lake, despite this exchange of bucketfuls. And their assertion would not imply belief in a stable, "core" lake, unaffected by such additions and subtractions. *Sameness* is more flexible than that. Analogously, if a Copernican removes "circled by the sun" from the meaning of *Earth* and replaces it with "circling the sun," people would probably say that he uses the word *Earth* in the same sense or with the same meaning as a non-Copernican, even—or especially—when they debate (non-tautologously) which body circles which. This assertion, too, would imply no stable core—that is, no core meaning unaffected by additions and subtractions. *Same,* once again, is a flexible expression. A different lake is, for instance, one to which you have to portage; a different meaning is, for instance, an analogous or equivocal one.

Chapter 9: A Paradigm Inquiry: Are Performatives True-False?

1. Graham, *J. L. Austin.*
2. See J. L. Austin, "Performative-Constative," in *The Philosophy of Language,* ed. J. R. Searle (London: Oxford University Press, 1971), pp. 13–14. Compare Justus Hartnack, "The Performatory Use of Sentences," *Theoria* 29 (1963): 138.
3. Graham, *J. L. Austin,* pp. 67–68; parenthetical references omitted.
4. Ibid., p. 72.
5. Compare Kent Bach, "Performatives Are Statements Too," *Philosophical Studies* 28 (1975): 229; E. J. Lemmon, "On Sentences Verifiable by Their Use," *Analysis* 22 (1961–62): 86–89; Geoffrey Warnock, "Some Types of Performative Utterance," in Isaiah Berlin et al., *Essays on J. L. Austin* (Oxford: Clarendon Press, 1973), pp. 79–82; Ingemar Hedenius, "Performatives," *Theoria* 29 (1963): 117–18.
6. Graham, *J. L. Austin,* p. 69.
7. Ibid., p. 50.
8. Wittgenstein, *Philosophical Investigations,* §117.
9. Ibid., §164.
10. See Patrick H. Nowell-Smith, *Ethics* (Harmondsworth: Penguin Books, 1954), pp. 167, 239–44.
11. Graham, *J. L. Austin,* p. 37.
12. See, e.g., ibid., p. 46: "There is this permanent possibility of conflict both between different *languages* or *conceptual systems* and within one *conceptual system.* When such conflicts cry out for resolution, the conservatism which the neo-Darwinian argument is used to justify will be worse than useless, for there is nothing at all to be said for the preservation of incompatible *theories*" (emphasis added).
13. Ibid., p. 38.
14. Compare Paul Churchland, *Scientific Realism and the Plasticity of Mind* (Cambridge: Cambridge University Press, 1979), p. 51: "What is it, after all, that permits two speakers to understand one another, to converse freely and efficiently with one another? Given that they share identical vocabulary, syntax, and dispositions to draw formal inferences, surely it is the systematic similarity in the sets of sentences they respectively accept, and the correlative similarity in the material inferences they are therefore disposed to draw." There is no mention of shared word meanings, nor are they included under "identical vocabulary."
15. Graham, *J. L. Austin,* p. 31.
16. See Hallett, *Darkness and Light,* pp. 92–97.
17. Compare his own examples, Graham, *J. L. Austin,* pp. 13–14, 17, 19, 48.
18. See Alan Montefiore, *A Modern Introduction to Moral Philosophy* (London: Routledge & Kegan Paul, 1958), p. 85: "It would be foolish to suppose that any account of such a central

term as 'true' could be both coherent and at the same time faithful to all the nuances of ordinary language."

19. See, e.g., Achinstein, "Rudolf Carnap, I," pp. 523–24.

20. According to Churchland (*Scientific Realism*, pp. 21–24), our "naive or common-sense conception of heat" involves us in contradictions. But for him this conception is a theory or set of beliefs, not a neutral word meaning. He acknowledges no distinction between theory and meaning.

21. Graham, *J. L. Austin*, pp. 31–32.

22. Ibid., p. 76. See also Hedenius, "Performatives," p. 119.

23. Graham, *J. L. Austin*, p. 78.

24. Ibid., p. 83.

25. Ibid., p. 79.

26. Ibid.

27. H. P. Rickman, *Understanding and the Human Studies* (London: Heinemann, 1967), p. 6.

28. Max Black, "Austin on Performatives," in *Symposium on J. L. Austin*, ed. K. T. Fann (New York: Humanities Press, 1969), p. 402.

29. See Hospers, *An Introduction to Philosophical Analysis*, pp. 21–22.

30. For a full, concrete illustration, see Hanson, *Patterns of Discovery*, p. 4.

31. See Richard Rudner, "Counter-Intuitivity and the Method of Analysis," *Philosophical Studies* 1 (1950): 87–89; Achinstein, "Rudolf Carnap, I," pp. 528–31 ("There is frequently a tendency not to spell out sufficiently what are the special purposes or contexts, scientific or otherwise, for which it might be important to employ the philosopher's concept"); Rudolf Carnap, *Logical Foundations of Probability*, 2d ed. (Chicago: University of Chicago Press, 1962), p. 7 ("Philosophers, scientists, and mathematicians make explications very frequently. But they do not often discuss explicitly the general rules which they follow implicitly").

32. J. Houston, "Truth Valuation of Explicit Performatives," *Philosophical Quarterly* 20 (1970): 149.

33. Ibid.

34. Should such surmises appear far-fetched, recall that disputes have arisen concerning the truth and falsehood of questions and commands, despite the clear verdict of usage.

35. Hallett, *Logic for the Labyrinth*, ch. 10.

36. Ibid., pp. 177–78. In analogous situations, not recognized as such, Alasdair MacIntyre speaks of "The Essential Contestability of Some Social Concepts" (*Ethics* 84 [1973]: 1–9).

37. Re similar debate concerning the truth of indicative conditionals, revealing similar disregard for usage, see Michael Dummett, "What Is a Theory of Meaning? (II)," in *Truth and Meaning: Essays in Semantics*, ed. G. Evans and J. McDowell (Oxford: Clarendon Press, 1976): p. 85.

38. Hallett, *Logic for the Labyrinth*, p. 176.

39. See Achinstein, "Rudolf Carnap, I," pp. 527, 533; Hempel, *Fundamentals of Concept Formation*, p. 54.

40. See, e.g., Mats Furberg, *Saying and Meaning: A Main Theme in J. L. Austin's Philosophy* (Totowa, N.J.: Rowman and Littlefield, 1971), p. 195.

41. Hartnack, "The Performatory Use of Sentences," p. 140. See also Georg H. von Wright, "On Promises," *Theoria* 28 (1962): 285; Erik Ryding, "The Truth Value of Promises," *Theoria* 33 (1967): 150.

42. Hartnack, "The Performatory Use of Sentences," p. 139.

43. Ibid., p. 140.

44. Ryding, "The Truth Value of Promises," p. 151.

45. See Peter Geach, "Kinds of Statement," in *Intention and Intentionality*, ed. C. Diamond (Ithaca: Cornell University Press, 1979), p. 226; J. L. Austin, *How To Do Things with Words*,

ed. J. O. Urmson (Oxford: Clarendon Press, 1962), p. 55; idem, *Philosophical Papers*, p. 234.

46. See Rundle, *Grammar in Philosophy*, p. 420.

47. Austin, *Philosophical Papers*, p. 130.

48. Compare, e.g., Carnap's account of a case "where the prescientific concept is not suffi-ciently discriminative": "Suppose I enter a moderately heated room twice, first coming from an overheated room and at a later time coming from the cold outside. Then it may happen that I declare the room, on the basis of my sensations, to be warmer the second time than the first, while the thermometer shows at the second time the same temperature as at the first (or even a slightly higher one) [sic]. Experiences of this kind do not at all lead us to the conclusion that the concept Temperature defined with reference to the ther-mometer is inadequate as an explicatum for the concept Warmer. On the contrary, we have become accustomed to let the scientific concept overrule the prescientific one in all cases of disagreement" (*Logical Foundations of Probability*, pp. 12–13). Here Carnap over-looks the distinction, even in prescientific talk, between *being* warmer and *feeling* warmer. The statement he cites is objectionable even by prescientific standards.

49. See ibid., p. 6.

50. Some relevant pages on questions: Henry S. Leonard, "Interrogatives, Imperatives, Truth, Falsity and Lies," *Philosophy of Science* 26 (1959): 179–83; David Harrah, "A Logic of Questions and Answers," *Philosophy of Science* 28 (1961): 40–45; J. M. O. Wheatley, "Note on Professor Leonard's Analysis of Interrogatives, Etc.," *Philosophy of Science* 28 (1961): 52–54; Henry S. Leonard, "A Reply to Professor Wheatley," *Philosophy of Science* 28 (1961): 55–64; C. L. Hamblin, "Questions Aren't Statements," *Philosophy of Science* 30 (1963): 62–63; Paul M. Hurrell, "Interrogatives, Testability and Truth-Value," *Philosophy of Science* 31 (1964): 173–82; Rodney P. Riegle, "The Logical Status of Questions," *Educa-tional Theory* 25 (1975): 380–84. On commands, see, e.g., Alf Ross, "Imperatives and Logic," *Philosophy of Science* 11 (1944): 35–36; Herbert G. Bohnert, "The Semiotic Status of Commands," *Philosophy of Science* 12 (1945): 306–08; Leonard, "Interrogatives," pp. 184–86; Edward Borchardt, "The Semantics of Imperatives," *Logique et analyse* 22 (1979):191–205.

51. Ralph M. McInerny, "Truth in Ethics: Historicity and Natural Law," *Proceedings of the American Catholic Philosophical Association* 43 (1969): 75.

52. Note the contrast with Forrester, *Moral Language*, p. 57: "We have seen that one of the problems with developing a logic for sentences which are not declaratives is that such sentences cannot be either true or false."

53. See Charles L. Stevenson, *Facts and Values: Studies in Ethical Analysis* (New Haven: Yale University Press, 1963), pp. 216–17.

Chapter 10: Moral Truth

1. Richard T. Garner and Bernard Rosen, *Moral Philosophy: A Systematic Introduction to Normative Ethics and Meta-ethics* (New York: Macmillan, 1967), p. 217.

2. Compare Kupperman, *Ethical Knowledge*, p. 63: "At the root of Ayer's denial of literal meaning to ethics is his view that ethics is too different from science and logic to constitute knowledge. Very broadly, a large part of the argument in the last three chapters of this book will be that there are important similarities between ethics and subjects which even Ayer would consider branches of knowledge, and that these similarities are important enough to justify speaking of ethical knowledge. This would lead to the complaint against Ayer that he made too much of the differences, and not enough of the similarities."

3. Forrester, *Moral Language*, p. 81.

4. Kai Nielsen, "On Moral Truth," in *Studies in Moral Philosophy*, ed. N. Rescher (Oxford: Blackwell, 1968), p. 25.

5. See Hallett, *Darkness and Light*, pp. 61–75.

6. D. S. Miller, "Moral Truth," *Philosophical Studies* 1 (1950): 45.

7. Ibid., p. 46.

8. Arne Naess, "Do We Know That Basic Norms Cannot Be True or False?" *Theoria* 25 (1959): 53.

9. G. E. Moore, *Principia Ethica* (Cambridge: Cambridge University Press, 1922), p. 147.

10. Ibid., p. 146.

11. Ibid., p. 25.

12. G. E. Moore, *Commonplace Book 1919–1953* (New York: Allen and Unwin, 1962), p. 330.

13. See Abraham Kaplan, "Are Moral Judgements Assertions?" *Philosophical Review* 51 (1942): 280.

14. See Nielsen, "On Moral Truth," p. 12.

15. G. E. Moore, "A Reply to My Critics," in *The Philosophy of G. E. Moore*, 2d ed., ed. P. Schilpp (New York: Open Court, 1952), pp. 545–46. For a critique of Moore akin to mine, see D. B. Terrell, "What You Will, or The Limits of Analysis," *Philosophical Studies* 3 (1952): 34–35.

16. For an especially suggestive passage, which evokes many another, see Baker and Hacker, *Wittgenstein: Understanding and Meaning*, p. 664.

17. Moore, "A Reply to My Critics," p. 547.

18. For a similar approach to the question of whether value judgments are "assertions," see Furberg, *Saying and Meaning*, p. 127.

19. See, e.g., Rudolf Carnap, *Philosophy and Logical Syntax* (London: Kegan Paul, Trench, Trubner, 1935), p. 24; Harald Ofstad, "Objectivity of Norms and Value-Judgments according to Recent Scandinavian Philosophy," *Philosophy and Phenomenological Research* 12 (1951–52): 44; Nielsen, "On Moral Truth," pp. 10–11; idem, "On Looking Back at the Emotive Theory," *Methodos* 14, 53 (1962):6: "Indeed, as Ayer points out, we do ordinarily say that moral claims are true or false, but here ordinary speech is misleading for what would it be like to know that they are either true or false?"

20. Austin, "Truth," p. 29.

21. Ibid.

22. See Stevenson, *Facts and Values*, pp. 214–15; White, *Truth*, p. 58; J. N. Findlay, "Morality by Convention," *Mind* 53 (1944): 146–47; William T. Blackstone, "On the Logical Status of Meta-Ethical Theories," *Theoria* 28 (1962): 298; the Declaration of Independence ("We hold these truths to be self-evident, that all Men are created equal, that they are endowed by their Creator with certain inalienable Rights").

23. Austin, "Truth," p. 29.

24. See Kaplan, "Are Moral Judgements Assertions?," p. 301: "Value properties seem to be *there*—in the object—only as the result of a fallacious inference from the fact of their givenness. Because valuations are not subject to the whim, the mere 'think-so', of the individual, it is supposed that there must be ineluctable value-properties present in the objects or situations valued."

25. Naess, "Do We Know," p. 34.

26. Arne Naess, "We Still Do Not Know that Norms Cannot Be True or False. A Reply to Dag Österberg," *Theoria* 28 (1962): 205. See also Baker and Hacker, *Wittgenstein: Understanding and Meaning*, p. 672, on Frege: "Everyday explanations of words are given short shrift . . . ; they do not meet the standards of completeness requisite for any adequate explanation. . . . As a consequence, Frege ignores their role in justifying or criticizing applications of words and in providing grounds for or against holding judgements to be true."

27. Feigl and Maxwell, "Why Ordinary Language Needs Reforming," p. 490.

28. Stevenson, *Facts and Values*, pp. 217–18. See also Carl Wellman, "Emotivism and Ethical Objectivity," *American Philosophical Quarterly* 5 (1968): 91.

29. Montefiore, *A Modern Introduction*, p. 86.

30. Wellman, "Emotivism and Ethical Objectivity," p. 95. See also Kaplan, "Are Moral Judgements Assertions?," pp. 294–98.
31. Richard G. Swinburne, "The Objectivity of Morality," *Philosophy* 51 (1976): 18.
32. See Robin Attfield, "The Logical Status of Moral Utterances," *Journal of Critical Analysis* 4 (1972–73): 78–84.
33. Swinburne, "The Objectivity of Morality," p. 19.
34. See Hallett, *Darkness and Light,* pp. 62–73.
35. See Garth L. Hallett, *Christian Moral Reasoning: An Analytic Guide* (Notre Dame, Ind.: University of Notre Dame Press, 1983), pp. 35–40.
36. Garth L. Hallett, *Reason and Right* (Notre Dame, Ind.: University of Notre Dame Press, 1984), p. 104.
37. Ibid., pp. 104–10.
38. Geoffrey Warnock, *Contemporary Moral Philosophy* (New York: Macmillan, 1967), p. 5.
39. Moore, *Principia Ethica,* p. 6.
40. Warnock, *Contemporary Moral Philosophy,* p. 13.
41. See G. E. Moore, *Commonplace Book,* pp, 19, 21.

Chapter 11: Empirical Truth

1. White, *Truth,* pp. 109–10.
2. See Carl G. Hempel, "On the Logical Positivists' Theory of Truth," *Analysis* 2 (1934–35): 49–59.
3. Ibid., p. 51.
4. Ibid., p. 53.
5. Otto Neurath, "Protocol Sentences," in *Logical Positivism,* ed. A. J. Ayer (Glencoe, Ill.: Free Press, 1959), p. 203. See also idem, *Philosophical Papers 1913–1946,* ed. and trans. R. Cohen and M. Neurath (Dordrecht: Reidel, 1983), p. 107.
6. Otto Neurath, *Foundations of the Social Sciences* (Chicago: University of Chicago Press, 1944), p. 12.
7. See Nicholas Rescher, *The Coherence Theory of Truth* (Oxford: Clarendon Press, 1973), pp. 23–27; White, *Truth,* pp. 110–11.
8. Moritz Schlick, "The Foundation of Knowledge," in *Logical Positivism,* ed. Ayer, p. 214.
9. Ibid., p. 215. See also Price, *Truth and Corrigibility,* pp. 23–24.
10. Hempel, "On the Logical Positivists' Theory of Truth," p. 57.
11. Ayer, *Logical Positivism,* p. 232, citing Price, *Truth and Corrigibility,* p. 19 (see also pp. 22–23).
12. Schlick, "The Foundation of Knowledge," p. 220. See also Price, *Truth and Corrigibility,* p. 29; Rudolf Carnap, *The Unity of Science* (London: Kegan Paul, 1934), pp. 47ff.
13. Schlick, "The Foundation of Knowledge," pp. 224–25. Compare Bertrand Russell, *Logic and Knowledge,* p. 130: "At any given moment, there are certain things of which a man is 'aware,' certain things which are 'before his mind.' Now although it is very difficult to define 'awareness,' it is not at all difficult to say that I am aware of such and such things. . . . If I describe these objects, I may of course describe them wrongly, hence I cannot with certainty communicate to another what are the things of which I am aware. But if I speak to myself, and denote them by what may be called 'proper names,' rather than by descriptive words, I cannot be in error."
14. See Wittgenstein, *Philosophical Investigations,* §§258–59; Hallett, *Companion,* pp. 314–15, 337–41.
15. Wittgenstein, *Tractatus,* 6.3751; idem, "Some Remarks on Logical Form," *Proceedings of the Aristotelian Society,* suppl. vol. 9 (1929): 167.
16. See Hallett, *Companion,* pp. 308–09.
17. Ibid.

18. Wittgenstein, *Philosophical Investigations*, §106.
19. "That the intension of a term of physical science is not any specific equation but the system itself *in its totality*, is confirmed among others by Pierre Duhem (*The Aim and Structure of Physical Theory*, Princeton University Press, 1954)" (Robert S. Hartman, "The Logical Difference between Philosophy and Science," *Philosophy and Phenomenological Research* 23 [1962–63]: 365).
20. See Charles Sanders Peirce, "Definitions of Truth," in *The Collected Papers of Charles Sanders Peirce*, vol. 5, ed. C. Hartshorne and P. Weiss (Cambridge, Mass.: Harvard University Press, 1958), pp. 394–98.
21. On the alleged falsity of all ordinary physical statements, and for a different response, see Hesse, *Revolutions and Reconstructions*, pp. 104–05.
22. Harold H. Joachim, *The Nature of Truth* (Oxford: Clarendon Press, 1906), p. 90.
23. Winston H. F. Barnes, *The Philosophical Predicament* (London: Adam and Charles Black, 1950), p. 31.
24. Ibid., p. 32.
25. W. H. Newton-Smith, *The Rationality of Science* (London: Routledge and Kegan Paul, 1981), p. 11.
26. Ibid., p. 161.
27. Thus PRS satisfies Newton-Smith's request for a theory which allows us "to determine the reference of singular terms of previous theories in such a way that on some occasions at least a singular term has a referent which is the same as the referent assigned to the corresponding term in our current theories," and on some occasions the terms' extensions at least overlap (ibid., p. 162). His account, lengthier yet less complete, than the present one (ibid., pp. 171–77), suggests reasons for "being charitable"—that is (I would say), for applying PRS.
28. See ibid., p. 160.
29. Putnam, *Realism and Reason*, pp. 199–200.

Chapter 12: Trans-empirical Truth

1. Antony Flew, "Theology and Falsification," in *New Essays in Philosophical Theology*, ed. A. Flew and A. MacIntyre (London: SCM Press, 1969), p. 106.
2. Ibid., pp. 98–99.
3. See Hallett, *Darkness and Light*, pp. 82–83; Ian M. Crombie, "Theology and Falsification," in *The Logic of God: Theology and Verification*, ed. M. Diamond and T. Litzenburg, Jr. (Indianapolis: Bobbs-Merrill, 1975), p. 325.
4. Kai Nielsen, *An Introduction to the Philosophy of Religion* (New York: St. Martin's Press, 1983), p. 36. See also Crombie, "Theology and Falsification," pp. 321–23; William P. Alston, "The Elucidation of Religious Statements," in *The Hartshorne Festschrift: Process and Divinity*, ed. W. Reese and E. Freeman (La Salle, Ill.: Open Court, 1964), pp. 440–41. James F. Ross, "Analogy and the Resolution of Some Cognitivity Problems," pp. 725–26, writes: "W. P. Alston, for instance, indicating that in religious discourse terms like 'wise,' 'good,' and 'person,' are applicable to God only if certain sorts of action terms, like 'does,' 'makes,' 'creates,' 'knows,' 'forgives,' and so forth, are also applicable, argues that in religious discourse the latter are used in ways that differ significantly from the ways in which those terms are used in empirically more accessible contexts." On the varied senses of *make* and *cause* in these "more accessible contexts," see Sherry, *Religion, Truth and Language-Games*, p. 154.
5. Hospers, *An Introduction to Philosophical Analysis*, p. 97.
6. Kai Nielsen, "Facts, Factual Statements and Theoretical Terms," in *Philosophical Studies* (Dublin) 23 (1975): 138.
7. Ibid., p. 139. Compare Freud: "If, for instance, we say: 'At this point an unconscious

memory intervened,' what this means is: 'At this point something occurred of which we are totally unable to form a conception, but which, if it had entered our consciousness, could only have been described in such and such a way'" (quoted in Abraham Edel, *Analyzing Concepts in Social Science*, vol. 1, *Science, Ideology, and Value* [New Brunswick, N.J.: Transaction Books, 1979], p. 78).

8. See, e.g., *The Standard Edition of the Complete Psychological Works of Sigmund Freud*, vol. 20 (London: Hogarth Press, 1959), p. 17.

9. See, e.g., Werner Heisenberg, *Philosophic Problems of Nuclear Science*, trans. F. Hayes (New York: Pantheon, 1952), p. 38. In "Facts," Kai Nielsen cites J. J. C. Smart's strictures on subatomic "particles," akin to his own strictures on God as a "person," then observes: "Smart could in turn reply, as in fact he does in a different context, that we could be realists about electrons and mesons without holding that electrons or mesons are particles or anything like particles. We only need to hold they are an *underlying reality* which can explain macroobjects and macrolaws and in principle can directly explain observations. We now have a claim of which it may be said that it is vague enough to be true" (p. 147). It may satisfy PRS, if particle talk does not.

10. See, e.g., Dorothy Emmet, *The Nature of Metaphysical Thinking* (New York: St. Martin's Press, 1961), pp. 86–87.

11. Only in one of the scores of articles and books I have read on the topic of this chapter—viz., in Swinburne's *The Coherence of Theism*—have I encountered any allusion to some such principle as PRS.

12. David B. Burrell, *Aquinas: God and Action* (Notre Dame, Ind.: University of Notre Dame Press, 1979), p. 68.

13. John E. Smith, *The Analogy of Experience: An Approach to Understanding Religious Truth* (New York: Harper and Row, 1973), p. 45.

14. Clarke, "Analogy," p. 85. Compare Sherry, "Analogy Today," *Philosophy* 51 (1976): 445.

15. Sherry, *Religion, Truth and Language-Games*, p. 155.

16. As Sherry himself observes, "there are many 'open-ended' attributes which are not applicable to God: Professor Geach has recently reminded us in this journal that virtues like chastity, courage, perseverance under temptation and gratitude cannot be so ascribed" ("Analogy Reviewed," *Philosophy* 51 [1976]: 344–45). See Peter Geach, "An Irrelevance of Omnipotence," *Philosophy* 48 (1973): 333.

17. See Wittgenstein, *Philosophical Investigations*, §67; Hallett, *Companion*, p. 149.

18. Kai Nielsen, "Language and the Concept of God," *Question* 2 (1969): 35.

19. Bernard Williams, "Has 'God' a Meaning?" *Question* 1 (1968): 51. See also Nielsen, "Language," p. 35.

20. Frederick Copleston, *A History of Philosophy*, vol. 2 (London: Burns, Oates, and Washbourne, 1959), p. 349, expounding Aquinas's position.

21. I need not here consider the intriguing problems raised by the fact that *simple* and *complex* are cognitive comparatives.

22. See Brown, *Do Religious Claims Make Sense?*, p. 92; Mary Hesse, "Talk of God," *Philosophy* 44 (1969): 345; George P. Klubertanz, *St. Thomas Aquinas on Analogy: A Textual Analysis and Systematic Synthesis* (Chicago: Loyola University Press, 1960), p. 146; Lewis, *Philosophy of Religion*, p. 128; Ninian Smart, *The Philosophy of Religion* (New York: Random House, 1970), p. 58; Swinburne, *The Coherence of Theism*, pp. 86–87; Donald D. Evans, "Differences between Scientific and Religious Assertions," in *The Logic of God*, ed. Diamond and Litzenburg, pp. 387–88; the responses to Braithwaite in *Christian Ethics and Contemporary Philosophy*, ed. I. Ramsey (New York: Macmillan, 1966), pp. 74–88.

23. Crombie, "The Possibility of Theological Statements," p. 84.

24. Sherry, *Religion, Truth and Language-Games*, p. 12. The quotation is from Paul van Buren, *The Secular Meaning of the Gospel* (London: Collier-Macmillan, 1963), p. 132. For a fuller

sampling and critique of such reductive views, see Hugo A. Meynell, *Sense, Nonsense, and Christianity* (London: Sheed and Ward, 1964), pp. 55–61, 90–136. Besides the authors there mentioned, see, e.g., Douglas Berggren, "From Myth to Metaphor," *Monist* 50 (1966): 547–52; and, more recently, Don Cupitt, *Taking Leave of God* (New York: Crossroad, 1981), e.g., p. 9: "What then is God? God is a unifying symbol that eloquently personifies and represents to us everything that spirituality requires of us."

25. Sherry, *Religion, Truth and Language-Games*, p. 12.
26. Antony Flew, *God and Philosophy* (London: Hutchinson, 1966), pp. 22–23. See Nielsen, *Introduction*, pp. 5–6, 75–79; Feigl and Maxwell, "Why Ordinary Language Needs Reforming," p. 498.
27. Clarke, "Analogy," p. 67.
28. See James F. Ross, *Portraying Analogy* (Cambridge: Cambridge University Press, 1981), pp. 19–22, 33–34.
29. Clarke, "Analogy," p. 68.

Chapter 13: A Comparison with Tarski and Davidson

1. Joseph F. Hanna, "An Explication of 'Explication,'" *Philosophy of Science* 35 (1968): 29.
2. For a similar version, similarly used in support of explication, see Quine, *Word and Object*, p. 259.
3. See Hallett, *Logic for the Labyrinth*, p. 39.
4. Tarski himself wrote: "I do not have the slightest intention to contribute in any way to those endless, often violent discussions on the subject: 'What is the right conception of truth?' . . . Disputes of this type are by no means restricted to the notion of truth. They occur in all domains where—instead of an exact, scientific terminology—common language with its vagueness and ambiguity is used; and they are always meaningless, and therefore in vain" ("The Semantic Conception of Truth and the Foundations of Semantics," *Philosophy and Phenomenological Research* 4 [1943–44]: 355). I too have complained of vagueness and ambiguity—for instance, in the Austin-Strawson debate. Yet I have seen no need to adopt a "scientific terminology." To Tarski I would suggest: *Datur tertium*. One may use ordinary language with greater care to make necessary distinctions—for instance, the distinction Tarski often blurred between an ordinary language (e.g., English) and ordinary discourse or employment of the language. After all, a scientific terminology or artificially constructed language would itself have to be explained by means of some familiar, natural language.
5. Haack, *Philosophy of Logics*, p. 99.
6. Tarski, "The Semantic Conception of Truth," pp. 342–43.
7. Ibid., p. 342.
8. "Tarski is clear that *sentences* are truth bearers in his theory. But when we ask the question: Does he mean token-sentences or type-sentences? we do not get a clear answer" (D. J. O'Connor and Brian Carr, *Introduction to the Theory of Knowledge* [Minneapolis: University of Minnesota Press, 1982], p. 179).
9. Tarski, "The Semantic Conception of Truth," p. 348. Many have held that natural languages like English are inconsistent; and many have so understood Tarski, with better reason, I believe, than is recognized by A. B. Levison, "Logic, Language, and Consistency in Tarski's Theory of Truth," *Philosophy and Phenomenological Research* 25 (1964–65): 384–92. See Alfred Tarski, "The Concept of Truth in Formalized Languages" and "The Establishment of Scientific Semantics" in idem, *Logic, Semantics, Metamathematics*, trans. J. Woodger (Oxford: Clarendon Press, 1956), pp. 153, 165, 402.
10. See, e.g., Yehoshua Bar-Hillel, "New Light on the Liar," *Analysis* 18 (1957–58): 1–6; idem, "Do Natural Languages Contain Paradoxes?," *Studium Generale* 19 (1966): 394–97; An-

derson, "Mathematics and the 'Language Game,'" p. 484; William C. Kneale, "Propositions and Truth in Natural Languages," *Mind* 81 (1972): 241–43; Rescher, *The Coherence
Theory of Truth*, p. 15.

11. In his defense of the meaningfulness of, for instance, "What I am now saying is false,"
Mackie overlooks this important similarity with meaningless utterances and asserts unhesitatingly that each word in such an utterance "is used in its standard way with its
standard meaning" (as though the construction of paradoxes were a standard use of words
and as though, in Wittgenstein's words, the meaning "were an atmosphere accompanying
the word, which it carried with it into every kind of application"). See Mackie, *Truth
Probability and Paradox*, pp. 242–43.

12. Tarski, "The Concept of Truth," p. 165.

13. See, e.g., Tarski, "The Semantic Conception of Truth," pp. 348–49.

14. See Wittgenstein, *Philosophical Investigations*, §70.

15. White, *Truth*, pp. 97–98. The sayings of Tarski, Russell, Graham, and others examined in
this study suggest a rough rule of thumb: the worse we understand everyday language, the
worse it looks; the better we understand it, the better it looks.

16. Ibid., p. 98.

17. Donald Davidson, *Inquiries into Truth and Interpretation* (Oxford: Clarendon Press, 1984), p.
70. See also ibid., pp. 35, 55, 74, 94–95.

18. Putnam, *Realism and Reason*, p. 80.

19. Ibid.

20. See Wittgenstein, *Philosophical Investigations*, §164.

21. Davidson, *Inquiries*, pp. 69–70. Compare my ch. 5.

22. Ibid., p. 70. Compare my ch. 3.

23. Ibid., pp. 43, 58. Compare my chs. 3 and 4.

24. Ibid., p. 43.

25. Ibid., p. 54.

26. Ibid., pp. 71–72. Since I see no menace in these antinomies, from a nonformal point of
view, one of many objections I shall bypass is the claim that Davidson's return to natural
languages involves him once again in paradox. See Charles S. Chihara, "Truth, Meaning,
and Paradox," *Nous* 10 (1976): 305–11.

27. Davidson, *Inquiries*, p. 51.

28. Wittgenstein, *Philosophical Investigations*, §81.

29. Davidson, *Inquiries*, p. 32.

30. Donald Davidson, "The Logical Form of Action Sentences," in *The Logic of Decision and
Action*, ed. N. Rescher (Pittsburgh: University of Pittsburgh Press, 1967), p. 82.

31. Ibid.

32. Davidson, *Inquiries*, pp. 51–52.

33. Wittgenstein, *The Blue and Brown Books*, p. 18.

34. Davidson, *Inquiries*, p. 36.

35. Ibid., p. 59.

36. See Hallett, *Logic for the Labyrinth*, pp. 167–68.

37. On various alleged exceptions to the norm of bivalence (future-contingent sentences,
sentences containing nondenoting terms, certain sentences in mathematics or quantum
mechanics), see, e.g., Susan Haack, *Deviant Logic: Some Philosophical Issues* (Cambridge:
Cambridge University Press, 1974), pp. 48, 55–56.

38. "For suppose '*p*' to be neither true nor false; then the left-hand side of:
    '*p*' is true iff *p*
will be, presumably, false, while the right-hand side will be neither true nor false. So the
whole biconditional will be false, or at any rate untrue" (Haack, *Philosophy of Logics*, pp.
101–02). This implicit requirement of bivalence is a second important respect in which

Tarski's analysis departed, without justification, from Aristotle's text. See Tarski, "The Semantic Conception of Truth," p. 343.

39. For analogous difficulties with regard to ambiguous statements, see Charles S. Chihara, "Davidson's Extensional Theory of Meaning," *Philosophical Studies* 28 (1975): 7–8; with regard to statements containing the word *any,* see Jaakko Hintikka, "The Prospects for Convention T," *Dialectica* 30 (1976): 61–66, and idem, "A Counterexample to Tarski-Type Truth-Definitions as Applied to Natural Languages," *Philosophia* 5 (1975): 207–12.

40. Davidson himself acknowledges that "the theory reveals nothing new about the conditions under which an individual sentence is true; it does not make those conditions any clearer than the sentence itself does" (*Inquiries,* p. 25). See also ibid., pp. 218, 221, 223.

41. Ian Hacking, *Why Does Language Matter to Philosophy?* (Cambridge: Cambridge University Press, 1975), pp. 144–45.

42. Esa Itkonen, *Causality in Linguistic Theory* (Bloomington, Ind.: Indiana University Press, 1983), p. 141. For further comments similar to mine, see ibid., p. 140; John McDowell, "Truth Conditions, Bivalence, and Verificationism," in *Truth and Meaning,* ed. Evans and McDowell, p. 43 ("It would be suspect to rely on an assumed prior understanding of 'true,' as used in specifying the form which the theorems would take"); Christopher Peacocke, "Truth Definitions and Actual Languages," in *Truth and Meaning,* pp. 162–64; Neil Tennant, "Truth, Meaning and Decidability," *Mind* 86 (1977): 371–72; Dummett, "What Is a Theory of Meaning? (II)," p. 69 ("The really elusive notion is that of truth conditions itself. What *is* it to know the truth conditions of a sentence?"), p. 78 ("As long as we take the notion of truth for granted, then it seems obvious that it is in terms of it that meaning must be explained. The moment that we cease to take it for granted, however, and start to enquire into the correct analysis of the notion, to ask where we get it from, this obviousness evaporates").

43. See, e.g., Davidson, *Inquiries,* pp. 24–25.

44. Joseph Butler, *Works,* vol. 2 (Oxford: Washbourne, 1850), pp. 31–32.

45. Should it appear contradictory to speak of a "standard meaning" which is "widely re-sisted . . . especially in speculative inquiry," recall the conflict noted in chapter 8 between Russell's everyday assertions of what he "saw," "heard," "touched," and the like and his speculative denials in book after book. The kind of inconsistency which characterized Russell's personal practice can be found, generalized and written large, in the culture he represented. (See, e.g., chapter 8's catalog of comparable cases.)

INDEX

Abstraction, 9
Accuracy, 21, 82–84
Achinstein, Peter, 215, 219
Adams, George, 206
Alston, William, 204, 207, 212, 223
Anaxagoras, 215
Anderson, Alan, 216, 226–27
Aquinas, St. Thomas, 8–10, 15, 181, 202, 203, 207
Arieti, James and Silvano, 215
Aristotle, 7, 8, 15, 16, 190, 202, 203, 227
Arnauld, Antoine, 208
Asymmetry, 61–69
Atomist conception of language and truth, 12–14, 15, 27–30
Attfield, Robin, 212, 222
Attributives, 194–95, 209
Augustine, St., 11, 15, 16, 20, 28, 203
Austin, John, 207, 208, 212, 218, 219, 221; on truth, 3, 58–60, 61–62, 63, 193, 195, 207; on performatives, 64–65, 154; Graham's critique of, 132, 135, 139, 140, 143, 145; on moral statements, 157–58
Avowals, 64, 66–69
Ayer, A. J., 51, 156, 206, 215, 222

Bach, Kent, 218
Baier, Kurt, 127, 215
Baker, G. P., 203, 211, 213, 221
Bambrough, Renford, 216
Barber, Agnes, 4
Bar-Hillel, Yehoshua, 225
Barnes, Winston, 173, 223
"Bearer" of truth, 32, 58–64
Belief(s), 52–53, 68
Benacerraf, Paul, 216
Berggren, Douglas, 225

Berkeley, George, 10, 22, 119, 120, 155, 156, 202, 214
Berlin, Isaiah, 218
Binkley, Robert, 203
Bivalence, 191–92, 197, 226
Black, Max, 3, 124, 201, 209
Blackstone, William, 221
Blanshard, Brand, 119–20, 216
Bohnert, Herbert, 220
Bohr, Niels, 174
Borchardt, Edward, 220
Borderline cases, 106, 133–34, 146–47
Boyd, Richard, 213
Braithwaite, R. B., 224
Brentano, Franz, 48, 50, 203, 206
Brown, N. J., 203, 224
Brown, Roger, 204
Brown, Stuart, 122, 212, 214, 216
Burrell, David, 224
Burtt, Edwin, 215
Butler, Joseph, 198, 227

Campbell, Charles, 212
Carnap, Rudolf, 166, 219, 220, 221, 222
Carr, Brian, 225
Cassirer, Ernst, 210
Causal: primacy, 53–55; extensions, 103–04
Chafe, Wallace, 205
Chappell, V. C., 214
Chase, Stuart, 214
Chihara, Charles, 226, 227
Chisholm, Roderick, 216
Churchland, Paul, 218, 219
Ciardi, John, 211
Clarke, W. Norris, 181, 185–86, 212, 224
Clement of Alexandria, St., 6, 201, 203

Cobitz, J. L., 214
Cognitive comparatives, 69, 70–85, 127, 196–97, 209; simple, 72–78; complex, 78–79, 81, 82; minority, 79–80; commendatory, 81–82
Cognitive content, 117–19, 121–22, 128
Cohen, L. Jonathan, 208
Commands, 146
Common sense, 114, 115–16
Compositionality, 92, 211
Contradictions, 94, 103, 209–10. See also Inconsistency; Paradoxes
Copi, Irving, 206
Copernicus, Nicolaus, 116, 122
Copleston, Frederick, 184, 202, 224
Correspondence, 201; isomorphic, 5–30; essentialist conceptions of, 7–10; empiricist conceptions of, 10–11; atomist conception of, 12–14, 27–28; linguistic, 34–45; degree of, 35, 36, 83–84, 91–106; norm of, 89, 109–29, 131, 148–49, 161–64, 189; importance of, 108–12, 113, 115. See also Principle of relative similarity
Cousin, D. R., 50, 206
Crick, Francis, 116
Criteria, 38, 40, 49, 52, 55, 58, 65, 69, 159–60, 164, 205
Crombie, Ian, 212, 223, 224
Cupitt, Don, 225

Danto, Arthur, 214
Darwin, Charles, 128, 215
Davidson, Donald, 4, 189, 192–99, 216, 227
De George, Richard, 208, 211
Demos, Raphael, 212
Dennes, W. R., 206
Descartes, René, 22, 214
Dewar, Lindsay, 215
Dewey, John, 85, 211
Diamond, Cora, 219
Diamond, Malcolm, 214, 223, 224
Dillenberger, John, 210
Ducasse, Curt, 211, 212
Dulles, Avery, 209–10
Dummett, Michael, 219, 227
Durfee, Harold, 207

Eddington, Arthur, 214
Edel, Abraham, 224

Emmet, Dorothy, 224
Emmet, E. R., 214
Empiricist conceptions of language and truth, 10–12, 15, 19–23, 29–30
Error, 22, 39, 122, 126–27, 152–56. See also Falsehood
Essentialist conceptions of language and truth, 7–10, 15, 23–27, 29–30, 134, 151–52
Etymologies, 135
Evans, Donald, 224
Evans, Garth, 219
Ewing, A. C., 206
Explication, 3, 219
Ezorsky, Gertrude, 208

Facione, Peter, 206
Falsehood, 14, 22, 25, 29–30, 45. See also Error; Lying
Fann, K. T., 219
Faricy, Robert, 216
Feigl, Herbert, 158, 216, 221, 225
Fetzer, James, 217
Feyerabend, Paul, 216
Findlay, J. N., 221
Finnis, John, 206
Flew, Antony, 177–78, 185, 209, 211, 223
Forrester, Mary, 214, 220
Franzen, Winfried, 201
Freeman, Eugene, 223
Frege, Gottlob, 204, 221
Freud, Sigmund, 223–24
Furberg, Mats, 219, 221

Galilei, Galileo, 128
Garner, Richard, 220
Geach, Peter, 208, 211, 219, 224
God, 96, 98, 103, 123, 125, 175, 177–87 passim
Goldman, Alvin, 201
"Good," 81–82, 162–63, 189, 210
Gorovitz, Samuel, 201
Graham, Keith, 132–46, 204, 210, 218, 219, 226
Gregory, Richard, 214
Grice, H. P., 206
Guthrie, William, 202, 214

Haack, R. J., 205
Haack, Susan, 189, 205, 225, 226
Hacker, P. M. S., 203, 211, 213, 221

Hacking, Ian, 198, 227
Hamblin, C. L., 220
Hamlyn, D. W., 206
Handy, Rollo, 216
Hanna, Joseph, 188, 225
Hanson, Norwood, 215, 219
Hare, Richard, 211
Harman, Gilbert, 216
Harrah, David, 220
Harré, Romano, 215
Harris, Roy, 203
Harrison, Bernard, 205
Hartman, Robert, 223
Hartnack, Justus, 144, 218, 219
Harvey, William, 116
Hasker, William, 208
Hayakawa, Samuel, 101, 213, 214, 216
Hedenius, Ingemar, 218, 219
Heisenberg, Werner, 224
Hempel, Carl, 165–69, 175, 208, 219, 222
Heraclitus, 214
Hesse, Mary, 100, 105, 212, 213, 215, 223, 224
Hilliard, Albert, 214
Hintikka, Jaakko, 211, 227
Hintikka, Merrill, 201
Hochberg, Herbert, 215
Hook, Sidney, 212
Hospers, John, 210, 215, 219, 223
Houde, Roland, 202
Houston, J., 142, 150, 219
Hurrell, Paul, 220
Huxley, Julian, 102–03

Images and imagine, 11–12, 19–24, 42, 179, 203, 204
Incompatible terms, 91, 95, 213
Inconsistency, 137–38, 225
Indefiniteness, 36, 75, 76–77, 188–89, 197
Interdependence, 36–37, 83
Isomorphist views, 5–30, 32, 203, 204
Itkonen, Esa, 198, 227

James, William, 3, 15, 19–24, 32, 48, 110, 158, 201, 203, 204
Joachim, Harold, 172–73, 223
Johnson, Elizabeth, 212
Johnson, Wendell, 214

Kamp, J. A. W., 210
Kanger, Stig, 211

Kant, Immanuel, 22, 155
Kaplan, Abraham, 221, 222
Keenan, Edward, 210
Kenner, Hugh, 211
Khatchadourian, Haig, 209
Kiefer, Howard, 209
Kincade, J., 208
Klubertanz, George, 224
Kneale, William, 226
Knowledge: and language, 38–39, 62–85 passim; and truth, 38–40, 62–85 passim; and thought, 70–71, 208. *See also* Cognitive comparatives; Cognitive content
Knox, John, 209
Knox, John, Jr., 208
Körner, Stephan, 215
Kripke, Saul, 205, 212, 216
Krishan, Daya, 94, 102, 212
Kuhn, Thomas, 95, 122, 212, 216
Kupperman, Joel, 216, 220

Language: neutrality of, 121–28; revision of, 126–28, 135–42. *See also* Atomist conception of language and truth; Empiricist conceptions of language and truth; Essentialist conceptions of language and truth; Knowledge
Lee, Harold, 215
Lee, Irving, 217
Lee, Patrick, 202
Lemmon, E. J., 218
Leonard, Henry, 220
Lepley, Ray, 215
Levison, A. B., 225
Lewis, David, 213
Lewis, H. D., 212, 216
Linnaeus, Carolus, 158
Litzenburg, Thomas, 223, 224
Locke, John, 8–10, 15, 202, 203
Loewenberg, J., 206
Lying, 10, 39

McClure, George, 216
McDowell, John, 219, 227
Mace, Cecil, 215
McInerny, Ralph, 146–47, 220
MacIntyre, Alasdair, 214, 219, 223
Mackie, J. L., 203, 226
McPherson, Thomas, 213
Malcolm, Norman, 208, 215

Mannheim, Karl, 215
Marrone, Steven, 202
Martin, James, 216
Martinich, A. P., 213
Mason, J., 215
Mates, Benson, 214
Maxwell, Grover, 158, 216, 221, 225
Maynard, Patrick, 203
Mayr, Ernst, 215–16
Meaning: speakers', 50; statements', 50; words', 70, 117–18, 121–22, 124, 168–70
Mendel, Gregor, 128
Metaphor, 100
Meynell, Hugo, 206, 225
Mill, John S., 51, 206
Miller, D. S., 221
Mitchell, Dorothy, 210
Montagu, Ashley, 216
Montefiore, Alan, 159, 218–19, 221
Moore, G. E., 16, 18–19, 28, 52, 150–52, 157–58, 162–63, 203, 206, 221
Moore, W. Edgar, 215
More, Paul, 211
Morgenbesser, Sidney, 214
Muirhead, John, 206
Mullaly, Joseph, 202
Munitz, Milton, 209

Naess, Arne, 150, 156–57, 221
Neurath, Otto, 165–69, 175, 222
Newton, Isaac, 214
Newton-Smith, W. H., 173–74, 223
Nielsen, Kai, 93, 179, 181, 182, 183, 185–86, 212, 220, 221, 223, 224, 225
Nowell-Smith, Patrick, 210, 211, 218

Objectivity, 77–78
O'Connor, D. J., 225
Ofstad, Harald, 221
Öhman, Sven, 211
Ortony, Andrew, 212

Palmer, George, 214
Paradoxes: mystical, 94, 213; semantic, 137–38, 190–92, 193–94, 226; of analysis, 188. See also Contradictions
Parker, Dewitt, 214
Parmenides, 215
Peacocke, Christopher, 227
Pearce, Glenn, 203

Peirce, C. S., 223
Pepper, Stephen, 206
Performatives, 64–66, 68–69, 76, 131–45 passim. See also Promise
Perry, David, 210
Personhood, 142–43, 161
Phelan, Gerald, 202
Picture theory, 12–14
Pitcher, George, 206, 207
Pitkin, Hanna, 214
Plato, 7–8, 18, 201, 202, 203, 214
Pletcher, Galen, 213
Port Royal Logic, 70, 71
Power, William, 212
Price, Henry, 203, 208, 215, 222
Primacy, 47–57, 59, 206; practical, 52–53; causal, 53–55; conceptual, 53–55; functional, 53–55, 207; statistical, 53–55; temporal, 53–55; valuational, 55–57
Principle of relative similarity (PRS), viii, 91–107, 165, 170–76, 177–87, 211, 223. See also Correspondence
Promise, 65–66, 133, 144. See also Performatives
Propositions, 51–52
Provence, Donald, 201
Putnam, Hilary, 99–100, 174–75, 192–93, 201, 212, 216, 223, 226

Questions, 146–47
Quine, Willard van Orman, 216, 225

Ramsey, Frank, 51, 206
Ramsey, Ian, 224
Randall, John, 215
Ratner, Joseph, 211
Rawls, John, 214
Ray, John, 158
Reese, William, 223
Reference: problem of, 13, 22–23, 24–25, 28, 29–30, 45–46; and linguistic correspondence, 40–41; of truth-ascriptions, 62–64; versus meaning, 74
Reid, Thomas, 214
Rescher, Nicholas, 209, 220, 222, 226
Richards, David, 215
Rickman, H. P., 140–41, 219
Riegle, Rodney, 220
Ringbom, Marten, 202
Rorty, Richard, 215
Rosen, Bernard, 220

Ross, Alf, 220
Ross, James, 104, 213, 223, 225
Ross, Stephen, 209
Ross, W. David, 18, 203, 210
Rudner, Richard, 219
Rundle, Bede, 208, 220
Russell, Bertrand, 202, 203, 205, 214, 215,
    226; on truth, 11–12, 47–48, 50–51; on
    language, 12; on thought, 12, 16; on
    sensation, 113–15, 120, 136, 138, 154,
    198, 227
Ryding, Erik, 219
Ryle, Gilbert, 207

Sagan, Carl, 214
Santas, Gerasimos, 203
Santoni, Ronald, 212
Scheler, Max, 214
Schiller, F. C. S., 217
Schilpp, Paul, 221
Schlauch, Margaret, 212, 213
Schlick, Moritz, 166–68, 175, 222
Schwartz, Stephen, 212
Scotus, Duns, 93, 212
Scriven, Michael, 217
Searle, John, 213
Sellars, Wilfrid, 51, 206, 210
Sherry, Patrick, 184–85, 209, 223, 224,
    225
Similarity: versus isomorphism, 5–6; and
    reference, 22, 25, 29–30, 45; and con-
    ceptual borders, 26, 97, 104, 140–41;
    not a sharp, uniform notion, 93, 94–95,
    186. See also Principle of relative sim-
    ilarity
Skinner, B. F., 214
Smart, J. J. C., 211, 216, 224
Smart, Ninian, 224
Smith, John, 224
Smith, Peter, 211–12
Sober, Elliott, 203, 204
Socrates, 18
Sommers, Frederic, 205
Sparshott, F. E., 214
Stace, Walter, 102, 213
Statements, 32, 59, 60–61, 63, 190, 193
Stebbing, L. Susan, 214
Stegmüller, Wolfgang, 201
Stern, Gustaf, 212, 213
Stevenson, Charles, 151, 158, 220, 221
Storer, Thomas, 203

Strawson, Peter: on truth, 3, 58, 59, 60–
    62, 63, 157–58, 193, 195, 207, 208
Stumpf, Samuel, 215
Sturtevant, Edgar, 211
Swinburne, Richard, 159, 212, 222, 224

Tarski, Alfred, 4, 189–93, 194, 199, 225,
    226, 227
Tennant, Neil, 227
Tennessen, Herman, 205
Terrell, D. B., 221
Thomson, Joseph, 174
Titchener, Edward, 21, 202, 203
Tlumak, Jeffrey, 206
Toulmin, Stephen, 215, 216
Truth: explication of, 3; isomorphic con-
    ceptions of, 3, 5–31; James's theory of,
    3, 23–24; essentialist accounts of, 7–10,
    23–27, 29–30; empiricist accounts of,
    10–12, 19–23, 29–30; Tractatus account
    of, 12–14, 27–29; linguistic, 31–57;
    bearer of, 32, 58–64; mental, 47–50,
    55–57; propositional, 50–52; impor-
    tance of, 55–56; Austin on, 58–60, 61–
    62, 207; Strawson on, 60–63; sufficient
    condition of, 91, 96–101; necessary con-
    dition of, 91, 101–106; of performatives,
    131–47; moral, 131–32, 148–64; of
    commands, 146–47, 220; of questions,
    146–47, 220; empirical, 165–76; co-
    herence theory of, 165–68, 169; trans-
    empirical, 177–87; not precisely defin-
    able, 188–89; Tarski on, 189–92; David-
    son on, 192–99; mathematical, 209; of
    conditionals, 219. See also Bivalence;
    Correspondence; Principle of relative
    similarity

Urmson, J. O., 211, 214
Usage, 112, 130, 133–34
Uses: established, 32–34, 95, 98, 122; of
    tools, 32, 35, 37, 42; of words, 32–34,
    42, 43–45, 92–93; stipulated, 34;
    "blind," 208

Van Breemen, Peter, 215
Van Buren, Paul, 184–85, 224
Vendler, Zeno, 209
Vesey, Godfrey, 202
Von Wright, Georg H., 219

Waismann, Friedrich, 32–33, 205, 209, 215
Wallace, John, 210
Warnock, Geoffrey, 60, 162, 206, 207, 208, 218, 222
Watson, James, 116
Weinreich, Uriel, 211
Weitz, Morris, 215
Wellman, Carl, 159, 221, 222
Wells, Donald, 209
Wheatley, J. M. O., 220
Wheeler, Samuel, 209, 210
Wheelwright, Philip, 206
White, Alan, 192, 206, 208, 209, 215, 221, 222, 226
Williams, Bernard, 183, 224
Williams, Ron, 201
Winch, Peter, 217
Wisdom, J. O., 209

Wisdom, John, 201
Wittgenstein, Ludwig, 64, 103, 112, 125, 187, 201, 203, 204, 205, 206, 208, 210, 212, 213, 215, 218, 222, 223, 224, 226; early views of, 5, 7, 12–14, 15, 27–29, 47, 126, 136, 166–68, 175; on truth, 12–13, 205; on concepts, 26, 99, 104, 159, 168–69; on method, 26, 31, 32, 44, 110, 116, 126, 134; on thought, 31; on speech, 47, 67, 71; on substitute languages, 126, 169
Wohlstetter, Albert, 201

Xenakis, Jason, 215

Yolton, John, 201

Zaehner, R. C., 102–03, 213